WEBSTER GROVES

CLARISSA START

WEBSTER GROVES

CLARISSA START

Pictured above: Constance Andrews Mathews, Walter Skinner,
Orpha Kendrick, Sidney Skinner, Julia Skinner.

Library of Congress Catalog Card Number: 75-30274

Printed in United States of America

This book was commissioned

by the

Council of the City of Webster Groves

in honor of

the Bicentennial Celebration

of the

United States of America

and

is dedicated to

all citizens, past and present,

who have made Webster Groves

a very special place .

Table of Contents

The Queen of the Suburbs.

Chapter One

A Very Special Place

A former resident of Webster Groves, returning for a visit, might be startled to see some of the changes in his home town. Driving up the hill of North Gore avenue, he would notice immediately that a long-time landmark, the turreted, turn-of-the-century building which housed a department store is no longer there. In its place, where Gore meets Lockwood avenue, is the sleek modern facade of a savings and loan company.

He might have noticed other changes as he drove along Gore. The one time feed and grain store across the railway tracks is a garden shop, spilling colorful blooms along the sidewalk in season. The train station has turned into a dress shop. The corner grocery is gone and in its building is a gift and antiques shop, one of several in that row.

There would be familiar stores on Lockwood but there would be unfamiliar ones, too, and the wide swath of Elm avenue, at the intersection where City Hall stands would be a change. All over Webster Groves he would see changes, from the youthful mod shops in Old Orchard to Highway I-44 cutting its ribbon through the south end of town.

And yet, after some initial disquietude, the former resident would begin to feel comfortable again. With all its changes, Webster Groves remains the same. The same — and different, different from any other suburb, perhaps in the world, certainly in the St. Louis County complex of more than 100 communities.

What makes Webster Groves unique? What gives it its special character?

Some would say it's the trees, the towering oaks, flaming maples, even some surviving full skirted elms, the "groves" which first gave the town its name.

Some would say it's the homes, especially the big old frame houses, set back from the street with large sweeps of lawn, homes of an age which might have deteriorated into shabby second class housing elsewhere, but here are lovingly tended and restored and maintained.

Some would say schools and some would say churches and others would sum it up with the word, "culture," and point with pride to Webster College with its Loretto-Hilton theater and the excellent library and symphony and Theatre Guild and the Artists Guild, newly moved to the area. And some would say tradition, the tradition of the Monday Club, the DAR, garden clubs, nature and bird clubs, the Historical Society and other bulwarks of any town.

But then others would argue with those pat answers, too, and say that it's more than that. It's people. Nice people. A kind of classless society in which you scarcely notice who's richer or poorer because your neighbor is accepted. After all, he lives in Webster, doesn't he? He must be nice because only nice people . . . well, it's kind of a circle. A friendly circle. A community in which there's little evidence of a struggle to exceed, to surpass, because everyone has already arrived. In Webster.

Whatever the reason, Webster Groves, population 28,000, has a personality and an image of its own, in contrast to any of its sister suburbs. Clayton is successful and Kirkwood is civic and Florissant is historic and Ferguson is mature and University City is intellectual and Ladue is fashionable and Lemay is solid . . . the list could go on and on.

The Old Bristol Building is gone.

But Webster Groves is . . . itself. A most significant fact is that a recent city survey showed that 43 percent of the residents have lived in Webster Groves more than 20 years and 85 percent have no intention of moving. In this day and age of a mobile, fluid, transient society, this is pretty remarkable.

Its residents may make a few suggestions for improvement, as they did in the survey. Fix those chuckholes, build a mini park, don't be a litterbug. But they don't really want things drastically changed.

People who live in Webster Groves love it as it is, which is pretty much the way it's always been. They're proud to live in Webster, which is a key difference in itself. As Texans are about Texas, Websterites are about Webster Groves.

In its place, the sleek and new.

Is it imagination or does the traffic move more politely in Webster, with one car giving the right of way to another and most cars pausing for pedestrians? Are the check-out clerks of the supermarket chains more patient and considerate in the Webster branches than in those of other communities? Do fewer people bump and shove and elbow you out of their path, or does it just seem that way?

People who live in Webster, people who lived there happily and have moved away, people looking forward to moving there, all feel there's no place like it. People who do not live there, never have and never want to, are sometimes a bit intolerant of this attitude.

"The trouble with Webster Groves," said a man from another suburb, "is that the people who live there think their town is better than any place else."

"I suppose we do," a long time resident admitted, then added as a mild afterthought, "That's because it is."

Without belaboring the point, Webster Groves is a very special place. This book may tell how it got that way.

Chapter Two

Early History

The Indians called it Dry Ridge, the area which extends west from St. Louis to the Meramec and Missouri rivers, a part of which is now Webster Groves. Many a gardener, struggling to maintain a lawn and flower beds while also trying to conserve water in late summer, can wryly appreciate this descriptive name.

They were the Osage, the Dakota and the Missouri tribes of Indians who inhabited this land before the white man came. History books tell us how Pierre Laclede Liguest, Auguste Chouteau and his mother, Mme. Marie Chouteau, came up from New Orleans and founded the village of St. Louis.

Soon they were followed by French, Spanish and English settlers in large numbers. Fur trading was the business of the day and St. Louis was a thriving post, the rivers from the little River des Peres to the mighty Mississippi serving as roadways to take pelts to the Eastern markets and thence to Europe.

The Revolutionary War and the creation of our nation itself were only a quarter of a century in the background when Charles Dehault Delassus, last Spanish lieutenant governor of the Louisiana Territory, began granting land to companies and individuals requesting it. Charles Gratiot, a St. Louis businessman, received a large tract just west of the city. Beyond Gratiot's Leagues, an area consisting of 7056 arpens (the Spanish measurement) or 6002 acres of land was assigned to a Frenchman, Gregoire Sarpy, who had married Pelagie Labadie, granddaughter of Mme. Chouteau.

After the Louisiana Purchase of 1803, this grant was confirmed by Congress in 1816 and surveyed in 1818. Because the tract was not one league square but rather an "L" shape, it was refused by the Federal Land Commissioner and litigation continued until Congress finally confirmed it in 1842.

The Sarpy tract was what is now Webster Groves. The litigation explains why settlement of this area was delayed until the 1840s.

By the time confirmation was complete, Sarpy had sold 4000 acres through Wilson P. Hunt to John Jacob Astor in 1817. This later was sold to Kenneth MacKenzie and became the MacKenzie tract, now part Shrewsbury, part Kenrick Seminary. The northern half of the remainder was acquired by John S. Sarpy, Gregoire's eldest son, and the south half by Pierre Chouteau Jr. The dividing line is now Lockwood avenue, the main street of Webster Groves.

Chouteau subdivided his portion into 36 forty-acre lots and many of the early streets of Webster developed along these lot lines. North to south, they are Old Orchard, Edgar, Selma, Plant, Elm, Gore, Gray and Rock Hill. East to West, they are Swon, Jackson and Glendale road.

Many of the early roads took their names from geography or from their function. For example, Big Bend road, cutting southwestwardly through the area, led to the big bend in the Meramec River where water was obtained. A narrow horseback trail in 1840, it was widened for wagons in 1850. Jackson road was the road to Sam'l Jackson's farm, now Algonquin Country Club. Bompart led to Bompart's farm. Elm was known as Farm road.

The main road in the area was the Osage Trail, later known as the St. Louis to Springfield road. Made a highway in 1835, it is now Manchester and Missouri Highway 100.

Names of Webster streets have changed with the years. Gore was Church street (the joke had it that there was one church and three saloons on the street in early days). Kirkham was known as Shady avenue. Lockwood was once First street. Rock Hill road, which led to Jefferson Barracks, was known variously as Old Military, Barracks and Reavis road, because it passed the Reavis property.

The Reavis ground was part of the earliest record of ownership of an individual homestead, in the form of a deed dated in the early 1820s to Noah Reavis. Reavis came from Georgia to Kentucky to Missouri, and he and his wife built a log house which they eventually expanded to a 10 room house on what is now Reavis place. The house is no longer standing, but must have been impressive in its day as the family had 17 slaves tending the gardens and tilling the fields.

In Captain Tom L. Gibson's memoirs, published in 1946, he told the story told to him 50 years earlier by Noah's son, Anson Reavis, who lived to be 107 years old.

"You see that big elm tree there," Reavis said to Captain Tom, pointing to a tree on the corner of Gray avenue and Big Bend. "One day, the Old Man and I were coming out of the big woods and right where that road is now (Big Bend) there were eleven Indians, all of them with bows and arrows, painted up red, for business. The Old Man said to me, 'Shst, Kid!' Then he shoved me right down by that old elm tree and we let them Indians go by. "

"I said to the Old Man, 'Why didn't you shoot them, Pop?' He said, 'This here gun of mine just goes off once and them bows and arrows goes off eleven times.' "

Believed to be the oldest house still standing in Webster Groves is the James Spencer home at 428 California avenue. Authorities on architecture have placed the construction of the rear portion of this house at about 1800.

It was acquired by Spencer, who came from Lancaster, England in 1830, as part of 40 acres he purchased from Pierre Chouteau, Jr. The property was bounded by Spencer (now Selma), Big Bend, Edgar and Oak (now Jackson) roads.

Settlement was sparse and scattered in the 1840s and 50s. In 1850, Joseph, Sylvester and Henry (sometimes spelled Silvestre and Henri) Papin purchased property and built a house in 1851. The Papins later had sizeable estates with 80 to 90 slaves.

Henry Papin is believed to have built the first brick house in Webster, hauling the materials along Big Bend road. By the time he had finished his home, the story goes, he was convinced that there were too many "redskins" in the area for his wife's safety so he took her back to St. Louis. She reversed the decision, however, and soon was living in her Webster home, turning out loaves of bread so fragrant that the Indians came from miles around to beg for a handout.

She settled this habit by putting the bread down a well and telling the Indians the well was inhabited by evil spirits. The Papins were bothered no more by hungry tribesmen.

Webster Groves folklore is filled with stories about the Papins, especially Miss Rita, reputedly a great beauty. The classic tale is told of a party on Vandeventer place in the city, where she met the famous poet, Sidney Lanier. According to story, he was so smitten by her that he waltzed her out onto the veranda through the French doors, telling her, "Come out, will you? I want to show you to the other flowers."

Another early resident was Thomas Jones, who purchased a lot from the Pierre Chouteau subdivision of the Sarpy tract in 1850. An exchange deed between Jones and S. V. Papin dated September 8, 1851, noted that whereas Thomas Jones had mistaken his south line and built a house on said line and had no ingress or egress from said house, that Jones would give the southern 75 feet of the west half of his lot to Papin who, in turn, would give the north 75 feet of the east half of his lot to Jones.

And this explains why Swon avenue jogs at Sylvester. If it did not, the street would run through the house that Jones built, which is now 318 E. Swon.

Before he could enjoy his home, Jones was killed, in December 1851, while fording the River des Peres on Big Bend with a wagon load of lumber to be used in constructing his property. His widow married John Richardson, a widower, on January 29, 1852, and they settled down in the house with their families of children. The marriage was the second for the bridgroom but the fourth for the bride who had been married to a Mr. Soutar and a Mr. Schwartz before marrying Jones and Richardson.

Notes from the Kate Moody papers at the Missouri Historical Society record that when B. F. Webster bought the property which later became the Loretto Seminary and then Webster College, Mrs. Richardson asked him to "save the grounds of the old cemetery" near Big Bend and Selma, "because," she said, "I have some husbands buried there."

The area around this house was a dense forest, judging from a story told by William Kerruish, son-in-law of Mrs. Richardson. He came from St. Louis on Big Bend road one day, arrived at a point near Sylvester avenue, but became lost and was unable to see the house two blocks away. He was forced to wedge his way through the underbrush with his hands clasped in front of his face.

Travel on foot was hazardous, by horse and wagon it was rugged and railroads were in their infancy, but steamboats were having a heyday and many of the residents of that period had something to do with the booming business.

Richard J. Lockwood was one of those who succumbed to the lure of the river as a young man in St. Louis. He obtained a position on the Steamer Irene, a small sidewheeler built in 1837, which ran on the upper Mississippi from St. Louis to Galena and Dubuque. The Irene had the honor of carrying Henry Dodge to Fort Snelling to negotiate a

Home built by Captain Swon. Four generations of Smyth family, later owners.

treaty with the Chippewa Indians.

Lockwood's rise in the steamboat world was fast. He became a captain the first year and left the Irene to become master of the Government Dodge. In 1842 he formed a partnership with James B. Hill and established a chandlery located at 517 North Levee street.

In 1853, Lockwood purchased two lots from the Chouteau property and built a home on First street, which was changed to Lockwood avenue in 1858. The home is now a dormitory for nuns at Nerinx Hall. In 1866, the prosperous riverboat captain gave some of this ground for Emmanuel Episcopal Church.

Captain John Swon was another riverboat man for whom a street is named in Webster Groves. He was just 16 years old when he took a trip up the Missouri River to Council Bluffs and was so fascinated that he decided to make boating his livelihood. His guardian was the owner of the R.M. Johnson, named for himself, as well as the Thomas Jefferson and the Expedition.

In 1821, Swon became a clerk on the steamer Calhoun. In 1824, he built the Big Missouri, which was greeted on her arrival in St. Louis by a huge cannon firing a welcome. It was longer than any other boat seen at the St. Louis wharf up to that time and cost $45,000. Four months after her debut, she burned in a fire, a total loss. Undaunted, Captain Swon bought out the Alexander Scott and then the J.M. White, legendary for its speed. In 1848, he decided to build one more boat, the Alec Scott, like the Alexander Scott, named for a captain from whom he had obtained his training. A jingle of the day went:

Fire up my furnace and get my boiler hot
And I'll give you fifty dollars if you pass the Alec Scott.

Captain Swon sold the Alec Scott and retired at age 51. Friends bought a handsome sidewheeler and named it the J.C. Swon in his honor. In 1857, Swon bought property and built his home in Webster Groves.

The year 1857 was notable for the building of homes which have become a part of Webster Groves history. One was the house built by Chris Hawken of the rifle manufacturing family, which originally stood at 9442 Big Bend road and now is the Webster Groves Historical Society restoration on South Rock Hill road.

Chris, the eldest son of Jacob Hawken, worked for his father, joined the '49 gold rush to California and returned to this area to open a livery stable. He married Mary Ann Kincaid Eads, daughter of Granville Eads, and built the house as a copy of her family home. A large Federal style brick building, it was constructed with slave labor on land purchased for 25 cents an acre.

Another residence built in 1857 was that of John Helfenstein, reputedly a German baron, who came to St. Louis to work for wealthy fur trader, Robert Campbell, and then went into business with Stephen Gore in the firm of Helfenstein, Gore & Co., wholesale grocers and outfitters. He married Mary Ann Gore, retired at age 44 with a comfortable fortune and later became a vice president and director of the Citizens and Union Railway Co. The Helfensteins had six children.

The architect for their home at 135 South Rock Hill road was Robert E. Mitchell, one of the architects for St. Louis' Old Court House. According to story, a railroad spur was built to transport bricks and building materials to the location.

Land prices were going up in the area. A few years before, it had sold at "a buck and a bit" an acre. Now, lots such as the Helfensteins were bringing $10 an acre.

The Helfenstein home. General Grant sat there.

John Philip Helfenstein.

Helfenstein was a Union sympathizer during the Civil War period and a friend of Ulysses S. Grant. Lore has it that when Grant was eking out a living on the farm which he called Hardscrabble, he would stop by to visit Helfenstein on his trips delivering firewood. A tree which stood near the driveway was known for many years as Grant's Tree.

Augustus Moody's general store.

There were other scattered settlers throughout the area which one day would be known as Webster Groves. In 1853, Dr. William Brown subdivided his farm into Brown's place, north of Brown street (now Newport) to Marshall and from Yeatman to Lafayette. Bompart bisected this area north to south and Central (now Tuxedo) from east to west. Later this area became known as Tuxedo Park.

Apparently there were enough people to justify the opening of a general store, as Augustus Moody did. A sign atop the building advertised, "A. Moody & Son, Dry Goods & Provisions." Later on, this building contained the local post office, doctor's office and served as a railway depot. It was located on North Gore next to the Missouri Pacific Railway tracks.

The settlers of the 1850s made their contributions and left their mark on the community in various ways, but of all the early arrivals, the ones who left the most lasting effects were the members of the Marshall family of Fairfax, Maryland.

Chapter Three

Artemus Bullard's Dream

James Collier Marshall, a Maryland merchant, native Virginian, grandson of a leaseholder of Lord Fairfax, first came to St. Louis to visit a cousin in 1819. The cousin, George Collier, whose daughters married Henry and Ethan Allen Hitchcock, was in the shot manufacturing business and wanted Marshall to join him. Marshall told him he thought he'd stick to farming, but he was impressed by the beautiful rolling countryside in the St. Louis area.

He went back to Maryland, talked to his brother, John Marshall and their two widowed sisters, and his enthusiasm was so contagious that they sold their holdings and made the trip to Missouri by wagon to the Ohio River, by flatboat to the Mississippi and then up to St. Louis and out the Ozark trail to Dry Ridge.

They settled on a tract of land of about 800 acres and built a log building on Manchester road in which they lived and operated a store. In 1840, James married and, in 1841, he built a weatherboard home modeled after his Maryland home and named it "Fairfax" for that home. Today an office of an architectural firm, the building at 9430 Manchester road still has the name on the doorstep.

It became residence, place of business and also a stopping place for the stagecoach bound for Kansas City, and the first post office in the Rock Hill area. James and his wife, Elizabeth McCausland of Georgia, had five children. John Marshall married Cynthia Berry; they had no children.

The Marshall family property was bounded by Manchester on the north, Lockwood on the south, Rock Hill on the west and an area called Fairview on the east.

The conditions of these early grants of land were that the land was to be improved and used agriculturally. Actually, the Marshalls and most of the other early settlers were not farmers but businessmen who acted

Original Rock Hill Church, a gift of the Marshalls.

as overseers for their land. Slaves built their homes and tilled the soil; but the owners themselves had other types of business, in the Marshall's case, trading in furs and operating a store and supply center.

The early settlers in the Webster area were, for the most part, country people who found little to attract them in the gay social life of the French settlers in the city of St. Louis. They were also religious people and it was significant that one of the first acts of the Marshalls was to give three and a half acres of land for a church site, the building to be constructed from stone cut in the area, in the year 1845.

Slaves built this building, too. In the 100th anniversary program of the church, the story was told that the overseer of the slaves, a man named John White, went to Marshall and told him the slaves wanted to make a contribution to the building of the church. When told that they were contributing their services, White replied, "Yes sir, but that's our job. We want to do something on our own." And so they decided to work on Sundays to construct the roof of the church as their special gift.

The church was dedicated in August, 1845. It was the visiting clergyman, the Rev. Artemus Bullard, minister of First Presbyterian Church, then located at Fourth and St. Charles streets in St. Louis, who gave the church and the area its name. Mindful of the trip from St. Louis, he suggested the name Rock Hill. And so the church became Rock Hill Presbyterian Church, the area around there was known as Rock Hill and Old Military road became Rock Hill road.

The visiting minister was also impressed by the beautiful rolling countryside around Rock Hill. He had been in St. Louis since 1838 and had built First Presbyterian Church from a small struggling congregation into a strong vigorous group. He was a remarkable man in many ways.

Born in Northridge, Massachusetts June 3, 1802, Artemus Bullard was the son of a physician who indoctrinated his children with the idea of service to God and man. All three boys became ministers and the two girls married ministers, one of them Henry Ward Beecher, brother of Harriet Beecher Stowe.

Artemus Bullard attended Amherst and Andover and was licensed to preach in 1828. He became a pioneer in the Sunday School movement and traveled throughout New England, urging churches to organize schools for the children. In 1832, the American Board of Commissioners for Foreign Missions sent him to the Mississippi Valley where he worked until his call to First Church. Six feet tall, with premature white hair, he was an eloquent speaker and soon had a substantial following.

His heart was still with children and young people and, as he looked around this new wide open area, he conceived the idea of a school for boys and young men, living in the area. He was able to interest the Marshalls and Carlos G. Greeley, a St. Louis businessman, in the project with the result that the Marshalls agreed to donate land and Greeley to give $10,000 for a school building.

It was built on a hill overlooking the surrounding country and was named Webster College in honor of Daniel Webster of Boston whom Bullard greatly admired. The building still stands, now known as Rock House, a part of Edgewood Children's Center at 330 North Gore avenue.

Other backers of the school were Henry D. Bacon, for whom Bacon avenue was named, Edward Hale, Henry Barron, Dr. John Bates Johnson, Samuel Glover, William M. Morrison, Morris Collins, Samuel C. Davis, Edward G. Gay and John Simonds.

Old Rock House, once Artemus Bullard's Webster College.

In September 1854, an advertisement announced the opening of the school. Tuition rates were quoted at $6, $8 and $10 per term, "payable in advance." Faculty members were the Rev. David Dimond, the Rev. James Darrah and Mr. John Worth. Prospective students were advised that board, including washing, fuel, lights and room, could be obtained "in the homes of good families in the neighborhood at $3 and $4 a week."

The first four students were Arthur Armstrong, Henry Bullard, Thomas J. Carr and John E. Worth. The school flourished and soon there were 36 students in a preparatory and a college section. Teachers from the East were attracted, among them Edward Morehouse Avery, a Yale graduate and lawyer, who became a professor of mathematics at the college and married Sarah Robinson.

A new advancement speeded both the development of the community and the college. This was the Pacific Railroad, for which a right-of-way had been purchased in 1851.

There was a great deal of pressure for a railroad, not only locally but on a nation wide basis. Asa Whitney of New York, who had an interest in Oriental trade, came to Missouri to meet with a citizens committee of which Pierre Chouteau Jr. was a member, his purpose to urge the building of a railroad that would cross the continent. A St. Louis lawyer, Mr. Loughborough, who wrote for the Western Journal, was another early proponent of the railroad. The choice of route was advocated by W. R. Singleton, engineer for the Independent and Missouri River Railroad, who pointed out that the geology of the Meramec Ridge showed the existence of lead, copper and stone, and railroads were needed to transport these valuable products.

After many speeches and debates, the Missouri legislature granted a charter to the Pacific Railroad on March 2, 1849. Surveys were begun under the direction of James P. Kirkwood, as chief engineer, in 1850. The first spadeful of dirt was dug ceremoniously on July 4, 1851, and on May 6, 1853, the road was opened for travel to Kirkwood, the town which took its name from the railroad's engineer. The train also made stops at Rock Springs, Cheltenham, River des Peres, Laclede and Webster College.

The railroad made the trip to and from St. Louis so much easier and faster that it spurred interest in the purchase of land around Webster College. A letter from the Rev. Mr. Bullard in the Missouri Republican of November 29, 1854, told how the college was only a few hundred yards from the station and advised those having sons or wards wishing to attend, to place their application. Artemus Bullard's dream was taking shape.

The reality was short lived. The Pacific Railroad completed construction of its line to Jefferson City and a gala celebration was planned with many civic, political and religious dignitaries invited to take the first ride on a special excursion train on November 18, 1855. As the train was crossing the Gasconade River, the trestles, weakened by heavy rains, gave way and many passengers were hurled to their death, among them Artemus Bullard.

Webster College went along for a while without its founder, but internal dissension broke out and both Dimond and Darrah resigned. A catalog of 1857-58 lists Edward Avery as acting president. But a few years later, the unsettled conditions which led to the Civil War proved the final blow and the school was closed.

But if nothing else, Webster College established an area for the early development of the town and gave its name — the name of the railroad station — to that community. Some time later, it was learned that there was another Webster in the state and so, because of the luxuriant trees, the word Groves was added.

It would be many years before Webster Groves would be officially incorporated, but by 1860 there was a village, a railroad station and a number of families who lived there.

As an early account put it, "Soon others came to make their homes and to live in the midst of pleasant lawns and gardens."

Chapter Four

The Civil War Years

On July 4, 1861, a girl named Lucy Robinson rushed breathlessly to the home of a neighbor, William Plant, to tell him that some men had threatened to kill her father if he did not "take that flag down." "That flag" was the Stars and Stripes, the Union flag, and feeling was already running high.

Lucy's father was Frederick E. Robinson, known to his neighbors as Father Robinson. He was given this name because, as his obituary put it many year later, "for 70 years he served God among the poor. . . an illustrious example of the true philanthropist."

From 1850 to 1860, Robinson had lived in a log cabin but then he built a house which was known as The Ark on the location where the Webster Cinema, formerly the Ozark Theater, stands. His diary which came to light a few years ago through a great grandson, Kenneth Shoulberg, gave glimpses into the life of the community in the early pioneer 1850s and 60s, especially into the interdependence of families on one another and their great dependence on the fickleness of nature as they attempted to wrest a living from the land.

Robinson was a farmer and woodsman and many of his entries are simple and terse. On Saturday, March, 1859: "Went to city with load wood. Brought home sack corn, sack meal. Sold wood $2.50." On March 11: "Went to James Marshall's to breakfast. Made arrangements to go to the Spencers this evening. Plowed for Mr. Gore." Plowing was done with oxen and there was frequent exasperation expressed over yokes and plows which broke and over the hours spent rounding up the oxen. Robinson had hired men but these seemed to come and go with rapidity.

A sale at "the college," presumably Webster College, on Friday, June 17, elicited a disgusted reaction: "All the men came in from work and

Life was hard for Father Robinson.

"The Ark"... Robinson Home.

went to sale. One too drunk to get home and another so far gone as to hardly get to bed. I would here record my opinion that it will be a lasting reproach to college trustees for furnishing material to get bidders drunk and many availed themselves of the privilege."

On one of his rare trips to the city, he observed, "I leave the city frequently with the sincere wish that I may never again have occasion to return to it."

In November 1859, a pathetic series of entries related: "Ma taken with chill very sick," and a week later, "Ma died at 20 minutes past 5 a.m. Present were Mr. and Mrs. Moody, Mr. J. R., Lucy Armstrong and A. A. Barnard. Here let me record with gratitude the kindness of our neighbors generally but especially Mrs. Charles S. Rannals, Miss Mary Ruth Rannals, Mr. William H. Gore, Mrs. Gore's elder, younger, and Mrs. Liversmore. What shall I render unto God for raising up a host of friends in the hour of need?"

In contrast to Father Robinson's record, the journal kept by Kate W. Gore reveals the life of a sheltered woman for whom each day was "a rather pleasant day" or, sometimes, "not a very pleasant day." She, too, records prayer meetings and dinners at the Marshall home but there are skating parties, a trip East and several pages devoted to her French lessons, with the beginner phrases, "J'ai le bon pain. J'ai le bon sucre. Avez vous quelque chose de bon? J'ai rien de bon."

On the last page is a verse, "To Kate From HWP," who was going away but apparently hoped to return, judging from the last stanza:

> *We soon shall part to meet again*
> *To meet with joy once more.*
> *Oh say not then, farewell, dear Kate*
> *But only Au Revoir.*

Neither the Robinson nor the Gore diaries make reference to pre Civil War tensions, but the Kate Moody papers tell the story of the flag incident, which apparently become folklore in later years.

As she described the scene, William and Alfred Plant and some of their clerks marched over to the Robinson house. There they found a man on horseback, holding the horse of another man who was in the house.

Inside, Father Robinson stood on the narrow staircase with a carving knife, defending the passage way to the roof. Ordered to take down the flag, he refused and the men left but later word came that they would be back to "clean out" the Plants. The men prepared by picking up small stones to fire from a cannon. (The cannon, another story relates, was smuggled into Webster Groves in a hay wagon.) Nothing happened that evening but many came out to celebrate and "consecrate the place for liberty." The flag stayed up throughout the Civil War.

J. Collier Marshall, a descendant of James Collier Marshall, made a sentimental journey to Webster Groves in 1959 to present Rock Hill Presbyterian Church with a set of chancel fitments honoring his grandparents. It was an occasion for retelling tales he'd heard in his youth.

"I always told my wife who was a Virginian that the south was in error in not calling the War Between the States the Civil War as the north did," he told a newspaper reporter. "In this part of the country, neighborhood, friends and family were split asunder and that is Civil War."

Rock Hill Church was split asunder, according to Marshall. Just after the outbreak of the war, a divinity student, son of a Northern sympathizing family, returned home and was asked to speak from the pulpit. His sermon was such a strongly worded attack on slavery that, one by one, members of the congregation walked out until Grandfather Marshall stood up and said, "Frederick, stop. Stop now." The young man stopped, but many of those who had left the church never returned.

According to J. Collier Marshall, some of them formed the nucleus of the Webster Groves Presbyterian Church in 1866.

A happier story concerns the brother of the Rock Hill divinity student who also returned for a visit after he had joined the Federal Army. He had been a caller on Miss Mary, eldest daughter in the Marshall family, and customarily had been invited to the Marshall home for dinner each Sunday. This time, fearful of a snub from slave owner Marshall, he slipped into church late, listened to Miss Mary sing her solo and then left early and stood on the sidelines.

"Years later," said Collier Marshall in relating the story, "he told me how he stood there in an agony of fear as my grandfather came out of the church. Grandfather Marshall looked at the young man in uniform and said, 'Luther, I'm glad to see you. Aren't you coming to dine with us?' And not a word was said about the war."

Ernest Marshall, son of James and father of J. Collier Marshall, was still a boy when the elder Marshall died, leaving his wife little money, much land and 33 slaves. When the Emancipation Proclamation was signed, Mrs. Marshall freed her slaves and gave each one a tract of land on Shady avenue, now Kirkham road. It was the beginning of the black community in that area.

The college which the first Marshall had given did not last long after the death of its founder, the Rev. Artemus Bullard. During the war, it was an orphanage for soldiers' children, operated by the St. Louis Sanitary Commission. In 1869, the Commission offered to unite the orphanage with the St. Louis Protestant Orphans Asylum, founded in 1834 by Mrs. Ann Perry, a friend of Dr. Bullard's. The new institution was called the St. Louis Association of Ladies for the Relief of Orphan Children and provided for the children of settlers going west who died without providing for their families. Later it became known simply as The Protestant Orphans Home and many long-time Webster residents remember it by that name rather than its present one of Edgewood Children's Center.

Despite the turmoil of the war and post war years, many a family settled in the new suburban area. Two major subdivisions were Alfred Lee's subdivision off North Rock Hill road and Mary Gore's subdivision south of Lockwood from Gray to Elm with Swon as its south border. In 1868, the 40 acres east of Mary Gore was subdivided by F. L. Plant, creating Maple and Cedar avenues. In 1865, Nathan D. Allen built a fine home, now Mittelberg Gerber Funeral Home on Lockwood.

In 1867, a St. Louis lawyer, John Fulton, and his wife Mary acquired three acres from the Marshall family through William and Clementine

John Fulton, early settler.

Porter and built a home at 300 North Gore avenue. Fulton's obituary many years later described him as "one of the first St. Louisans to build a home and reside in Webster Groves." He was also an interpreter for the Mexican consul's office and a writer on Mexico.

Henry Prehn came to Webster Groves from Germany in 1857 to work for Edward M. Avery of the college. His daughter, Carrie, later recalled her father's description of Webster then as "a vast woods." In 1865, he bought land extending from Pacific to Kirkham along Gore for $500 and, in 1867, opened a country store.

Prehn served as a sergeant in the militia for home protection during the war and later was postmaster. Married twice, he had 10 children and Captain Tom Gibson's memoirs referred to Congregational Church prayer meetings as "Prehn meetings."

The other store in the area was that of Augustus Moody, who was killed by a mailbag thrown from a passing train in 1870. His son, S. A. Moody, continued in his business. A daughter, Carrie, married Charles Connon, a florist who built greenhouses along the Pacific tracks at North Gore in 1862.

Jotham Bigelow and Peers Griffin, cousins of the firm of Griffin and Bigelow, architects and builders, both built houses for themselves in this period, Bigelow on what is now Claiborne place and Griffin on College avenue.

Bigelow, the story goes, suffered financial losses and sold his house to Col. Nathaniel Claiborne, whose daughter Jennie married Robert McCormick Adams, grandson of the inventor of the McCormick reaper. They inherited the house, raised a large family there and for many years the residence was known as "the old Adams house."

Summer at the Alfred Lee home, circa 1887. Mrs. Alfred Lee (Sarah Gardner Thayer) with her daughters (left) Miss Mary Augusta Lee and (right) Miss Ellen Barbara Lee, (later Mrs. Louis F. Booth, Sr.). At front left is Cousin Norah who, with her infant daughter guarded on the horse by the family yard man, had come to visit in healthful Webster Groves, away from New Orleans' annual yellow fever epidemic.

A handsome home was built by Edward and Nancy Jackson, at the head of Jackson lane, now 133 Gray avenue. It is dated 1868. During the war, Jackson was a member of the St. Louis militia. One night, coming home from church, he tried to stop some soldiers from fighting a Negro and in the fracas was struck a blow which took the sight of one eye.

Other homes built in this 1860s period include the Alfred Lee house, 519 Lee, the William D. Butler home, 5 Marshall place, the A.B.M. Thompson home on Thompson place, the Leverett Mills home, 19 E. Lockwood, the house at 621 Lee which later belonged to Dr. Henry Barron and houses at 524 Lee, 55 Marshall place and 465 Foote avenue.

The extent of involvement in the war is indicated by the number of stories, none too well documented but all fascinating, about the underground railroads for runaway slaves. The Fulton house, Helfenstein house and others in the vicinity have been described throughout the years as sites for underground activities. The owner of the Fulton house at 300 North Gore was surprised one evening in the 1950s by a small boy who asked for permission to examine the basement. He walked around, tapped on walls and finally admitted he had heard about the underground railroad and was seeking traces of it.

Fact or fiction as these stories may be, Webster Groves was involved in both sides of the war and the reliving of the fighting went on for many years. Many of the German born were Northern sympathizers and fought under Gen. Franz Sigel of the Union Army. It was the custom in later years for one German meeting another to ask, "Fit you mit Sigel?"

Captain Tom Gibson told of William Yaeger, one of Sigel's men who loved to reminisce and, in his stories, had killed more Southerners than anyone on the Northern side. In memory, he would charge up a hill, black with the enemy, and with his trusty bayonet would clear the hillside so the rest of the Army could come up.

"I remember once," wrote Gibson, "that Fritz Schneeburger said to him when he was in the gory stages of his reminiscences, 'Uncle Bill, you had better stop now and take some of those Rebels off of your bayonet so you can keep on using it.' "

But that was many years later, when the war had become legend and a subject for jesting. While it was going on, it was serious, deadly serious, and, near the end, simply deadly.

A letter to Kate Gore from Frederick Bone, who had been a Sunday School pupil of hers, deplored the conduct of the soldiers as he saw it:

"Cussing, stealing, drunkenness are constantly seen and heard. I thought it strange that men should ever .become lost to all that is good. . . . Yesterday the news arrived of the fall of Charleston . . . The soldiers all hope that the war will end soon."

Chapter Five

Churches—The First Four 1866

"Webster had churches before it had public schools — another illustration of the character of the people." This observation was made by Velma Benner in her history of Webster Groves, published in 1950.

Actually, the two institutions were fairly contemporary, the churches in 1866, the first school board in 1868. Four churches shared the honor of being first, the First Congregational Church, now United Church of Christ, the Webster Groves Presbyterian Church, Emmanuel Episcopal Church and First Baptist Church. All four participated in a glorious centennial "service of witness" at Memorial Field on Sunday, May 29, 1966.

Two of them, the Congregational and the Presbyterian, were formed by members of Rock Hill Presbyterian Church, in part out of tensions arising over Civil War issues, in part from sheer geographic necessity. The statement dated January 31, 1866, by the Congregational Church founders begins:

"Whereas it having been for some time the opinion among several of the Christian brethren at Webster Groves that a Church should be organized near the Depot in order to better accommodate its growing population. . . ."

A statement clearly indicating that the residents in the settlement around the Pacific Railroad station were finding it increasingly difficult, especially in severe winter weather, to travel over Church road (North Gore) and Rock Hill road by carriage or wagon or, in many cases, on foot, to the church on Manchester road.

Early in 1865, John P. Helfenstein, Robert P. Studley and William Plant jointly erected a small frame building just south of the station and began a private school for their children, taught by a Mrs. Margaret Nevius and Miss Sarah Mills. The building was offered to Rock Hill Presbyterian Church for a branch Sunday school and for prayer meetings but the offer was declined on the grounds that it was "so far from the present center, it might lead to a subdivision" of their society.

In an early church history, Alfred Plant, brother of William, wrote:

"In this same winter of 1865, on a Sunday morning, a party of five or six men, among them William Plant, R. P. Studley, Charles Connon, William Porter, James Martling and Alfred Plant, were ascending from the then deep hollow, up the steep Rock Hill road on the north side of College Hill. While conversing about the long and tiresome walk and the growing difficulty of getting all the families from about the station to Sunday school and church and regretting that the Rock Hill Presbytery declined to do anything to relieve the situation, one of them exclaimed, 'Why not form a Congregational church?' Another replied, 'That is just what I have been thinking,' and another said, 'I can join such a church.'

As Plant continued, it was discovered simultaneously that the same thought had been in many minds. "There were as many as three denominations represented in this group and another not a professing Christian, but out in the forests of Webster Groves, they proposed to organize a Congregational church."

At that time, the Studleys were living in a two-story log house near the site of what is now Nerinx Hall. Charles Connon was living in a cabin east of the Connon greenhouses with his father-in-law, Augustus Moody, near Church (Gore) and Pacific avenues. William Plant had built a barn on the site of what is now the Masonic Temple and had fitted it as a temporary dwelling.

Their choice of denomination indicates something of the political persuasions of these men, since Congregationalism was not too welcome in many parts of Missouri. Many Missourians with Southern sympathies looked with disapproval on an institution which was thought to be a propagator of free thought, loose views and most heinous of all, promoters of abolitionism. The Rev. Dr. Ervine Inglis once said the founders had been known as "black abolitionists."

Apparently the winter months solidified their resolve, for in late January a covenant was signed by Plant, Connon, his wife Caroline, Jane A. Martling, Studley and his wife Mary, James and Margaret Monroe and Porter and his wife, Clementine.

Only two months after this statement, the First Presbyterian Church of

Webster Groves was established on March 29, 1866. On October 12, 1866, the cornerstone was laid for Emmanuel Episcopal Church and later that year, in the black community on Shady (Kirkham) avenue, the First Baptist Church was established.

"Thus 1866 became a significant year in the religious history of the community," wrote Sylvia Stevens Schmid in the centennial history of First Congregational Church, "with the establishment of four churches which still exist and which, from the beginning, have exemplified the ecumenical spirit of Christian unity and brotherhood."

On February 18, 1866, the first public worship of the new First Congregational Church of Webster Groves was held in Chapel Grove Seminary with 42 present. The sermon was preached by Dr. Julian M. Sturtevant, president of Illinois College. This small frame chapel stood under massive oak trees on Lockwood, opposite what is now Jefferson road. Later a bell tower was built and a bell, in part the gift of employes of the Plant Brothers seed store, was installed to call worshippers to service. The bell is still in use.

At the first Sunday school session on March 25, 1866, a Sabbath hymn book was adopted, a communion service was ordered, and a committee appointed to assist the black people living nearby in acquiring a lot for a meeting house. On April 2, 1866, the ten members of the church subscribed $1350 for a minister's salary and expenses and $2775 toward a parsonage to be built on five acres of land donated by Mr. and Mrs. Alfred Plant, at Gray and Swon avenues. William Plant gave $2500 for the parsonage building. In that first year, $11,343 came into the treasury of the small group. The first minister was the Rev. H. M. Grant.

William Plant did not live to see the parsonage completed. He died at age 46 and his close friend, Robert P. Studley, took over the leadership of the church. The Plant property on the northeast corner of Jefferson road and Swon avenue is now a bird sanctuary.

The Congregational Church withstood many adversities in its early years, including two financial crashes in the 1870s which reduced both membership and treasury.

A new pastor, the Rev. James Cruikshank, came in 1871 but by 1874 there was no pastor, only visiting ministers. During this time the first wedding was held in the new church, that of Mr. and Mrs. Stanley Wheat. The story is told that relatives and friends were gathered for the service, the bride and bridesmaids arrived but where was the groom? And the flowers which he was to bring?

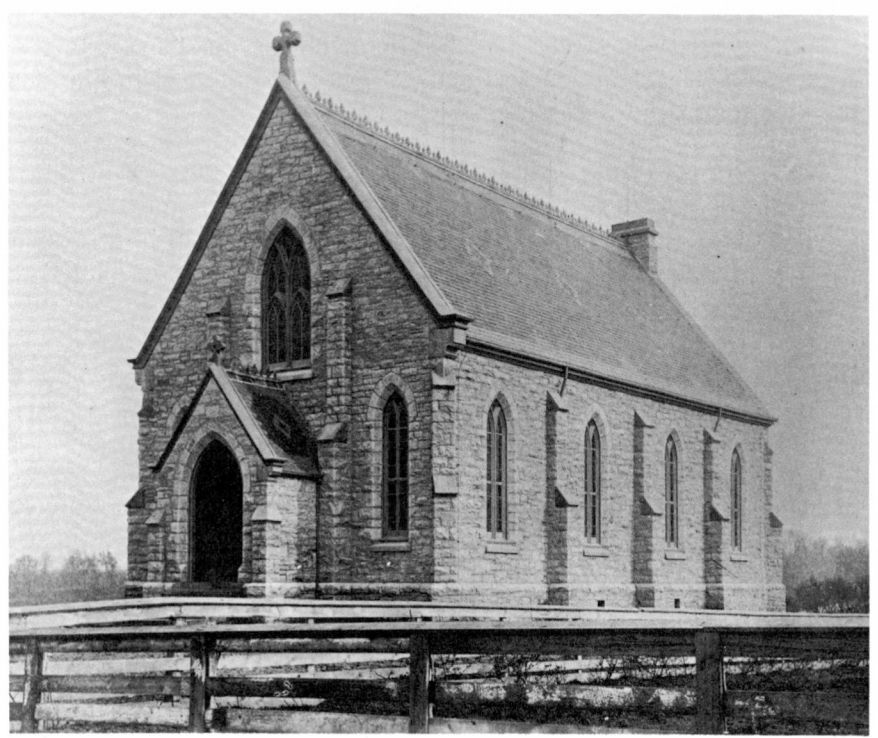

First Congregational Church of Webster Groves, 1870.

The father of the bride said he'd go down the road and see if perhaps he was coming up from the station, as the train whistle had blown half an hour ago. Sure enough, he found a very flustered bridegroom hurrying toward the church. The "Railroad War" of the time had resulted in the curtailing of commuter service and orders from the general manager of the Missouri Pacific to eliminate Webster as a regular stop. The bridegroom had signaled for a special stop but the conductor said he had his orders and the first stop would be Kirkwood. The frantic young man hired a rig to drive him back to Webster Groves.

By 1878, the railroad problems began to drive people back to the city and the situation had its effect on the churches. The Rev. Robert Kerr, minister at that time, tried to get by on his salary of $1200 a year, and records show that he "cleaned and darned a discarded old hat himself and bound it with an old silk necktie in order to appear without shame at meetings." His children and wife could not attend services because they lacked shoes. Finally the church had to tell Mr. Kerr they could no longer pay a fixed salary and he left.

A $6000 debt was slowly paid until only $2300 indebtedness remained. At a meeting in January, 1880, Alfred Plant offered the resolution, "Resolved that we now proceed to pay the debt." A committee of five went to work and a year later the church was free from debt. Apparently this was with help from the other churches as minutes of a meeting at that time state:

"We wish to record our thanks to our Episcopal, Baptist and Presbyterian friends who have, in this case, proved again that church walls and sectarian partitions are no barrier to the overflow of Christian love and sympathy."

The membership grew; in 1883 a manse was erected on what is now the site of City Hall, and a reading room in the Moody Building on Church and Lockwood provided "a place for men to go of an evening instead of a saloon."

Memoirs of Miss Carrie Prehn told of a pipe organ installed by the B. F. Websters in memory of their son, Benny, that Miss Carrie Allen was the first regular organist and that Professor Otten, director of the St. Louis Symphony Orchestra, formed a "singing school" for the first choir, with a quartette composed of Franklin Knight, William Jager, William Rhodes and Clarence Becker. Miss Prehn also recalled her first Sunday School teacher, Mrs. James F. Allen, who would frequently say, "It is not enough to be good – we should be good for something."

Many ministers and moderators guided First Church, as its members call it, through the years. Among the ministers were the Rev. Charles L. Kloss, 1898-1904 and 1911-17; The Rev. Dwight Bradley, 1920-29; the Rev. George M. Gibson, 1930-38; the Rev. Dr. Ervine P. Inglis, 1939-62; the Rev. Dr. Martin L. Goslin with the Rev. A. Greig Ritchie, the Rev. Edward Nolting and the Rev. John Thompson, 1962-65; and since 1966, the Rev. Paul R. Davis as senior minister, assisted by the Rev. Floyd Davidson and the Rev. Gerald O'Connor; and, at the present time, the Rev. Charles A. Rota and the Rev. Robert D. Mutton.

First Church was the setting for two widow-widower romances in the clergy. In 1954, Dr. Ervine Inglis was married to Mrs. Frances Littlefield, and in 1967, the Rev. Floyd Davidson was married to Mrs. Peg Coffman; in the latter case, it was a real family wedding with the bride's son, the Rev. Ford Coffman performing the ceremony, the ring designed by her daughter, Nan Knight, and other children of the pair as attendants.

The Webster Groves Presbyterian Church has a similar story of establishment in the days of 1866, when, as one of their histories puts it, "To the little stone church (Rock Hill Presbyterian) led a dirt road over which zealous Christians trudged or rode in horsedrawn vehicles on each Sabbath Day. Of the one hundred people scattered through this little wooded hamlet, sixteen met in the home of Mrs. Martha Moody (southwest corner of Gore and Pacific avenues) and prepared a petition for presentation to the Presbytery of St. Louis on March 8, 1866, asking for the organization of this church." The petitioners were: Edward M. Avery, Sarah R. Avery, Edwin Barnard, Charity Barnard, Maria Moody, Martha E. Moody, Mary Gore, Katharine M. Gore, George B. Parsell, Mary S. Hamilton, Horace Wright, Esther D. Wright, Arthur McBirney, William Kerruish, Mary Kerruish and Malissa Watson.

The Presbytery granted the petition and appointed a commission with the Rev. Henry A. Nelson, pastor of the First Presbyterian Church in St. Louis as Chairman. The commission met in Chapel Grove Seminary, the same building used by the Congregational brethren, and constituted a church with the charter members listed above and ten others: Sarah F. McCracken, Leverett H. Mills, Sophia G. Mills, Sarah Mills, Charles W. Mills, Sarah M. Mills, William M. Pierce, M. F. Pierce, Martha Parsell and Cyrus E. Robinson.

Services were held in homes until a lot was obtained and a church built. The first building, which faced "Lockwood's Road" was a frame structure with two octagonal towers and was built in 1866 largely by manual labor of the congregation. The first regular pastor, the Rev. Raphael Kessler, was installed September 15, 1867, and William Groshon and Edwin Ticknor were consecrated as deacons.

In 1890, the church building was destroyed by fire of unknown cause. A new stone church costing $25,000 was erected in 1891, a building which later became the chapel of the church.

Early ministers were the Reverends James J. Marks, Ormund Wright, Jr., Howard Nixon, William L. McEwan, H. A. Hymes and W. H. Bates. Then, on February 20, 1902, began the long and fruitful ministry of the Rev. Dr. David Miller Skilling. Under his leadership, the membership grew from its initial 200 to 2000, a manse was purchased, a large sanctuary built and what was a village church became one of the nation's leading Presbyterian congregations.

In 1935, Dr. Skilling tried to retire but the congregation unanimously rejected the request. In 1937 he became minister emeritus. On Sunday, March 23, 1941, the church observed Dr. Skilling's fiftieth anniversary

PRESBYTERIAN CHURCH OF WEBSTER GROVES.
ORGANIZED, MARCH 29TH, 1866, WITH 25 CHARTER MEMBERS.
CHURCH BUILDING ERECTED, APRIL. 1867.
DESTROYED BY FIRE, MARCH 1ST, 1890.
FIRST PASTOR—REV. R. KESSLER, 1867 TO 1872.
REV. J. J. MARKS, D. D., 1873 TO 1875.
REV. O. WRIGHT, 1876 TO 1877.
REV. P. H. K. McCOMB, 1877 TO 1887.
REV. J. H. NIXON, D. D., 1888

of ordination and its own seventy-fifth anniversary.

His successor was another much loved minister, the Rev. Dr. Harry T. Scherer, who led the church for twenty more years of growth. His successor, the Rev. Dr. Reuben Field Pieters, had his ministry cut short by his own untimely death in 1958, a year after he came to Webster.

"In each instance of a change of minister," said one member of Webster Presbyterian, "we were sure we would never find another of the stature of the man who was leaving, but in each instance, God supplied us with a leader who came into our church and into our hearts."

The next minister was an outstanding speaker and writer, the Rev. Dr. George E. Sweazey, for a time national Presbytery moderator. His assistants were the Rev. Dr. C. C. Carnahan and the Rev. Donald Weems. The present staff consists of the Rev. Dr. Daniel C. Thomas, with associates, the Reverends Donald J. Barnes, Thom H. Hunter and John Spangler.

On New Year's Day 1958, the church and all Webster suffered a loss when the Elizabeth Holloway Woods Memorial chapel portion of the church was destroyed by fire. But it was repaired and this cloud had a silver lining, too. An old bell, found sealed off, was brought back into service and pealed out on New Year's eve of 1959.

Both of the first two churches of Webster have been noted for their music and for the high caliber of musical leadership and participation. At First Congregational, Miss Esther Replogle, the dynamic director of the Webster Groves High School choral work, was choir director for many years. At Webster Groves Presbyterian Church, Alfred Lee Booth started as organist when he was, in his own description, a "22 year old stripling who, with the nerve of youth, stepped in where angels would have feared to tread." He was to remain at the post for more than fifty years. A composer as well as musician, Alfred Lee Booth wrote the Webster High Alma Mater song while he was a student there, collaborated with F. Scott Fitzgerald on the Princeton Triangle Show, and wrote a special centennial hymn for the four-church observance in 1966.

Webster Presbyterian also has had an active choir director in Mrs. W. F. (Gene) Symes, whose husband was a soloist at the Congregational church; and in many fine soloists through the years, among them two well known radio-television performers, Bob Hille and Nancy St. James.

Its musical productions have been memorable, among them "Amahl and the Night Visitors," and "Noye's Fludde" with its animals, two by two.

Office workers, caretakers and cooks have had long time, distinguished careers as important in their spheres as the occupants of the pulpits, and many of them have been honored in church histories. Miss Orpha

Kendrick, for instance, was the much loved secretary of both the Presbyterian and Congregational churches at different times. Ken Holaday has been a long time pillar of strength at "First Church".

Mattie Wilkins, for many years janitress at First Church is pictured in their history. The Presbyterian annals make special mention of Raymond Wilkinson who died on duty in his fortieth year as caretaker of their church and Josephine Elazer who served for twenty-nine years as kitchen manager. And each church has its own long honor roll of laity.

Emmanuel Episcopal Church had one family above all others to name in its centennial history – the Lockwoods. Richard J. Lockwood and his second wife, Angelica Peale Robinson, had built a summer home in Webster in 1853. (His first wife, Jane Morrison, died giving birth to their son, William.) On a stroll one evening in 1857, they chose a knoll and promised themselves that some day they would build an Episcopal church there. The nearest Episcopal churches at that time were at 17th and Olive street in St. Louis and Grace Episcopal Church in Kirkwood.

It was almost 10 years before they could keep their promise because of the financial panic of 1858 and the hard years of war. But by 1866 their fortunes had improved and they gave the job of planning a church building to Henry Isaacs, with Mrs. Lockwood's expressed hope that the church would be similar to the one in Shepherdstown, Virginia where she had grown up.

A tin box sealed in the cornerstone contained a Bible, a Prayer Book, the Southern Churchman, the Missouri Republican, and currency and coins of the day. A bell in the tower was inscribed for Jane Lockwood, their small daughter, and a metal cross atop the church was made to be just her height at that time.

The new building was consecrated a year after the cornerstone laying, on October 24, 1867, by Bishop Hawks. The first rector was Philip Nelson Meade, who served first as layreader and was just 21 when he began his official duties in 1871. He married Mrs. Sallie Daggett, a member of the Rannells family who were on the first communicant list of the church. Rannells avenue is in Maplewood today and it is assumed that families came from this distance to attend church. In addition, Mr. Meade started a mission near "Georgetown," now the Affton-Sappington area, and held monthly services there.

Emmanuel Episcopal Church, 1867.

Mr. Meade left in 1872 and the Rev. George K. Dunlop of Kirkwood's
Grace Church came to help with weekly services, a generous gesture
when one considers that he had his own growing parish, missions in
Eureka, St. James and Rolla and a family of nine children! A full time
minister, the Rev. John Gregson arrived in August of that year, and in
December the Church News announced the completion of the new
rectory, built on a lot given by Mrs. Lockwood along with $1000

toward the cost of building. The parish at that time had twenty-six families.

The Rev. Algeron Batte followed, and a Ladies Aid Society was organized. During Lent, weekday services were held in the rectory as they could not afford to heat the church and Mrs. Batte, state early records, should be given special commendation as she welcomed the congregation, muddy feet and all, into her parlor.

A theological student, Charles H. Gauthier, spent two years at the early Emmanuel and contributed this little gem to church annals, a letter to Church News dated December 15, 1881:

"To the Editor, Church News: I come demanding satisfaction. The cause is this. My family and self had been spending the day of Thanksgiving last at the residence of one of those hospitable families whom God hath raised up to care for poor ministers, when on approaching the rectory its windows seemed all ablaze with 150 candle power. One of the noble order of Vestry pretended to arrest me . . . I enter the gate and a burly Presbyterian meets me. I am carried into my parlor. The din deafens. More Presbyterians, a 'right smart' sprinkling of Congregationalists, Methodists, Christians and Baptists. . . . The Episcopalians were outnumbered 2 to 1. Besides the assistants appeared all armed with ammunition in plenty. What could a poor deacon do? Now the batteries began to play: pickled tongue, corned beef, peaches and tomatoes, sugar, tea and coffee, preserves with sundry lots of flour and crisp greenbacks. Our poor table used only to frugal johnny cake and purest rain water (!) fairly groaned beneath such fowl proceedings such as chickens, turkey, ducks, cake and jellies. There fell into my hands most of the camp-equipage, all the ammunition and a big bundle of loving kindness unmeasurable, and may God bless all such beleaguers. 'He that hath pity upon the poor lendeth unto the Lord and what he layeth out it shall be paid him again.' And now Mr. Editor, I ask you to publish this that the world may know the ways of Webster Groves, and the struggle of, Very truly yours, Charles H. Gauthier, Missionary."

Gauthier finished building the church at Affton, started a Sunday School at Glendale and held some services called Cottage readings. He was called "that zealous and earnest Christian," in notes of the time. Unfortunately, from an Episcopalian point of view, he came to a sad end, as Bishop Robertson's Journal of 1884 notes that he had left the ministry and was working with the Congregationalists, and concludes, "Have to depose him." Ecumenicity had its limits.

The rectors who followed were C. E. D. Griffith, 1883 - 1887; G. H.

Sterling, 1887-1894; Jefferson Davis Ritchey, 1894-1900; J. M. Northrup, 1900-1902; J. Courtney Jones, 1903-1931; J. Manly Cobb, 1931-1942; James M. Lichliter, 1942-1954; Alfred B. Seccombe, 1954-1961; Pitt S. Willand, 1961-1966; Esty Denkinger, 1966-1972; and Robert Skinner, 1972 to the present time.

The musical history of Emmanuel began again with the Lockwood family. Their daughter, Mrs. George Robinson was the first organist, followed by her daughter and later her son. Another daughter, Angelica Robinson Jenkins wrote in later years that there was a small cabinet organ and no regular choir but everyone who could "turn a tune" was expected to gather around the organ and sing the hymns and chants.

"Sometimes my sister would be a little late and we had to manage the opening hymn without her. But when it came to the Venite, we would give despairing glances toward the door. Could we possibly manage the Venite without the organ? But we never had to try, for she always came breathlessly in at the last second, and, needing no notes, started just in time."

The Church News of 1889 announced that a new $2000 organ would be in position for Easter services, the biggest and best in the state. This organ had to be pumped by a boy and Mrs. Jenkins tells of one named Peter who would "sometimes forget to work the bellows while he gazed out upon the lawn."

William Jenkins, organist and choir director from 1899 to 1903, kept a scrapbook. One clipping lists choir members, among them two longtime churchgoers, Percy Ludlow and Adah Straszer. Miss Straszer who was 17 when she joined the choir in 1898 lives at the Old Folks Home in Kirkwood, is bright as a button and well remembers her days in the choir and the fact that her mother, a Methodist, wasn't too approving when her daughter accepted an invitation to sing and later joined the church. Miss Straszer became a school teacher the same year, taught in Webster schools, many other states and finally, just before retirement, at Kirkwood's Nipher Junior High.

Jenkins' son, Gordon, well known Hollywood musician, later paid tribute to Emmanuel Church and its bell in one of the sequences of his composition, "Seven Dreams."

Since 1958, Emmanuel members have used a chalice made of old silver donated by parish members from teething rings to candle sticks, all melted down by Webster craftsman Dwight Dillon. Since 1949, a self supporting day nursery school has been in existence. Long time employees at Emmanuel have included Page Wright Aydlette and

Louise Ewing. This church, too, has sent many missionaries and young people out into the world to follow Emmanuel's early teachings.

Records of First Baptist Church note that it was established "on the Third Lord's Day in November, 1866," at a location just west of North Gore on Kirkham, then Shady avenue. There were just nineteen members; among the founders were William Wright, Allen Brown, Mrs. Allen Brown and Mrs. Louise Bolden. Mr. and Mrs. Allen contributed $25 toward the building.

Early pastors were the Reverends Simon, Lott, Burton, Cartwright, Carruthers, Lyles, Langford, Thompson, Cole and Purnell. In the fall of 1914, the Rev. E. J. Buckner began his pastorate of four years and during this time the church began to grow. In 1919, he was succeeded by the Rev. R. E. Lee. At this time a baptistry was installed and the original church was remodeled.

Most of the members lived so far from the church that they found it difficult to attend, and so on October 15, 1923, the present location at 159 E. Kirkham was purchased. The Rev. and Mrs. Lee paid the first note of $100 on the new building. Sadly, this pastor preached only one sermon in the new church, on Easter Sunday, 1929. He was stricken with illness and never recovered.

The Rev. J. L. Cohron took over and worked under great difficulties as the depression of the 1930s had an effect on the economy of the church, too. In September 1942, he was succeeded by the Rev. J. J. Blackburn as interim pastor until the Rev. W. D. Thompson Jr. came in December 1942. Under his guidance, membership increased with high attendance and in 1949 the church paid off its property debt.

The associate pastor, the Rev. J. A. Hill, served as interim pastor when the Rev. Mr. Thompson left, until July 1951 when the Rev. Neal J. Haynes came to the church, first as part time and, a year later, as full time pastor. The Rev. Mr. Haynes told the church they must carry forth their plan to build a greater sanctuary for the Lord, and urged them to, "Attempt great things, expect great things."

All branches of the church cooperated. Mrs. Christine Stepney and Mrs. Fannie Beasley, women's chairmen; R. A. James, men's chairman, worked to bring the sanctuary to reality. Ground breaking ceremonies were held June 14, 1954 and on May 17, 1955, the congregation marched into the new edifice, singing "We're Marching to Zion" and offering prayers and praises.

First Baptist Church, as it appears today

The mortgage on the church was burned in May 1958. In 1964, through the sale of gold seal bonds, a second unit over Fellowship Hall was financed with the help of 56 members whose names were written in the church remembrance book in gold ink.

In the church's ninety-eighth year, the names of the oldest living members – Mother Cornelia St. James and Mr. George V. Walker–were recorded, the youngest member being Debra Hollis. In 1965, the oldest woman member was Mother Consuela Austin.

In the church's centennial year, the Rev. Mr. Haynes served as pastor of the day at the four-church celebration. In 1969, Pastor Haynes was honored by the men of the church by being sent on a tour of the Holy Lands and came back to share his observations and pictures with the congregation.

In 1975, First Baptist Church sent its pastor as a missionary to Africa, the first black church of St. Louis County to participate in such mission work. In September 1975, during the National Baptist convention, its foreign mission board awarded a plaque to First Baptist Church for its pastor's work.

In later years, a total of 27 churches were in operation in Webster Groves, but these four – First Congregational, Webster Groves Presbyterian, Emmanuel Episcopal and First Baptist – were the pioneer churches with a special place in Webster's history.

Chapter Six

The Schools — 1868

"Throughout the hundred years of the School District of Webster Groves, there has been a peculiar bond between the school and the community. Typically the residents of the school community have been people who valued education, and who have expected a special quality of excellence from their schools."

George W. Brown, superintendent of schools, wrote those words for the history, "100 Years, 1868-1968." They succinctly state one of the factors that makes Webster Groves a very special place.

This rapport began on August 25, 1868 when a group of citizens met at the Missouri Pacific Railway Depot to discuss the possibility of organizing a school district. The notice for the meeting read: "The qualified voters of the village of Webster Groves, St. Louis County, State of Missouri, are requested to meet at the railroad depot on Tuesday, August 25, 1868, at 7½ o'clock p.m. to decide by ballot, for or against the adoption of the proposition of chapter 47 of the general school laws of the state as amended March 17, 1868." The notice was signed by John Keller, Charles Connon, William B. Butler, August Moody, John Percival, M. S. Gerould, William M. Kinney, Frank Stark, Henry Prehn, F. B. Howe, T. L. Slocum, W. D. Allen, William Porter, Anton Stadelmann and John M. Fulton.

Following the unanimous vote to organize, Allen, Butler, Connon, Slocum, Porter and H. B. Thompson were elected to the first Board. At its initial meeting in September, the Board directed that a census be taken of all children; the census reported that there were 225 white children over 5 and under 21 years of age, and 30 black children of the same age.

T. L. Slocum resigned from the board to become the first teacher at a salary of $1400 a year. Miss Augusta Murfelt was employed at $550 a year, and Miss Emma Babcock, a white teacher, volunteered to donate

Webster Room 5, 1889.

Webster School, later Bristol

her services to teach the black children and was paid money for her transportation. These three began teaching on October 11 in quarters leased from the Congregational Church.

In March 1869, the board moved to have citizens meet to discuss a school building and a one percent tax rate was established. The Board accepted William H. Gore's offer of a lot of over an acre for $1600 and made a $300 downpayment, the remainder to be paid in 90 days at 8 per cent interest. In 1870, the total bill was presented. Including the cost of the lot, it came to $12,570.45. This sizeable sum included desks, blackboards and the grading of the lot.

It was called the Webster School and was a grade school with, later, two years of high school. Bristol School stands on its site today. As the number of students increased, additional space was required and rented quarters were used in the Congregational Church, the Bristol Building and the Brannon Building.

Geographically the district grew, too, from its small core area. In 1901, it took in the Old Orchard School District, which brought in Shrewsbury, the Old Orchard School (Lockwood) and the Tuxedo Park School (Avery). Old Orchard (Lockwood) classes had been held in a frame building near Big Bend and Laclede Station roads from 1868 to 1890 when a brick building was erected. In 1909, a new school was built on Newport and Page.

Avery began as the Tuxedo Park private school at the home of Mrs. Gilbert Fox on Forest avenue. A four room frame building was built on the Avery farm at 909 Bompart avenue, and in 1902, a four room brick building was added. In 1915, another addition went on. In early days, mothers of pupils sent hot food for the teachers' lunches, delivering it by walking carefully over the board sidewalks which led to the schools.

Douglass school classes were first held in a room on a lot west of First Baptist Church, with a Mrs. Dotwell teaching. School was at that time dismissed during the harvest season but remained in session for nine months. When the school district took charge, Miss Emma Babcock began teaching and in 1870, the first black teacher, a Mr. Busch, was appointed. In 1872, the school board rented more space for the growing school. Teachers from 1872 to 1890 are listed in early records as: Mrs. Swayner, Mr. Masterly, Mr. Perry Momatt, Mr. Needle, Mr. Mitchell, Mr. Morris, Mr. Johnson, Mrs. Clancey and Mrs. Jennie Davis. Mrs. Davis resigned in 1883 to become a missionary to Africa.

The school building burned in 1890 and temporary classes were held in

Douglass High School class, 1910. Thomas Moore, teacher.

the Baptist Church. A school law held that teacher contracts could not be legally issued if a school had burned, so teachers were employed without contracts until a school was built in 1892. A building was erected; the first principal was Mr. Agee.

At the request of school patrons in 1895, the name of the school was established as Douglass, for Frederick Douglass, a Maryland slave who escaped and attained fame as an anti-slavery orator. He was present at Lincoln's inauguration reception and later became minister to Haiti. Later Douglass High School was added and teen-agers came from towns as far away as Ferguson and House Springs to attend.

Goodall was the second of the original Webster schools. First called Selma School, it was later Mark Twain and then was renamed for Margaret M. Goodall, principal of the school from 1917 to 1929. Plans for its erection were laid March 20, 1896.

Tom Chestnut, who was developing a subdivision named for his daughter, Selma, sold the site. Mrs. H. D. Viser was the first teacher at a salary of $40 a month. Later Selma DeYong was hired at $55 and Sallie Watson at $45 a month.

The school was a four room frame building. Outside the door was a wooden bucket filled with cistern water and a dipper from which everyone drank. Early students remembered the teacher who fell in love with a farmer who plowed the field behind the school. Each day she would step to the window and shyly wave her handkerchief. The story had a happy ending! they were married.

In 1911 Goodall's new building was put up. For many years, these five schools made up the Webster Groves school system but then the district was increased to take in territory on its borders and with this move came the other schools in the district: Washington Park in 1940, Schall and Hudson in 1948, Clark School in 1949 and Edgar Road School in 1951. The Bristol Primary School was added in 1955.

The high school increased in size and status from its original one room in the original frame school and its makeshift quarters in the Bristol Building and Brannon Building, on Gore, north of the Missouri Pacific tracks.

Women's lib made itself known in Webster Groves many years before it was a national movement, even before the suffragette activities which led to the nineteenth amendment. The high school bond issue election of 1901 was a battle of the sexes, men against women.

"The women desired a new high school building," a story in the St. Louis Post-Dispatch, October 2, 1901 related. "The men objected to an addition to the present high rate of taxation. The men won."

The newspaper account admitted, however, that Webster's first high school teacher, Miss Sarah Milligan, had made a "masterly speech" in favor of additional facilities. Her words set off a "petticoat push" which let to "pretty women in pretty gowns" working all day, bringing voters to the polls in their traps and surreys. By noon, all the votes were in that could be brought in until the men returned from St. Louis on the evening trains. The account relates, "During the afternoon, the clerks and judges took naps, played checkers and drank soda pop."

Despite the petticoat push, the issue was defeated twice. Finally a contract was let for the new high school facilities in December 1905. The new school, built in 1906, consisted of a two story brick building with three classrooms and an auditorium which was used for a study hall. Six teachers including the principal, George L. Hawkins, made up the faculty. Mr. Hawkins taught six classes daily and supervised the study hall.

Principal Hawkins' daughter, Helen (Mrs. Paul A. Pickel), has, among her possessions, correspondence to her father from a teacher. Mr. Hawkins was in Columbia, Missouri at the time; the teacher had been persuaded to leave the Festus (Missouri) school and come to Webster and was either homesick or was finding her work in new surroundings frustrating. It may be a bit of a blow to the Webster ego to read her words about her new situation:

"The parents are very indulgent and mothers do nothing but lounge around and the children are lacking in industry. They were positively bad, noisy and unruley." (The spelling is hers.) "I worried until I was a nervous wreck but finally decided that the only thing to do was to use very strenuous means for securing order. They are a very great deal better now but by no means perfect. This third grade was further behind than my second grade at Festus. They knew nothing about multiplication, not even the twos, couldn't write an intelligent story, beginning and closing, and merely called words when reading and not doing that very well."

However, she concluded, she would make the best of things for "I owe it to these people and I have concluded that we are happy only as we share our lives with those around us, or sacrifice our lives for others. 'Happiness was born a twin.' "

Two graduates of the Webster High class of 1927, Robert Phemister and his wife, Nora Savinac Phemister, read of the compilation of this history and sent a copy of "Our School 1891-1927" written by Mrs. Phemister for The Echo yearbook. Among her notes was an informative letter from Mark Moody, a graduate of the first high school and the school's second principal. He was succeeded by Mr. Thurston, followed by Mr. Hawkins and then by James T. Hixson in 1907.

Mrs. Phemister's history told of the adding of two front wings to the high school building in 1913; these provided a gymnasium and a new auditorium.

"With the war came another change," she wrote. "The Armory, built for our home guards, was erected in 1917. A few years later, a basement was dug and the lunchroom was moved from the second floor. After the war, the Armory was given over to the high school to be known as the Webster High School Gymnasium.

The most conspicuous thing to come down through the years, her account concluded, is the "Spirit of Webster High, which is known throughout the county and state. Early graduates still feel that 'their'

New high school; built in 1924.

school was the finest of its kind. May we continue to keep 'our' school the finest."

Others who attended the early high school have memories of it, too. Miss Frances Dewey, who started the four year high school in 1906, recalled what a change it was to go from Tuxedo school where pupils were called by first names to high school where one became "Miss" and "Mister."

Girls wore bloomers in those days and stockings had to meet the bloomers without a trace of bare leg showing. Each Monday morning at high school a minister came to talk. Mrs. Olive Benson, another early student, recalled that discipline was maintained and dismissal from school was the result of pranks such as letting a mouse loose in study hall. Smoking was a problem in early days, too, but not cigarettes or marijuana. Then it was cornsilks.

Football came to Webster in 1903 and an early player recalled they often had to borrow boys from Smith Academy and other schools to make up an eleven man team. Boys did not have complete uniforms but played in overalls. The first Webster-Kirkwood competition in football was in 1907. W. Scott Smith, who lived in Clayton, which had no high

The dance. . . an ideal exercise.

school then, and traveled to Webster by streetcar and on foot, played in that first memorable game and carried away a lasting memento – a broken nose.

Football gear was much lighter than it is today. Smith's recollection is that he caught the ball on the kickoff and went tearing down the field. A boy of five feet seven, he looked up to see what he thought was a giant – "one of the Kirkwood fellas, who weighed every bit of 225 pounds" – charging down on him. He tried to duck but the tackler made connection and Smith's nose hit the hard frozen ground. His football career was over – all three minutes of it.

The high school's first graduation class of 1907 consisted of fifteen students. Exercises were held in the hall on the third floor of the Bristol Building. The next five classes had their graduation at the Holy Redeemer building on the second floor. It was at one of these that Alfred Lee Booth played the Alma Mater song for which he composed words and music.

Classes varied in sizes according to the times. The 1919 class was only 49 graduates because of the war and the influenza epidemics. Early classes generally were a far cry from the seemingly endless line of students who assemble now at Memorial Field.

Many changes have come in facilities and curriculum through the years. The fall of 1909 saw the addition of manual training with workbenches, saws, chisels and hammers for the students to make footstools and magazine racks. A companion class was domestic science.

Physical training for girls was added to the curriculum in 1914, with

Mr. James T. Hixson,
Principal of the high school,
1907-1943.

aesthetic and folk dancing, military marching, and work with Indian clubs, wands, dumbbells. By 1927, girls were playing baseball.

With changing times, electronics and electricity and drivers education became part of the curriculum. In 1966, the Herbert Schooling Library was added, named for the superintendent of schools who later became chancellor of the University of Missouri.

Superintendents, in order, have been:

W. D. Grove	*1902-14*
H. M. Gilmore	*1914-15*
Wm. Robertson	*1915-17*
Frank Hamsher	*1917-24*
W. A. Gore	*1924-29*
Willard E. Goslin	*1930-44*
Leonard E. Steger	*1944-56*
Herbert W. Schooling	*1957-63*
George W. Brown	*1963 —*

James T. Hixson was principal of the high school from 1907 to 1943, Howard Latta from 1943-68. His successor was Gerald E. Kusler, and the present principal is Jerry Knight.

The high school was named for Frank Hamsher; the gymnasium was dedicated to Charles A. Roberts in 1947. Coach Roberts had died in

The Track Team of '26. From left, back row: McMillan; Greene; Thornton; and Woods. Front row: Coach Roberts; Ward; Joe L.; Sample; Billups; Ass't. Coach Tudor.

1946 after 39 years at Webster High. His enviable record consisted of victories in 95 percent of the football games and 92 percent of the basketball games before 1915. After that date, his football teams won 12 county championships and football and track teams won state honors. Swimming teams have ranked high, as well.

From 1910-30, Webster won all the traditional Turkey Day games against Kirkwood except one. In 1917, the score was Webster 75, Kirkwood 0. Carl Stadelhofer was captain of that team and Allan Lincoln starred, scoring six touchdowns and kicking 10 out of 11 extra points.

Wrote L. C. Davis in his Sport Salad column:

> *The Websters put a crimp in Kirkwood High*
> *Who, from the kick-off, didn't stand a show;*
> *The Kirkwoods battled gamely, but were pie*
> *For Allan Lincoln's educated toe.*

An outbreak of overzealous partisanship caused a cessation in the traditional Webster-Kirkwood game for a few years, but in 1940 the rift was healed and the Friendship Dance initiated, with the winner receiving the Frisco "Bell," the loser the "Little Brown Jug."

Webster teachers have received honors through the years. George Brucker, high school mathematics teacher, was named one of the 10 best in the United States by Yale University in 1963. Mrs. Buena Stolberg was a member of the first Commission on the Status of Women in Missouri, and with her sister, Corinne Jackson, has attracted nationwide attention for their role in helping restore the Missouri community of Arrow Rock.

Many teachers and principals have been honored for long years of service — Miss Miriam Sander of Bristol, Egbert Nowlin, Bristol principal, King Barnett, principal of Clark school, Howell B. Goins, Douglass school principal, and others.

Junior high schools came to Webster in 1955, the first one built on South Elm and named for James T. Hixson. Among its innovations was the teaching of Spanish and French in seventh grade.

There was considerable community controversy over the building of the next two junior high schools. At first, only one was proposed and debate ensued as to whether it should be in the north or central part of town. The dispute was resolved with the building of two schools, Steger Junior High, named for Superintendent Leonard Steger, on Rock Hill road and Brownbert lane, and Plymouth Junior High near the high school on Lockwood. Both were opened in September 1960.

Webster schools were integrated as soon as the law indicated. The all black high school was phased out of existence. As a result of declining enrollment, Washington Park School was closed in 1973. Then, in the 1975 district reorganization, two more schools were closed: Schall School in Rock Hill and Goodall, long a south Webster landmark.

Looking over the histories, formal and informal of the educational process of Webster, it is obvious that education and the building of schools has always been a controversial subject from the petticoat push to today. But it is also obvious that one generation's controversy becomes another generation's amusement. As exhibit A, there is this document, a stirring issue in its time, entitled, "Keep The Boys and Girls Pure!" Circa 1901.

Keep the Boys and Girls Pure!

Do you know that the boys **and girls** are mixed promiscuously in the seats of the Webster schools? Think how you would like to sit five hours every day, surrounded on every side by the opposite sex in two feet of you, then think how much worse it is for boys and girls with their unformed habits. It is bad for their Comfort, their Morals, and their Attention to Work.

The Practice is Condemned by Educational Experts!

"It is generally agreed among teachers of experience that in mixed schools promiscuous seating of boys and girls is not advisable. Good discipline and good work require that they be separated."—W. T. HARRIS, United States Commissioner of Education (The greatest living authority on public school matters).

"Few schools of any standing practice it."—F. LOUIS SOLDAN, Superintendent St. Louis Schools.

"I should not seat the boys and girls together promiscuously."—W. T. CARRINGTON, State Superintendent of Schools.

"I would not have a boy of mine sit with other people's girls if I could help it; I will not allow a daughter of mine to sit with any other man's boy. I will take her out of school first."—JOHN R. KIRK, Former State Superintendent of Schools, now President of Kirksville State Normal School.

"I have very good reasons to think that they should not be seated together."—E. B. CRAIGHEAD, President Warrensburg State Normal School.

It is Condemned by the Clergy, who are Moral Experts!

"Their separation is clearly an aid not only to the individual morals but also to the discipline and attentiveness of the school."—REV. H. BLUNT, Old Orchard Congregational Church.

"Separation would contribute to good order and more polite behavior."—REV. P. J. KANE, Church of Our Holy Redeemer.

"I am glad to second your efforts to secure separate seating of the sexes in our public schools. I know from experience that not only is the practice detrimental to morals, but it has been almost entirely eliminated from all the schools of my acquaintance."—REV. C. L. KLOSS, First Congregational Church.

"I have seen boys placed for punishment among girls. Their natural timidity soon disappeared and with it the respect due the girls, and there came in place of these boldness and freedom of speech and act which neither girl nor boy were ashamed of. I think you will find the opinions of the best educators to be that the promiscuous seating of boys and girls is at least not conducive to a good moral tone. I think it is not too much to say it IS conducive to a distinctly immoral tone. Delicacy in thought, word and act between boys and girls is something greatly to be desired; something indeed, that is necessary if we are to have good moral men and women."—REV. J. M. NORTHROP, Emmanuel Church.

"I believe that the morals of the scholars will be more securely guarded by having the boys and girls seated in different parts of the room."—REV. DAVID M. SKILLING, Presbyterian Church.

Yet in spite of this evidence, the Board of Education voted to continue the practice. If you have never attended a school where the sexes are thus mixed, talk with those who have and learn what goes on. As one lady expressed it, LET THE MOTHERS SPEAK on this question. After the expressions quoted above, you need not hesitate to do so.

A PARTIAL REMEDY!

Superintendent Grove has consented to separate the sexes where parents request it; so if you care to take the trouble you can get relief for your own children. The separation requires but a moment, takes no more desks, will not interfere with the studies, and you need have no fear that your request will make the teacher angry.

AUGUST BUESSE, DIRECTORS
CH EVANS,

Chapter Seven

Joy in Old Orchard
1880s-90s

As the church histories indicated, railroad problems in the 1870s dealt a setback to suburban development. Some homes were built — George R. Robinson's Annefield, which later burned, was built at Big Bend and Laclede Station road in 1870, and the George A. Holloway house at 119 South Gore dates to 1878, but Pitzman's Atlas of 1878 shows no great increase in the early families.

In the 1880s, things picked up. There was additional railway service by this time in the form of the Frisco, at first a part of the Pacific Railway known as the South Pacific and later the Pacific Southwest. It used the same tracks as Missouri Pacific in the city but in 1884 began using its own line from Cabanne Station (near what is now Spring avenue) to the town of Pacific. It ran through the Lockwood farm and so officials asked permission of Mrs. Lockwood to name the stop for her family.

There was a Missouri town named Lockwood, however, so Mrs. Lockwood suggested that, since the stop was near their old apple orchard, it be called Old Orchard. Stations beyond Old Orchard were Selma and Shady Side where the present Frisco station stands.

Shady Side Acres was developed at the south end of Gore avenue by John Smith who, with his brother Charles, came from England. After a successful business career, he retired as Englishmen often did in those days, at 45 years of age, and began buying land. At each subdivision, he would plant an apple or peach orchard.

The Smiths were bachelors with a widowed sister, Mrs. Henry Atkinson Stine. Henry Stine had been a passenger on the ill fated train which went into the Gasconade River in 1855. A young man, he'd been given a pass by his uncle, Madison Miller, president of the Iron Mountain

The Gore Family waves goodbye.

Railroad. It was his good fortune that he was not seated up front with the dignitaries; he was in a back car and so survived the wreck. But he did not have a long life and left his wife with teen age children. Her brother John Smith told her he would give her a lot if she would build a house on Shady Side Acres. She said she would if he would supervise the building. He supervised it well and "by mistake" — on purpose, her granddaughter Adele Stine is convinced — the house was situated in the middle of two lots. A two story house, it still stands. William Stine grew up there and married Mary Catherine (Mamie) Harper; they were the parents of Adele and Janet Stine.

Miss Kate Twining Moody, for many years Webster's unofficial historian and a St. Louis public librarian for 50 years, moved to Webster Groves as a girl in 1875 and first lived in a home her grandfather, William Twining had built at 709 Laclede Station road. Later the family moved to Twining place. From her notations, we get this picture of life in Webster in the 1880s:

"Lockwood avenue," she wrote, "was distinguished chiefly by a single plank walk. It was about three feet wide, and made of cross boards. Every so often, one of them would work loose and fly up and you never quite knew what would happen."

As a child, she rode the Missouri Pacific trains to school. For the student, the shopper, the businessman, commuting was the only way to travel. Most families rode to the station by carriage, leaving the vehicle for a boy to take to the nearby livery stable. However, Mrs. William Jenkins, descendant of the Lockwood family, once recalled that it was her father's custom to ride his horse to the station and then, when he reached the tracks, to send the horse home by itself. One day he started the horse out on Laclede Station road but it never arrived and was assumed stolen.

The memoirs of Mrs. 'Jenkins also recalled the thrill of early mail deliveries by train to Webster Groves.

Her brother would be sent on horseback for the mail and for yeast for bread baking. On the day that the Youth Companion magazine came, he would become so absorbed that he would arrive home without the yeast and would be sent back, on foot.

In 1883, James F. Allen, who lived on Marshall place, bought six acres of ground and the remains of a burned-out house and built a home on the old stone foundation. The house faced Lockwood and was approached by a long winding drive. The house still faces Lockwood but its present address is 29 Plant avenue. Its owners, Oscar and Audrey Anderson, have the original specifications including directions to save the old bricks and clear rubble from the cellar. The Allens had three children, Sylvia Henry, Helen (Mrs. Lon) Harper and Mildred Allen, long time school librarian. It was in this house that the Monday Club was founded.

Another residence of this era was built by Clifford Darby at 216 North Elm. It adjoined the J. P. Dawson estate (now Epworth School) and the two families were close friends.

Friends and partners in a firm which became the successful Penny-Gentles Dry Goods Company were Alexander Penny who built a home at 2 Roseacre lane in 1885 and John Gentles who bought 220 South Gore from the Presbyterian minister, P. H. K. McComb, in 1890. By 1893, the latter house had an enviable modern feature, a cistern which pumped water into a tank on the third floor providing running water in the kitchen.

In 1886, Patrick J. J. O'Connor purchased 40 acres bounded by Selma and Glendale and built a home for himself and his widowed sister, Mrs. Mary Waddock. A native of Ireland, he called it Innisfail.

Two buildings which became landmarks were constructed during this

Mr. Joy,
the father of Old Orchard.

Beautiful Old Orchard.

Views at Old Orchard Park,

Located on St. Louis & San Francisco R.R. } Fare. Eight Cents.
Eight Miles from Union Depot.

St. Louis County, Missouri.

One Hundred and twenty Acres in the Park. Streets MacAdamized and Sidewalks made. Houses and lots for sale on usual terms, or monthly payments. For particulars, call on or address

E. JOY, Old Orchard, St. Louis Co., Mo.

period. The Bristol Building at Lockwood and Gore was started in 1889 when a group of citizens headed by Dr. Benton Bristol decided there was a need for a building to provide space for community meetings, dances and concerts. Its first floor was shared by the Ambrose Mueller Drug Store and William A. Straub's new grocery.

Nearby, at 17-19 North Gore, Parker's Livery Stable started up in 1889. Down the street, Henry Schulz, who had come from Sappington to Webster Groves, bought a saloon on Gore and Pacific, tore it down and built a large brick building for his feed business. It is now Rolling Ridge nursery, operated by Schulz' granddaughter, Harriet, and her husband, Jim McMillan.

Thus, individual projects for residential and business purposes were going on in all parts of Webster Groves. But the big effort was the work of one family, the Joys, and especially Edward Joy, known in later years as "the father of Old Orchard."

Joy and his son, Justin E., came to the area of Lockwood's apple orchard in 1885, looking for a home site. With a prophetic eye for the future, they ended up purchasing 128 acres to subdivide. The House That Joy Built was to become a well known slogan for fifty years.

A couple from Salem, Ohio had moved to St. Louis and were interested in finding a home outside the city. They read the Joy ad which promised them a free ride on a train and luncheon served to anyone who would like to see what Old Orchard had to offer.

The Ohio couple bought one of four houses just alike, on Spring avenue, a street which followed an old cowpath which ran to a spring. They moved in March 1890, and in August their baby girl was born, the first child to be born in the new area. She was to be named Alice Louise Hutton but Mr. Joy asked the family if they would give her the middle name of Joy instead. At a public christening at the Episcopal church, she was named Alice Joy Hutton, the name engraved on her silver christening cup.

Joy Hutton Flint (she dropped the Alice) and her husband, Ray Flint, still live in the house on Spring, a graceful high ceilinged home with a beautiful tree and flower circled yard which extends 200 feet up a grassy hill.

"We've always lived in Webster Groves," Mrs. Flint said. "Never thought of living anywhere else. We love it here."

Joy Hutton Flint. Old Orchard's first baby.

Both she and her husband have memories of life in early Old Orchard. He lived at 854 Newport when it was one of four houses between Big Bend and Summit. His father was Sunday School superintendent of the

Old Orchard Congregational Church, which branched off from First Church in 1890. Both Flints remember carrying lanterns on their way to Christian Endeavor Society and prayer meetings. Both remember attending Old Orchard school, a two story, four room building with two grades in each room. They recall that everyone had outdoor plumbing, their own cisterns and that most people owned a cow. The Hutton girls were fortunate; they had Indian ponies sent them by their grandfather in Kansas.

Her father was one of 16 men from the Frisco Railway who went to Alaska during the gold rush of 1898 and from then on, he spent much of his time in Alaska, working his mine, coming home only a short time each year.

Mrs. Flint remembers going up to Summit avenue to see the first street car go by. (The United Railway Company acquired its first right of way in 1896.) She remembers when the house she lives in had red velvet carpets, lace curtains and a rose bowl sitting on the floor in front of the long window. She still has the walnut furniture of her youth, her grandmother's platform rocker and other treasured heirlooms.

Once she took a trip to the Smoky Mountains. At a stop on the way back, she spied a tiny pine seedling, hanging by one root from a rocky ledge. She disengaged it, put it in a Dixie cup and carried it home and planted it. It's 100 feet tall now. It thrived — and grew and grew and grew. Like the Old Orchard area.

The first 60 houses were only the beginning for the Joy family. Years later, in 1938, Marguerite Martyn, a Webster resident and feature writer for the St. Louis Post-Dispatch, interviewed Wilford Joy, grandson of Edward, and asked him how many houses he had built.

"Somebody counted 400 once," he replied, "but that was a long time ago."

"Let him advertise a new house open for inspection," wrote Marguerite Martyn, "and he has a procession of sightseers that often blocks traffic."

Headquarters for the Joy real estate company was on Log Cabin lane, so named because in 1890 Edward and Justin Joy purchased General Grant's log cabin home for $5000 and moved it to Old Orchard to attract attention to their company. For 12 years it stood on the west side of Log Cabin lane, serving as an office for the firm. It was later sold to the Blanke Coffee Company for $8000 and moved to the St.

Grant's Cabin on Log Cabin Lane

Louis World's Fair in 1904 to advertise coffee. In 1907, August A. Busch bought it and took it to his estate, Grant's Farm, though not to its original site. Originally the cabin stood in what is now St. Paul's Churchyard on South Rock Hill road; on its site is a marker put up by the D.A.R.

In the early days of his enterprise, E. Joy advertised as follows:

Beautiful Old Orchard

"If you want a Home in the suburbs, don't fail to secure one of the ten new Modern-built Houses now being completed at Old Orchard. They range from six to nine rooms — all on MacAdamized streets, good side walks and large grounds. Only eight miles from Union Depot, St. Louis, on the great St. Louis & San Francisco R.R. FARE 8 cents. . ."

The ad went on to detail the other attractions — churches, schools, post office, grocery, meat shop, 2000 forest trees, 2500 evergreens, and No Saloons.

"You can buy direct from the owner, on as liberal terms as you can make with any well managed Building Society," the ad encouraged. "By making a liberal cash payment, balance monthly payments, you can be made independent of the seller in five years, if you choose to do so.

"If you want to make an investment that will do you good, this is the place, and now is the time. No visionary scheme. Come and see. Call on or address

E. Joy
Old Orchard, Mo."

Many came, saw and were won over to the delights of living in Old Orchard. Presumably Edward Joy acquired a great deal more land as his obituary (at age 84 in 1905) listed him as "one of the largest property holders in St. Louis County."

In 1896 he made the news in another way. A story prominently headlined told of his romance.

"It was two years ago that gossips of Old Orchard first noticed it and of course they talked," the 1896 news story began. "This is not to be wondered at for when a gray haired old widower who has seen 75 winters gets to riding around a little country town with a maiden lady who for 50 years has lived in single blessedness, it becomes a legitimate matter for comment.

"Everybody in Old Orchard knows Grandpa Edward Joy. He is the big man of the town and when you strike a house out there which he doesn't own, it's like catching the zero on the roulette wheel. Miss Ellen Twining is also prominent. One time she was Postmistress so everybody knew her.

"If they had been youngsters, it would have been bad enough but having reached the wintry side of life, people chucked each other in the ribs and grinned and smiled all the more.

"The aged lovers kept right at it and last Wednesday they sprung a surprise on the community in the shape of a marriage. And now 99 percent of the Old Orchardites are saying, 'I told you so.' "

The story went on to enlarge on the background of both Joy and Miss Twining, who had been appointed by President Harrison as a good Republican and served until the "hungry Democrats" of President Cleveland's regime took her job away.

The ceremony was performed in Grant's Cabin, with the bride's sister Mrs. Catherine Moody and niece, Miss Catherine Twining Moody (Kate Moody, the historian), present. The bridal couple took an extended honeymoon to New Orleans and California, and returned to make their home — where else — in Webster Groves.

Webster was indeed the idyllic spot painted by Edward Joy in his advertisement, but no place is perfect and occasionally crime invaded even this garden spot of St. Louis County.

Miss Adele Stine grew up hearing the stories of the burglar scare in the 1890s. House after house was struck.

"No one was able to catch the intruder," she remembers being told. "When the family would go down to breakfast there would be no food in the pantry, it was completely bare. People bought in quantities in those days — a barrel of flour, sacks of potatoes. Authorities could not catch the burglar and people took to locking their bedroom doors. One morning the Stine family awoke and found candle grease at each door on the upstairs hall carpeting.

"It was about two years before the adroit burglar was finally caught," said Miss Stine. "He turned out to be the proprietor of a small grocery store in another suburb and it was learned that he kept his shelves stocked with other people's groceries."

From time to time, a group of Webster citizens would get together and propose that the town incorporate in order to have a more efficient system of crime control and other advantages of an organized community. The first petition for incorporation was presented in 1883 but failed.

The main reason was that the majority of residents simply didn't want incorporation. They had moved to this sylvan paradise to get away from city restrictions, went their argument. They liked it just the way it was. No changes, please.

Thus it was that incorporation plans were pushed out of the way again and again, until 1896. Then something happened which brought home the fact that, even in paradise, evil can exist.

Chapter Eight

Webster Faces Life.
Incorporation —1896

It was a dark and stormy evening when the stranger from the big city arrived in town by train. He was on his way to visit his sweetheart but he never reached her house. Three men conspired in the saloon near the station and, while one of them acted as his guide, the other two hid in ambush to rob him. He pulled out a gun. So did they. And the stranger was dead.

This melodramatic tale would seem to have little in common with Webster Groves and the image it has attained through the years. But it was because Bertram E. Atwater, of Chicago, was murdered on Lee avenue in January 1896 that the loosely knit together communities which made up Webster Groves took steps to incorporate and insure law and order.

It was also because Brennan's saloon had played a part in providing the setting for the plotters that the sale of liquor was prohibited for many years in Webster Groves and is still allowed only in eating places, causing detractors to say scornfully, "You can't even buy a drink in that town."

The best way to recapture the spirit of the times and the drama of the event which acted as catalytic agent for the town's incorporation is to go back to the microfilmed newspapers of the day and read about it as it first burst on the consciousness of the St. Louis area.

MURDERED BY HIGHWAYMEN
Bertram E. Atwater Foully
Slain in Webster Groves

The headline was over the top news story, right hand column, page one

Artist's interpretation of the Bertram E. Atwater Murder of 1896.

of the St. Louis Post-Dispatch for Friday, January 24, 1896. The story began:

"Webster Groves is wildly excited over the terrible tragedy of Thursday night when Bertram E. Atwater, a young Chicago artist who had gone to the pretty little suburb to visit his betrothed, was waylaid by highwaymen and foully murdered.

"One of the robbers, wounded to death by the plucky Chicagoan, will probably die before the sun goes down. The other thugs, Sam Foster and "Cottonhead" Smith who arranged the trap into which Mr. Atwater was unsuspectingly lured and then slain, are in custody."

The stories in both the Post and the Globe-Democrat of that day were substantially the same, although the Post referred to the assailants as "highwaymen" and the Globe as "footpads."

Both agreed that Bertram Atwater, age 30, a designer and artist whose work appeared in leading magazines of the day, had come from Chicago to St. Louis on business with the Terminal Railway Company. From St. Louis, he telegraphed Miss Genevieve S. Orton, daughter of M. C. Orton, "a capitalist" of Webster Groves, telling her he would arrive for a visit.

He arrived via Missouri Pacific on the 8:08 p.m. train. Peter, nicknamed "Cotton" or "Cottonhead" Smith, ran up to him at the station and offered to carry his "grips," as luggage was called then, and lead him to his destination. Atwater, unaware that the 17-year-old boy was recently released from jail under $1000 bond on a charge of robbing the driver of a Moll's Grocery Store truck, agreed. But first, he said, he wanted to go to the barber shop down the street for a shave and shoeshine.

While Atwater was in the barber shop, Smith (as he later confessed) hurried to Brennan's tavern.

There he talked to his cousin, John Smith. (By the second day of the story, the name Smith had become "Schmidt" but in the early version, it was consistently Smith.) The Smiths, both white boys, prevailed on a black friend, Sam Foster, to go along on the job.

"Every detail of the crime," reads one news story, "indicates that Mr. Atwater was selected as a likely victim the minute 'Cottonhead' Smith first accosted him at the depot. He was a stranger, richly dressed, had a valise and was en route to the home of a wealthy citizen.

"Such a man would naturally have a well filled purse. That he might also have arms and the courage to use them the highwaymen took but lightly into consideration. If he showed fight, they would have every advantage."

The thoroughfares of Webster Groves, as the news stories pointed out, were boarded with plank walks about three feet wide.

"In front of the house of H. L. Wilson, County Treasurer of St. Louis County," they continued, "the plank walk is divided by a trestle bridge which spans a ravine through which a tiny stream winds to the River des Peres. . . . On one side there is a fence. On the other there is a growth of trees just thick enough to afford a perfect cover."

Rain was falling as Atwater reached the bridge and started across. The two men stepped out in his path, one with a revolver. Atwater, the story theorized, reached for his pistol and fired, the shot striking John Smith. The robbers fired two shots each, one killing Atwater instantly.

Peter Smith dropped the valise and ran toward town to notify the constable, John Fieldson, that Atwater had been accosted and shot. Before Fieldson reached the scene, the bodies had been discovered by M. R. Strickland, "a young man of the village" on his way home.

Strickland fell over Atwater's body. He struck a match and "saw in the flickering light the form of a young man, a stranger to him, laying prostrate upon the water soaked ground, his face upturned against the drizzling rain. . . .

"Knowing that a crime had been committed," the Post story continued, "Strickland was about to go back to the main street when the smothered cry of another man attracted him to the hedge fence. There he found a man suffering great pain, face down. Upon turning him over, he was surprised to recognize John Smith, a man known about Webster Groves and whose reputation had been considered by no means that of a desperado."

Constable Fieldson arrived and the Orton family was notified. Orton ran out of the house, bareheaded. His daughter followed.

"She saw the body of her dead lover by the dim light of the lantern," the story related, "and her grief was unbounded. With tears streaming down her cheeks and shaking with sobs, she followed the corpse to an undertaker's rooms, where it was borne on a rude stretcher improvised by the Constable and his posse."

The wounded "highwayman" also was moved and taken to Dr. Bristol's office where Dr. A. Eichler determined that the bullet had missed his heart by an inch. Stimulants were administered and he made a statement to Justice of the Peace John Prehn, implicating the other two men. Soon they were picked up.

As news of the crime spread throughout town, "every male citizen of the place and many women gathered on the streets, in the stores and at Carvell and Parker, undertakers," the story went on.

"The propriety of lynching Smith was freely discussed, and a plan was formulated to take him from his bed and swing him from a tree at the bridge where the murder was done," according to the Post-Dispatch.

"It was not carried out, because no one assumed the leadership and because some conservative citizens opposed it.

"Still the crowds did not disperse. The two drug stores remained open all night and the dawn found many a sleepless eye in the little town."

It was not this crime alone which had aroused them, the newspaper pointed out.

"For months," it read, "there has been a reign of terror throughout St. Louis County. A number of burglaries have occurred in Webster Groves, Kirkwood, Benton, Clayton and other towns in the county. There have been frequent hold-ups and in some of them the robbers have manifested a desperate disregard for human life.

"In nearly every instance where a description of the robbers was given, they were described as a negro and a white man."

And so the stories continued, playing on every emotion possible and drawing out the utmost in human interest. It was noted that Atwater and Miss Orton were "probably engaged" and that his visit "was prompted by the tender sentiment of love." The young lady was described as "a beautiful brunette of 20, of rather small stature and winsome disposition."

Webster Groves was described as "an aristocratic little suburban village 10 miles out from the city." The scene of the crime lent itself to dramatic description — the dark night, "with rain and sleet and a cold piercing wind."

There was a pen and ink sketch of Atwater, a handsome young man with an upturned coat collar, and sketches of the two Smith or Schmidt boys and of Sam Foster. One citizen said:

"John Smith is one of those people who live in the dark. No one knows much about them and no one cares. They are accepted as part of the scheme of society but are not considered important."

Feeling continued to run high. The Globe-Democrat story of January 25 related how a lynching party attempted to seize the accused men but were outmaneuvered by John Fieldson, the constable.

Efforts began when Sam Foster and Peter Schmidt (the name appeared this way now) were put into a carriage in Webster Groves to be taken to the county jail. A mob surged up to the carriages but the skittish horses reared and bolted and ran away with the carriage as men on the street ran after them, firing shots.

67

Fieldson started for Kirkwood, but, as he was hurrying along, urging on the horses which needed no urging, a man stepped into his path. It was not the forerunner of a mob as he at first assumed, but a single citizen warning him that a mob was forming in Kirkwood. Fieldson's deputies abandoned him. It was a few minutes later that Fieldson realized that, in the excitement, he had given one of them his gun and he was unarmed.

Concealing this fact from his prisoners, he started for the Woodlawn station, then reasoned this would be what he was expected to do and changed his destination for the Ellendale station. He ordered his prisoners out of the carriage and they traveled the last 10 miles on foot, stumbling through stubble. The prisoners begged to be allowed to rest but Fieldson roughly ordered them on, well aware that they could escape and he would be powerless to stop them.

They arrived at Ellendale station just before the 11 o'clock train was due. Fieldson ordered the men to lie down in the weeds for the final 10 minutes of waiting. He later described this as "the most enjoyable part" of the journey.

The three men got on the train, to the startled surprise of passengers who realized who they were. Fieldson telegraphed St. Louis police to meet them, which they did.

The story continued for many columns, describing the condition of the wounded Schmidt, who did not die as predicted. Sam Foster was pictured and described as "burly with a countenance that is at once cunning and repulsive." It was emphasized that he had already served a term in prison.

John Schmidt was described as the son of a teamster who "while generally regarded as a shiftless sort of boy was never considered desperate." Peter Schmidt on the other hand had "the appearance of an apt pupil in the criminal line."

Within a few days, after the manner of big stories, it had disappeared from the metropolitan front pages, but it was literally only the beginning of Webster Groves.

On March 16, a petition for incorporation was presented to the County court, bearing the signatures of two-thirds of the taxable inhabitants of the area. On April 2, a favorable decision was handed down.

And so Webster Groves was incorporated as a city of the fourth class and the court appointed W. Scott Fleming, a druggist, as its first mayor.

He was later elected and reelected, serving five terms in all, his tenure of office ending in 1901. Writing later from his home in Greencastle, Pennsylvania, he reminisced:

"I moved to Webster Groves in 1892, bought a home on Marshall and served several years on the school board before I learned that we had no town or city government. There was little thought given to politics in Webster Groves, the school board being the only thing we had to vote on. But when a young Chicago artist named Atwater was killed in our city, we took a deeper interest."

The first city meetings were held in the building housing the real estate office of Alan S. Moody. Space was rented for $10 a month and Moody was appointed city clerk at a salary of $15 a month.

The handwritten minutes of the meeting of April 8, 1896 list the following participants: Nathan D. Thompson, Albert B. Kauffman, James F. Dawson, Edward S. Hart and John T. Gruet, aldermen; James R. Trembly, collector; Louis F. Booth, assessor; and Robert L. Bush, marshall, all sworn in by Justice of the Peace John Prehn.

Rules and regulations were set up and some business was transacted, such as approval of a bid from the Pauly Jail Building and Manufacturing Company of St. Louis for furnishing "two Iron Jail cells capable of accommodating two Prisoners each, for the sum of $165." An estimate was presented to maintain, equip and operate an electric power house at a probable cost of $13,000. This vast expenditure was deemed worthy of further study.

A communication was presented from R. A. Allen, offering a room in the Allen Building for jail purposes at a rent of $30 a month for a term of one year. The proposal was referred to the Committee on Buildings. Also, a communication from J. W. Bellaire to erect a building for jail purposes at a cost of $144 was referred to the same committee.

Mayor Fleming wrote to the St. Louis Police Department and asked for the best man they had to "clean up Webster Groves and keep it that way." They supplied Officer Edward Nace, and apparently his work was good because a news item in the Webster Times of Octoer 10, 1896 reads as follows:

"Webster Groves enjoys the distinction of being exempt from street brawls and after dark cussedness. This is due largely to Mr. Nace, our efficient nightwatchman. Under Mr. Nace's reign, the hoodlum element has vanished and disreputable characters make themselves scarce in the city. During the summer, many arrests were made and many notorious characters made to leave town. The gentleman walks his beat during the night hours and is watchful in a marked degree. He has almost abated the tramp nuisance and otherwise purified the city. Mr. Nace was 15 years a member of the St. Louis police force and is a genial gentleman."

This particular issue of The Webster Times waxed eloquently on the virtues of Webster Groves, describing it, in one line as "A Flower Strewn Garden of the Gods." Besides that, it was "an ideal suburban city with all modern improvements and the business interests are growing."

There were, in addition, various shorter news items which in another era would be described as "puffs," lauding the various merchants in town — George Schefferling, a "first class barber" who "guarantees fashionable work," Mrs. L. Dodd who had "neatly furnished rooms," F. W. Theatenhorst who had "one of the nicest hardware stores" in the city, the Grove Pharmacy, J. Z. Rogers dairy lunch, Frank Watkins livery stables, Knickman and Sons coal business, Braun's Market, Bate sadler, C. J. Kalb shoemaker, W. M. Curtis retailer and, of course, E. Joy real estate.

The Webster Times of December 19, 1896 had less fluff and more news, in particular, two items of interest.

One was a news story relating that the Atwater murder weapon had been found by none other than his honor, the mayor. While inspecting the grading on Marshall avenue, he had discovered a revolver wrapped in a scarf and hidden under the sidewalk in front of the "Campbell residence." It was identified as the weapon belonging to Sam Foster, who had said he remembered wrapping it in a scarf and hiding it somewhere. It was .38 caliber which corresponded to the bullet taken from Atwater's body.

The story concluded, "The finding and identifying of the weapon, it is thought, removes all hope of the defense of saving young Foster from the death sentence."

The other story was a report by the Executive Committee of the Webster Groves Incorporation Association, signed by Charles W. Ferguson, secretary-treasurer, and it described its work as being "largely accomplished."

Its objects, the report continued, had been to secure incorporation, to furnish assistance to the state in bringing the murderers of Bertram

Atwater to justice and punishment, and to provide temporary police protection.

Incorporation has been secured, the report continued. Attorneys R. L. Mudd and Zach J. Mitchell had assisted the state's attorney in the Atwater case and on August 4, all three suspects were convicted and were (in December) under sentence to be hanged, awaiting the decision of the Supreme Court, to whom appeal had been taken in each case.

City government had been set up, the report went on, with 34 meetings of the Board of Aldermen and the passage of 46 ordinances, among them laws relating to vagrants, street and sidewalk obstructions, nuisances, health, repair and construction of sidewalks, merchants licenses and taxes, and other matters. The Police Department showed 26 arrests for minor offenses only, since incorporation.

Then, too, another milestone had been passed. This one must have brought joy to the hearts of the W. C. T. U., which a news item in the same issue described as holding its Social Purity Meeting, at the Congregational Church parlor, on Wednesday, December 9.

"On November 3rd," said the report, "the last saloon passed from our midst and when we look back upon the history of these institutions, what an objective lesson they furnish! The young people they have debauched, the crimes they have hatched, the sorrow they brought to so many hearts and homes, the damages they have inflicted upon the fair name of our town are beyond description. Who would wish for disincorporation, proposing to bring our city to an untimely end?"

This presumably was a rhetorical question, for the report eloquently continued:

"It may be that saloons will continue to exist elsewhere and do their deadly work and therefore we cannot wholly escape the evils they produce, but it is also true, and bear this always in mind, that the heaviest part of such burdens fall upon the immediate community where the saloons are located. Therefore, the farther away from us, the better we shall be morally, physically and in our pocket books."

Quoting Alexander Pope, the committee observed:

> *"Vice is a monster of such frightful mien*
> *To be hated needs but to be seen;*
> *Yet seen too oft, familiar with her face,*
> *We first endure, then pity, then embrace."*

The report concluded:

"We build not alone for the present. In the future many good people will be seeking homes in the suburbs and what more convenient and beautiful place can they find than Webster?

"Do we want them to make their homes with us, to the benefit of property, our society, churches, and local business houses? Then we must restore our fair name for love of order and as a Christian community, thus making our city as attractive morally and socially as it is physically."

The postscript to the Atwater murder was written a few months later. On February 16, 1897, Peter Schmidt and Sam Foster were put to death by the means considered a deterrent to juvenile delinquency in that day, a public hanging. The news story was on page one and, in the tradition of fearless journalism of the time, pulled out all the stops, recording the event, literally to the last gasp.

"With a smile on his face, 'Cottonhead' Schmidt, a boy in his 17th year walked onto the gallows at St. Louis County Tuesday morning and atoned with his young life for the murder of Bertram Atwater," the story related.

"He was the youngest man that ever stretched hemp in Missouri but he died with absolute indifference. He was as careless of his own life as of the life he aided in taking away. . ."

Sam Foster was hanged after him, and the reporter observed, "The double execution passed off without a hitch and reflected great credit on Sheriff Peter Kerth, a novice in the act of capital punishment."

The light was gray, the air cold, and the waiting crowd shivered as the men were brought into the place of execution, a passageway between the courthouse and the jail, known as the Bridge of Sighs. The hangman's rope hung from an iron ring in the ceiling. Below it was a double trap door that opened by a lever.

The reporter observed that Peter Schmidt, fair haired as his "Cottonhead" nickname indicated, looked delicate after his period of incarceration and that he was "a pretty lad, far too tender for the hangman's noose."

Both Schmidt and Foster left farewell letters, warning other young boys to beware of falling into their ways. Wrote Schmidt:

"Now boys, you see what I have come to by falling into evil ways. . . Had I done as my parents told me I would not have been in the fix I am now. . . Do not spend your evenings in running around but stay at home or go to some reading room or religious meeting. . ."

John Schmidt, who had been wounded by Atwater and presumably had not been the one who fired the fatal bullet, was scheduled to be hanged on March 10. Petitions were signed by a required number and his mother visited Governor Lon V. Stephens to plead for her son's life. On March 8, it was reported that Schmidt had "lost all hope" for a pardon. But on March 9, front page headlines read, "John Schmidt Will Not Hang." His sentence had been commuted to 25 years.

On March 8, a less conspicuous story on an inside page, read as follows:

"All loyal citizens of Webster Groves are urged to rally to the support of the town and save it from the flighty influence of those who want to sink back into the Rip Van Winkle sleep from which the little town has lately been awakened by its more progressive and business like inhabitants."

The slightly editorializing news story went on to announce that a meeting would be held at Allen Hall to discuss whether or not Webster Groves should be reduced to village status in order to lower taxes, a step which would mean an economic saving to the residents but the relinquishing of "independence."

The "progressive and business-like inhabitants" prevailed. Like Rip Van Winkle, Webster Groves had been awakened and, like it or not, was moving into the twentieth century.

The Park in the Queen of the Suburbs.

Chapter Nine

Webster— Queen of the Suburbs

"Let us consider the means of perpetuating good family stocks in a Democracy."

President Eliot of Harvard began an article in the Forum of November 1890 with that sentence. He continued:

"The first is country life. In this regard, democracies have much to learn from those European aristocracies which have proved to be durable. All the vigorous aristocracies of the past centuries lived in the country a large part of the year. The men were soldiers and statesmen for the most part and lived on detached estates sparsely peopled by an agricultural and martial tenantry. They were oftener in camp than in the town or city. Their women lived in castles, halls or chateaux in the open country, almost the whole year, and their children were born and brought up there.

"The aristocratic and noble families of modern Europe still have their principal seats in the country and go to town only for a few months in the year. These customs maintain vigor of body and equability of mind. In American society of to-day the conditions of professional and business life are unfortunately not ordinarily favorable to the establishment of families in the country. The fact is to be lamented."

President Eliot's words appeared as the preface to a charming booklet entitled, "Webster – Queen of the Suburbs," its subtitle "Webster Groves – Webster Park," an advertising brochure designed to interest prospective home owners in the new and lovely residential area being planned at the turn of the century. Its arrant snob appeal may startle us a bit today but it suited the tenor of the times.

There was more to it, too, than the allure of the exclusive. As the Eliot piece pointed out in length and in depth, country life was healthier.

Many of the professional classes were forced "of dire necessity" to live in the city, but their lives were consequently of brief duration. The statistics might jolt us a bit, too.

"From 1850 to 1880, the average age of persons who died in Suffolk County, an urban county in Massachusetts, was 23½ years," wrote President Eliot. The corresponding age in Barnstable, a rural county on the seaboard, was 37 and in Nantucket, a secluded island county, an elderly 46, almost double the age of Suffolk residents. Moreover, a study of business leaders showed that a vast majority had grown up in the country.

"Country breeding," he concluded, "gives a vigor and endurance which, in the long run, outweigh all city advantages."

True, he admitted, it was not possible in America to follow the European pattern of two homes, country and city with the employment of governesses. But the American substitute, suburban living in which a family man worked in the city but lived 15 to 20 miles away, could be an attractive alternative, so that his family could have "better air, more sun and a more tranquil life."

President Eliot encouraged the idea of exercise, somewhat avant garde for his day, and emphasized that, "All children in well-to-do families should be taught to walk long distances, to swim and to row and to ride on horseback. Girls need these accomplishments as much as boys."

Suburban life could be dull and monotonous, the Webster Park brochure admitted, but it need not be so. The first consideration should be accessibility to a city.

In this respect, Webster Groves was most fortunate, being on the Missouri Pacific, the "only double track railroad leading out of St. Louis," with 32 accommodation trains daily, "not only for business commuters" but with afternoon trains "run practically for the convenience of Ladies" and four night trains operating until 11:30.

Webster Park consisting of 160 acres, laid out by Elias A. Long of Buffalo, N.Y., a landscape architect of national reputation, had land which was "gently undulating, with commanding building sites and excellent drainage." . . . drives sweeping around in graceful and ample curves. . . . three thousand shade trees were being planted and building lots were large with frontages of 100 to 150 feet and an average depth of 250 feet. An attractive train station with comfortable waiting rooms was within a few minutes walk.

Early homes in The Park.

As for the town of Webster Groves itself, it was described as a charming suburban town of 2000 inhabitants, "composed largely of the families of the most wide-awake, intelligent and prosperous businessmen of St. Louis". There was a public school only half a mile from the Park, which employed ten teachers and ranked with schools of St. Louis. Four churches — Presbyterian, Congregational, Episcopal and Catholic were nearby.

There was the new center, Allen's Hall (this burned in the early 1900s) plus a post office, telegraph and telephone offices, drug store, grocery stores, Connon's greenhouses, meat shops, bakery, tin and stove stores, shoe stores, dry goods and notion stores, a barber, carpenter, blacksmith, harness maker's shops, and livery stable. "And," the advertisement concluded triumphantly, "what cannot be obtained in Webster Groves can be sent out from the city without cost, as all the leading drygoods and other stores make daily free deliveries." As a clincher, "The Suburban Electric Light Company has been granted a franchise" for a plant.

Aristocracy and electricity, too! The appeal was irresistible, and so it proved to many families. Webster Park has always been one of the lovely areas of the town, but when one looks at the early photographs, it is apparent that its sweeping vistas might have reminded viewers of European estates.

"Webster — Queen of the Suburbs" emphasized both the lyrical and the practical.

"Every breeze bears the invitation, 'Come, let us wander abroad.' . . . burdens of business and cares of home are forgotten. . . in the burgeoning and leafy spring the air is laden with balm of trees and song of birds; in the gorgeous and jewel-decked autumn the sumac and dogwood are aflame; the golden rod lifts its shining scepter. . . the sugar maple, sassafras and hickory gleam like burnished gold."

And when rains temporarily closed country roads, there were macadamized roads leading to places within an easy evening's drive — Forest Park, Sulphur Springs, Brown's famous orchid houses or Sunset Hill.

The healthfulness of Webster was proven conclusively. Many residents had come from the city expecting to spend a single summer but experienced such positive benefits they refused to leave.

"There are no malaria breeding spots and the entire surroundings are conducive to health. . . If sickness does come as come it will everywhere, there are experienced and skillful physicians at hand in Webster Groves. The death rate of the neighborhood has always been small."

Thus the Webster Real Estate Company (McCormick-Kilgen-Rule, agents), while not exactly promising heaven on earth, guaranteed lovely surroundings and a longer stay among them.

The American Gardening magazine for January 1892 had a similar rhapsodia description of Webster Park, describing its tree lined drives as "equal in beauty and grace to any found in our best public parks."

"Webster — Queen of the Suburbs" listed some of the well known businessmen then residing in Webster Groves, among them N. D. Allen, capitalist, L. R. Blackmer, Professor William M. Bryant, high school teacher, A. DeYong of Drummond Tobacco Company, John Gentles and Alexander Penny of Penny and Gentles, Alfred Plant, Charles Salveter, Henry Salveter, Havelock Simmons, and Charles Skinner.

The George K. Andrews house at 405 Orchard avenue was the first house built in Webster Park, in 1892. The daughter of the original owner, Mrs. Lewis Thomson, still lives there; she is the mother of artist Louise Taussig.

Nearby, 415 Oakwood was built in 1894 by Charles A. Baker. It was damaged by fire in 1901 and rebuilt for W. C. Rumsey. Other houses of the area include 406 Hawthorne, a Tudor style house built for Andrew Deacon, president of Lambert Pharmaceutical Company and one of the founders of Algonquin Country Club. Built in the mid-1890s, it has 18-inch stone walls, leaded glass windows and black beam and white

Homes had lavish interiors.

plaster gables. Others are 319 Oakwood, built for the Weir family in 1900, 30 Joy avenue, built for the Leonard Martins in 1901, 312 Hawthorne, built in 1902, and 100 Orchard avenue built for Edward Lemoine Skinner.

Some of the early families used the natural rounding winding paths as a track to try out horses. Later, the same land was converted into the first Algonquin Country Club golf links. When Algonquin moved to its location on Berry road, the caddy and club house became the Missouri Pacific station house and continued in use until 1950. It had the same ticket taker, Mrs. Annie E. Door, from 1896 until its closing date.

The borough of Webster Park was restricted from the very first against anything commercial. Its streets were private until 1925 when an association made up of residents took over control. An early map of the Park shows some street names which are unfamiliar today. Rosemont was then called Maiden Lane, Spencer and Spring road.

One by one, the small boroughs — Old Orchard, Webster Park, Tuxedo Park and Selma — merged with Webster Groves, forming a green border around the town, insulating it from urban areas. Little by little, the conveniences of the urban areas came to Webster.

Kate Moody's reminiscences observed with a touch of impatience that around the turn of the century "the town seemed to be continually torn up," as utilities were put in. One year, "the sewer people dug trenches all over and put in pipes." Another year, "the electric company dug up the streets, then the water company, and finally the streetcar tracks were laid."

All the modern conveniences coupled with those flaming dogwoods and the song of the birds. Small wonder that many agreed with the quote from Ingersoll on the back cover of "Webster — Queen. . .:"

"It is no advantage to live in a great city where poverty degrades and failure brings despair. The fields are lovelier than paved streets, and great forests than walls of brick. Oaks and elms are more poetic than steeples and chimneys.

"In the country is the idea of home. There you see the rising and setting sun; you become acquainted with the stars and clouds. The constellations are your friends. You hear the rains on the roof and listen to the rhythmic sighing of the winds. You are thrilled by the resurrection called spring; touched and saddened by autumn, the grace and poetry of death. Every field is a picture, a landscape; every landscape a poem; every flower a tender thought, and every forest a fairy-land. In the country you preserve your identity — your personality. There you are an aggregation of atoms; but in the city you are only an atom of an aggregation."

The cynical might detect the hard sell through the poetry. The sociologist might decry the undertones of class appeal. The ecologist of today would be the most understanding. But more than any of these, today's loyal Websterite would read and nod and agree. It was a wonderful place to live.

It still is.

Webster's Name

When did Webster become Webster Groves? Dates are a little vague on that subject. Most histories mark the beginning of the post office as 1884 but Marion Smith, retired Webster Groves postmaster, recalled seeing a postcard in a stamp collection postmarked Webster Groves and dated 1851.

It is a matter of record that there was a conflict between the use of the word Grove and Groves in the beginning. In 1887, John Henton Carter, who wrote under the name of Commodore Rollingpin, was inspired to write a poem about the correct name of the town. It is in his book, "Log Cabin Poems," and goes like this:

WEBSTER GROVES

Just outside of St. Louis, an hour's ride or so —
By the new trolley lines or by steam you may go —
Enthroned on the hills, like a queen in her pride,
Looms a suburban town where a number reside.
      Dear Webster Groves
      Quaint Webster Groves!
Where the birds build their nests and the tame squirrel roves.

In pronouncing the name, do not leave out the "S"
Such a breach of decorum would cause much distress;
For the limits are broad, there are ravines and coves,
Therefore, sound it in full, as the subject behoves
      Say Webster Groves!
      Groves! Groves! Groves! Groves!
If you wish to partake of the fishes and loaves.

For a grove is a thing that a farmer might own
And manage the whole institution alone.
But give it the "S" and it then becomes plain,
You may look for a much more extended domain.
      A grove's a grove,
      A stove's a stove.
It's the plural that makes all the difference, by Jove!

We've a Mayor and a Council, a Marshall and, more,
We've a rock-pile to work with a lock to the door;
And whenever His Honor is called to a case,
The defendant is sure of a permanent place —
      "Rat, tat, tat, tat;
      Bat, bat, bat, bat" —
Before the incumbent knows just where he's at.

For our Fleming's a daisy and rides a fine horse —
Isn't given to moping or fits of remorse —
And a tramp is a thing he's inclined to detest,
And of all recreation claims work is the best.
>> That's why so few
>> Of these are blew
Into town on the winds that are constantly due.

Then in morals as well we have climbed to the top,
And are running so dry we've dispensed with all sop,
Even beefsteak and pudding is served to us plain,
And we've nothing to moisten our stomachs but rain.
>> That's why the Groves
>> Smell so of cloves
When the trains bring us back to our shady alcoves.

To be sure, we're ambitious — propose to extend
Our limits, and thereby our neighbors befriend,
May take in the County, and Carondelet, too,
And it's hinted our Mayor has his mind on St. Lou —
>> Teach 'em to walk
>> The Webster chalk
With an eye on 'em, too, that belongs to a hawk.

But the glory of Webster's the people themselves,
In their neat, cozy homes, with good books on the shelves;
And the high moral tone that pervades the whole place,
Giving charm to the speech and ennobling the face;
>> Where grocers trust
>> Years, if they must,
And a poet's not expected to live on a crust.

So here's to the Groves that we all love so well!
Oh, to name them's enough our emotions to swell!
Where the lanes are so long, and the shadows so dense,
And the ladies (God bless them!) have beauty and sense.
>> Long may they live
>> Pleasure to give
Nor remind us too soon of the water and sieve!

The last line, one may translate to mean you may not hold onto life's joys any more than you can hold water in a sieve (an expression of that day). Even with this melancholy note, Commodore Rollingpin conveyed with joy a resident felt then — and feels now — at living in Webster. Webster Groves!

Chapter Ten

Churches — The Next Group

As the Old Orchard, Webster Park, Tuxedo and other areas built up, there was a need for churches in those neighborhoods and by the turn of the century, more had been formed.

The fifth church, chronologically, was Holy Redeemer Catholic Church, started in 1886 when a committee called on Archbishop P.R. Kenrick to ask for a parish to serve the 45 Catholic families in the community. The nearest Catholic churches were St. James in the city and St. Joseph's in Clayton.

The Reverend Cornelius F. O'Leary was transferred from DeSoto to take charge. The first Mass was said on Sunday, November 1, 1886 at the old Lockwood school in Old Orchard and from then on every second Sunday, as Father O'Leary said Mass in Fenton alternate weeks.

The first parish baptism was on December 5, 1886, Thomas Murphy, the son of Thomas F. and Mary Ryan Murphy who was born on November 13. He was ordained a Jesuit priest in 1928 and said his first Mass at Holy Redeemer. The first church marriage was that of Frederieck G. How and Elizabeth DeYong, the first funeral that of William Broderick, in 1887.

The site of the new church at Lockwood and Selma was purchased from Alfred H. Geen for $500 in December 1886 and a frame building was erected for $2800. The Rev. P. J. Kane, succeeding Father O'Leary, said the first Mass in the new church on April 17, 1887, an occasion attended by only 20 persons because of heavy rains.

But the dedication on June 10 was a gala affair. The Very Rev. Vicar General Brady, St. Bridget's young men's sodality band and the choir from Annunciation parish took part. After the ceremony, it was

Holy Redeemer building, 1887.

recorded that, "The entire assembly repaired to the adjoining woods where a bountiful repast was served by the ladies of the congregation, the Wolfe-Tone Rifles gave an exhibition of drilling and St. Bridget's Band played the greater part of the afternoon."

On July 17, a contract was awarded to Clemens and Swanston, "two young men from the city who were anxious to introduce themselves in Webster," to build a rectory adjoining the church at a cost of $2650. In 1889 and 1890, Father Kane purchased land from Edward Joy on the corner of Lockwood and Joy avenues for a total cost of $1550, and plans were made for a new church. By January 1891, there were 110 families but then a new parish was established in Shrewsbury for German speaking members which reduced the membership to 90 families.

Ground was broken on June 12, 1895 for the new church which cost $40,000 without furnishings and was built of stone from the quarry at Meramec Highlands. This church was dedicated on May 2, 1897 and Mass celebrated by Archbishop Kain for 1200 members and guests. In 1901, a new school room was erected and in 1909 a contract for building a school building was let for $40,000. In September of that year, the Dominican Sisters took charge of the parish school, using four rooms for classes and the rest for living quarters.

On August 11, 1925 Father Kane died and the following October 15, Father Peter J. Dooley became the pastor. In March 1926, the parish association voted an improvement program, a new rectory was built on

Holy Redeemer Catholic Church, 1948.

Joy avenue and the Harding home at 20 Mason avenue was acquired for a convent.

Holy Redeemer celebrated its golden jubilee for three days in October 1936, culminating in a big gathering at the Knights of Columbus recreation center. The Catholic Youth Association was organized in May 1943.

In 1948, fire damaged the church, necessitating repairs. A new church

Holy Redeemer Catholic Church today.

was started in 1962 with A. F. and Arthur Stauder as architects. It was dedicated by Cardinal Joseph E. Ritter on Sunday, May 9, 1965 with ministers from neighboring Protestant churches marching at the head of the procession. Its total cost was $653,934.32. It was the first church of the diocese designed to take advantage of the liturgical changes approved by the Second Vatican Council and is beautiful in its simplicity.

The Rev. J. E. Ernst was pastor from 1949 until his death in 1960. In

October 1960, the Rev. Joseph L. Gottwald became pastor, with the Reverends Robert Lampert and John Lightle currently his assistants.

Blackwell Chapel, A.M.E. Zion Church, at 511 North Elm, traces its beginnings back to 1889 when members worshipped in a little store front church on Gore and Moody avenues. The Rev. J. B. Bunch was their leader. Among the "faithful few" were James and Susie McElroy, Jacob Esaw, Grant Morrison, S. Esaw and Nancy Morrison.

A better location was sought and ground purchased on Shady avenue, now Kirkham. From this site, worship was held for 30 years under 20 different ministers. In 1914 the indebtedness of long standing was paid and the mortgage burned. The Rev. D. C. Canty was minister at the time. His successor was the Rev. C. F. Collins. It was during his time that the present building was acquired in September 1916. The pastor, officers and members celebrated their first Sunday by marching from Shady avenue to the new Blackwell Chapel, singing, "We are marching to Zion." The present minister is the Rev. Dr. Robert R. Bowie.

In 1890, members of the First Congregational Church who lived in the Old Orchard area decided to form a church of their own.

The Joy family who were among the developers of Old Orchard were early members as were the Charles O. Twinings, Samuel Slawson and others. The Rev. F. W. Burrows was the first pastor. Services were first held in the Village Hall on Big Bend, but later the congregation moved to the church on Amelia and Fairlawn avenues. This congregation disbanded some years ago.

A community church in Tuxedo led to the establishment of both the Methodist and the Christian denomination churches in Webster Groves.

The farm of Dr. William H. Brown occupied the area which is now bounded by Newport, Marshall, Yeatman and Lafayette, and when the railroad cut through his land in the 1850s, he subdivided the area into 56 lots known as Brown's Place.

He continued to live in the brick farmhouse, on what is now the northwest corner of Bompart and Tuxedo. In 1889, he was struck and killed by a train and Brown's Place was sold at public auction on the courthouse steps in the spring of 1890.

In June, 1890, Tuxedo Park Lane and Improvement Company platted its new subdivision, which included most of Brown farm except for a section between Greeley and Newport which was subdivided as Fairview Park and a small area west of Bompart, called Clark's addition.

By 1893, about twenty families lived in Tuxedo Park. Some belonged to city churches, which meant going to St. Louis on the 9 a.m. train on Sunday morning and returning at 2 p.m. Clearly, a church in the area was needed.

Mrs. Edward Joy, a member of the Congregational church of Old Orchard, enlisted the help of a Mrs. Miller of Tuxedo Park and together they canvassed the neighborhood for Sunday School pupils. On Sunday, October 22, 1893, the first session of the nonsectarian school was held at the home of J. D. Lang. The next week, with an enrollment of ninety-two, classes were held on the second floor of a new barn behind the home of Henry Lenson on the southside of Fairview west of Cornelia.

Here, the Tuxedo Park Union Sunday School was organized, its trustees William Jamieson, C. C. Harris and Walter S. Roff, with B. G. Bridges secretary-treasurer and F. Benton Miller, superintendent. It was determined that the institution would never become denominational except for a majority vote of all adult resident members. Miller maintained neutrality by using the quarterlies of the Presbyterian church for three months, those of the Methodist for the next quarter and so on.

The Tuxedo Park and Land Improvement Company donated a lot on the north side of Atalanta near Margaret and a building was put up at 667 Atalanta with a local carpenter, Mr. Beckard, donating much of the labor. On September 1, 1894, services for adults began to be held on Sunday afternoons with volunteer ministers. The plan was to keep these sessions non-sectarian, too, but some ministers where willing to donate more time than others.

On January 3, 1895, a group met at the home of Walter S. Roff and organized the Tuxedo Park Methodist Episcopal church, with Dr. O. M. Stewart presiding elder and the Rev. Lenig minister. Eleven charter members were present: Mr. and Mrs. B. G. Bridge, Mr. and Mrs. Henry Lenson, Miss Emma Leese, Miss Frances G. Powell, Mr. and Mrs. Walter S. Roff, Mrs. Delia Roff, Mrs. Charlotte Rhodes and A. H. Reeves.

The Sunday school continued its non-denominational activities but here, too, differences ensued and a group under the leadership of the Rev. Mr. Bartholomew organized the Tuxedo Christian Chapel. On March 21, 1895, plans were made to erect a building.

The existence of the two denominations raised the question of building ownership. An election was held, the Methodists won and on May 18, the deed was transferred to Tuxedo Park M. E. Church.

The small church grew under the leadership of the Rev. William Lee Gray, and by 1907, membership was 80, but it dropped drastically to 45 within the next two years. It was a low point for the Methodists.

One year later, a transformation had taken place. The congregation was installed in a new building with ten times the valuation of the old, membership had climbed to 84 with Sunday School enrollment over 100, and ministerial support had more than doubled.

The transformation had come about through the Christian zeal of 80 year old Dr. Thomas H. Hagerty. Dr. Hagerty who was serving as chaplain for city institutions, heard of the troubles of the Tuxedo Park congregation. Each Sunday, he made the trip from his Grand avenue home in the city, unlocked the church building, built a fire in the stove, and then went from house to house in the neighborhood, inviting people to come to church. He would then return to church, ring the church bell and preach the sermon.

Under his leadership, the congregation took heart and took some courageous steps. The first was the decision to move from the rather isolated site on Atalanta to a more accessible spot.

On May 1, 1909, two lots were purchased for $1900 at Fairview and Bompart avenues. The old church was sold to another congregation. Then Dr. Hagerty stepped in and made a gift of $1000 to complete the purchase of the ground. In gratitude, the church called itself Hagerty Memorial Methodist Episcopal Church.

That summer they worshiped in a temporary building with a tarpaper roof and no floor, later from a basement level. Another gift from Dr. Hagerty for $7000 made it possible to build. A high point was the worship service on Palm Sunday, April 16, 1916 with Bishop William A. Quayle, an outstanding orator, preaching, and Dr. Hagerty conducting the service of dedication.

The $15,000 cost of the building was met from several sources, some anonymous. Dr. Hagerty died in 1917 at age 89, virtually penniless, having given all of his savings to the church.

Between 1910 and 1930, church membership increased tenfold, from 45 to 450. The Rev. T. Ross Hicks was reappointed in 1930, to the First Methodist Episcopal Church of Webster Groves, members having decided on a more explicit name. With unification in 1939, the word "Episcopal" was dropped and in the late 1960s, "United" was added.

Extensive improvements were made in the 14 year administration of the Rev. Wilburn S. Yoder (1943-57). In 1950 Bishop Ivan Lee Holt led in the ground breaking ceremonies. The new building was dedicated in June 1955 and by 1961 was free of debt. In 1973, Fellowship Hall was remodeled, and at present the church is "free of debt and in excellent repair."

But, as its present pastor, the Rev. Berlyn V. Farris wrote, "The building is only a tool in which a church does its work. The real history of a church is written in the hearts of the generation of children, youth and adults who find a community of fellowship which brings them into a life-changing relationship with Christ and sends them out into the world to do their part in bringing the Kingdom of God into being on earth as it is in heaven."

The other half of the Tuxedo community church also had its hard times but also had a happy outcome.

When it was no longer possible to use the building which had been occupied jointly, W. S. Hull donated ground for a church. In 1895 while Sunday School rooms were being built, meetings were held in the Hull home.

In 1908, the church sanctuary was completed at a cost of $4500. This building, on Tuxedo and Bompart, is now occupied by a Chinese church. Early preachers included O. A. Bartholomew, E. N. Tucker, Luther Moore, W. W. Hopkins and G. M. Billett. Some preached without remuneration, some for whatever the congregation felt it could afford to give them.

The church grew in membership but there was a discouraging turnover in ministers, twenty-four in forty-five years. Then in 1939, a young man who had just been married and needed money for housing and tuition to get through Eden Seminary, took the job of pastor on a temporary basis, intending to stay, perhaps three years at most. In 1975, the Rev. Dr. Raymond F. McCallister retired after thirty-six years with the church now known as Webster Groves Christian Church.

In those years, the only Disciples of Christ church in the Webster area grew from a few hundred members to 1800, its budget going from $5000 a year to $200,000. And Dr. McCallister became a civic, community and religious leader in the St. Louis area.

In 1954, a new church was built, carved into a corner of Westborough Country Club's golf course at 1320 West Lockwood avenue, a handsome building for one of the major churches of its denomination in the

United States.

In an interview before his retirement, Dr. McCallister indicated that he felt the church might have come full circle and again assumed a role as a community church, with "probably 30 denominations represented on a Sunday," and a minimum of denominationalism.

Noted for his eloquence, Dr. McCallister expressed at this time his views on the future of religious awakening which were optimistic.

"I think for years we treated the Bible as a beautiful piece of literature and didn't see it as the food and nourishment for souls," he said. . . "Some Sundays, I think, as I stand in the pulpit, people are thinking, 'Don't give us a book review or tell us about a TV show. I can read and I have a TV set, too.' No, they're thinking, 'Preacher, do you have a word for us from the Lord?' "

The Lutherans, to whom Dr. Hagerty's Methodist church sold their building, were first organized on March 14, 1897, when a group of families gathered at the home of Albert H. Buser, at 787 Big Bend road, and went in a body to the Royal Arcanum Lodge Hall on the second floor about a grocery store on the southeast corner of Big Bend and Log Cabin lane to hold services. The Rev. M. S. Sommer, then pastor of Grace Lutheran Church in St. Louis, conducted the service, preaching from 1 John 5:4, "And this is the victory that overcometh the world, even our faith."

Arrangements were made to continue services at this location and the Rev. Frederick Bente, a Concordia Seminary professor, was called as first pastor with student assistants.

An early member of the congregation recalled that Mr. Buser would reach the lodge hall at 6 a.m., carrying fire wood from home, would build a fire in the stove, sweep and dust the hall and return home for more wood so the congregation would be comfortable. Families making up the early congregation were named Buser, Rasmussen, Jensen, Larsen, Grauer, Lauenborg and Wolfram.

By 1900, the congregation was known as Old Orchard Lutheran Church. Then at the suggestion of Peter Rasmussen, the name Christ Lutheran Church was taken. The first confirmation class had one member, Lillian Lauenborg. In the next were Edna and Florence Buser, Palm Lauenborg and Ella Wolfram. In 1904, Lillian and Ferdinand Larsen were confirmed; in 1906, Lillian Buser, Flora Larsen, Mary and Martin Rasmussen and Helena Wolfram.

The church moved from Royal Arcanum Hall to the Village Hall, then to Suburban School of Music Hall at Summit and Newport, and in 1909 to the building at 667 Atalanta. Their first altar there was made from an old office desk by one of the members.

By 1910, there were 52 members and a Ladies Aid. In 1915, a full time resident, the Rev. George Luecke, Jr., just graduated from Concordia, came as pastor. In 1920, a lot was purchased on the southeast corner of Lockwood and Selma. The cornerstone was laid in August 1923, the building completed in 1924 at a cost of $30,000. Early records mention the zeal and generosity of Robert C. Napier at paying off the indebtedness.

By 1930 a new building was needed. The Sunday School had grown under Mrs. J. S. Lake and was using space in the nearby high school. By 1934, two services were held. In 1940, Herman Gall, board president, began an expansion program. The Church property was sold to the Webster Groves school board and the present lot on the southwest corner was purchased. The new church was dedicated on November 15, 1942. The present pastor of this church is the Rev. Warren W. Gritzke.

Bethany Evangelical Lutheran Church was organized in 1897, too. Its charter members are listed as Abel Nielsen Winthers, Anders Petersen, Jens Anderson, H. C. Anderson, Jens Nissen, Hans Bock, Peter Hansen, L. P. Hansen, Hans Hansen and Jacob Braroe. The Winthers family gave free board and lodging to the Rev. J. K. Jensen, the first pastor, and the others pledged one dollar a month.

This group joined the United Evangelical Lutheran Synod that year. Its second pastor, the Rev. N. Bentsen, helped build the church at Fairview and Pacific avenues; it was dedicated in November 1904. Later pastors included the Reverends L. Johnson, M. T. Jensen, Pastor N. Bentsen a second term, Pastor Weismann, Pastor N. Bentsen a third time (1929-40) and the Rev. Axel Andersen.

Bethany is now a member of the American Lutheran Church; its present pastor is the Rev. David Ylvisaker, and its location is at Fairview and Glen road.

Chapter Eleven

Turn of the Century —
Turn Toward Growth

The census of 1900 gave Webster Groves 1,895 inhabitants, an increase from the 1,783 listed in 1890, but not a tremendous addition considering the building promotions which had been going on. But with the turn of the century came the turn toward growth. By 1910, there were 7,080 residents in Webster Groves. It had passed its neighbor, Kirkwood, and was hailed as the fastest growing city in Missouri for that decade, with a population increase of 300 percent.

The year 1900 saw the establishment of the Bank of Webster Groves in an office at North Gore avenue and the Missouri Pacific tracks. Incorporated with a capital stock of $25,000, its first officers were: W. C. Rumsey, president; N. D. Thompson, vice president; C. O. Evans, cashier; Henry Prehn, Charles L. Martin, Dr. Marshall Baker, Kent Jarvis, Charles W. Ferguson, George L. Edwards and C. L. Merrill, directors. Another 1900 development was the first Bell Telephone Exchange, set up in a small building shared with a barber on North Gore and Moody. Miss Mary Gaine presided with a kitchen table as her desk. This was a great advance in telephone service. A few years before, there had been just three telephones in town, all on the Kinloch system, one in the L. P. Douglas Drug Store, later called the Webster Groves Pharmacy, one in the Krausnick home on Bompart, and the other, a public phone. For a while, there were phones on both the Kinloch and Bell systems which led to great confusion as persons on one system could not telephone those on the other.

The first automobile, the Oakland "6", made its appearance in Webster in the early 1900s. Its sole county agency, managed by Walter Scott, was in the Brannon building, in place of the saloon where the Atwater holdup was plotted. This later was the location of the first filling station, perhaps an apt successor for a saloon. The second floor of the

Horse and buggy days at the Henry Schulz home.

Brannon Building was used for the high school and the late Tom Ward, a councilman, recalled that there was a fence along the railroad tracks to which boys tied their horses during school hours.

There is no dearth of reminiscence about this period in Webster history; in fact, it is the very period that Webster "old timers" recall in moments of nostalgia.

A fine source of local color is contained in the published reminiscences of a resident of that period, Captain Tom L. Gibson's "Memories of The Old Home Town," first published as columns in the Webster News-Times and, at Christmas 1946, in paperback book.

In a foreword, he quoted Longfellow:

> *Often in thoughts I go up and down*
> *The pleasant streets of that dear old town*
> *And my youth comes back to me.*

Captain Tom's book goes "up and down the pleasant streets" of Webster Groves, recalling first one family, then another, relating anecdotes about this character and that, and recapturing an era.

The Will Dyer home, he recalled, was a place where "festivities took place, such as home talent shows, church festivals and other like affairs." There was always a crowd at the F. D. Booth place and "their hospitality knew no bounds." It was great sport to roam around that farm, "slide down the strawstack, swim in the Booth pond, ride Nellie, the horse, around and when dinner time came, what a meal. . ."

It was "quite a stretch from the Booth farm to town" (Lee avenue to Lockwood) and midway was Hester Foster, a black woman who gave a barbecue once a year and invited all of her white friends.

"How I remember her laugh," Captain Tom wrote. "It was the most hearty I ever knew anyone to have. She was part of our family. One day her boy, Bob, and I upset her tub of blueing water and she caught us both. As she whipped me, while holding Bob's hand between her knees, she said, 'The white folks fust.' Then came Bob's turn and she warmed him up even more than she had me."

On the western skirts of town was the Brownell home. They used to come in with their span of croptailed horses with a coachman and "there was something very 'scrumdunctious' about their coming. . . we all felt we really knew somebody who belonged to royalty."

Dr. Marshall Baker, who lived on the southeast corner of Gore and Lockwood, "was so kind at all times and had a way in a sick room, or a sort of curing by his philosophy." Next door was Mrs. Hattie Fletcher and across the street was the Tichnor headquarters. He was the builder of Tichnorville, the houses on small lots between Lockwood and Cedar and up the east side of Gore.

There was John L. Sutton, an outstanding auctioneer, and the Thompson estate and the Blackmer home, and the Sylvester Watts on Oak Terrace. And the old Gheislin home between Jackson and Swon, which sat in the middle of a ten acre grove.

Tom Gibson was active in city politics in those years and recalled one obstinate citizen, Bill Yeager, who felt his taxes were too high and put up a sign in front of his house which read, "FOR SALE BECAUSE OF TAXES BEING SO HIGH IN WEBSTER." The City Fathers didn't care much for this so Mayor Ed Hart (1903-11) sent Tom over to visit Yeager and a reasonable adjustment was made.

It's a wonder we ever grew up. Orpha Kendrick (on dog), Walter Skinner (left) and Herbert Baker.

In the Gibson narrative, men who later were dignified civic figures are known as "Lemon" Skinner and "Bun" Booth and "Rabbit" Lewis. There's a Tom Sawyer-Huck Finn quality about some of the episodes, such as the time he and two other little boys decided the men who had robbed the Frisco train had hidden their loot in one of Webster's many sinkholes near Rock Hill road and climbed down with a bull's eye lard oil lantern, a torch and some candles to search. They got lost underground, their lights went out and it was three very scared kids who sighted a glimmer of light and shoved their way up through the tiny opening. Said one of them, Wallace Gruet: "I know a lot of better ways than that to get money. It would be a lot better and safer for us to rob the Frisco ourselves."

There was plenty of adventure for children in the small town that Webster was then. Orpha Kendrick, who grew up in the Webster Park area, once reminisced that it was amazing that she ever grew to be an adult. Much of her childhood was spent in the tops of trees, walking the rafters of every house to be built in the park and deliberately poking bumblebees out of the board walks.

Games in those days were hide and seek, cops and robbers, and battles were fought with homemade swords and old clothes boiler lids.

"The most of all fun was exploring the off limits culverts, trestles and sinkholes where the mosquitoes and rattle snakes held sway," she recalled. "There were always pretty flowers in those sinkholes as well as tin cans. Somehow we all must have led a charmed life for not one of us ever was bitten or cut. Needless to say, our parents knew nothing of these ventures nor did they know of the initiation each new child had to go through when a family moved into Webster Park."

Orpha Kendrick went to three grades of Bristol School and then attended a private school operated by Mrs. Wilda Mills in the Mills home which was on Lockwood avenue.

Webster residents today think of Lockwood avenue as a business district but in the early 1900s it was primarily residential. Mrs. Edward F. Wilson, who was Adele Trembley then, could name the residents house by house in her reminiscing moments.

" There was the Presbyterian manse and then there was the Rod Allen home and then the N. D. Allen home -- she taught music. Then there was the Ferguson home (now Parker-Aldrich), the Alcotts, the Sievers and the Mills."

Mrs. Wilson remembered Mrs. Kendrick's private kindergarten on Elm avenue, Mrs. Sutton who taught primary at Presbyterian church, entertainments at the Allen building, high school classes in the old Brannon building.

Just about everyone of that era remembers Straub's in the Bristol building. William A. Straub began his business in 1901, making deliveries by horse and mule. There were two other grocers and he was told there wasn't room for a third but he excelled in service.

Mrs. Richard (Rose Mary) Wessells remembers a family story told her about a woman who bought all of her groceries at another store and only her meat at Straub's but Straub's politely delivered both orders.

"Straub's was noted for their courtesy," Miss Adele Stine said. "When a small girl paid the bill, Miss Lulu Straub saw that one of the clerks gave her a bag of candy. One day the clerks were busy and the little girl went home without her candy. Miss Lulu noticed and had it delivered to the house."

Prehn's grocery is remembered too by the old timers, but it is Prehn's Hill they recall with most fondness, the steep slope on North Gore from the tracks down to Kirkham which was closed off for sledding in snowy weather.

There were 27 trains operating through Webster Groves on the Missouri Pacific line in the early 1900s. Trains which took the men to work at several early morning hours. A shoppers special later in the morning and then the 1:30 matinee train and the ones returning late in the afternoon with the shoppers, the theater goers and the workers; then a theater train which went into St. Louis at 7:30 in the evening and the late night trains which brought the last travelers home.

Trains weren't the only means of transportation by this time. Street cars were getting much business and old timers remember the Kirkwood line which ran along Shady (Kirkham) avenue. During the World's Fair of 1904, it was the custom for young matrons to take the street car to the Fair grounds in Forest Park and then their husbands would join them after work.

Students took the street cars, too. Miss Ethel Sprague whose family lived in a house built by Charlotte Holmes, more familiarly known as "the Coggeshall house" on North Gore near Kirkham, remembered walking -- or more often running -- through the big pasture to catch the car to get to Washington University. That was also in the 1904-05 period.

These wide open spaces are remembered by all of the generation who were children in the 1900-10 era.

"The house where I was born was the end of this street. There were no other houses beyond or across or anywhere. It was all woods. Dewberry patches and ponds and fields, a crabapple lane -- and snakes. There was a spring down there; we carried our water up the hill. It was a rugged life but it was a healthy life."

The speaker is Luther St. James, who, with his sister, Mrs. Della Brown,

Children at Douglass School, Luther St. James is in group.

was recalling life on Holland avenue in North Webster at the time their school pictures were made. . ."that must have been 1910 because Luther was about six years old then. . ."

At one time the St. James family owned all the area from Ravine avenue to Thornton along Holland and farmed the ground down to Kirkham where a shopping center now stands. The two story house covered with red brick shingles at 702 Holland avenue is "the old homestead" to them, where all six children were born -- Mrs. Ida Johnson (now dead), Henry who lives across the street, Della, Margaret Moore, Edna McCarey and Luther. Plus the two who didn't live through infancy.

Their memories, bittersweet, are of life in the then very segregated part of town where black people lived. Their grandparents were the children of slaves who came up from Virginia.

"A man named William Long gave my father's father a job sharecropping on Grant's Farm and that's where my father was born. My mother came from the Lovejoy Farm, that was on Laclede Station road and Highway 66. When my mother was eight years old (about 1878) she came to this area with her father; she had no mother. Our parents were married in some judge's house on the corner of Oakwood and Fairlawn."

They're not sure how old the house at 702 Holland is but Henry, who is 78, was born there and it wasn't a new house then.

Their father farmed on a large scale -- a big rhubarb patch, peas, string beans, potatoes, sweet potatoes, butterbeans, tomatoes, corn, watermelons, "mushmelons". . .all that plus hogs and chickens and horses and three cows. Apparently it was a healthy life, for their mother lived to age 92, their father to 94 and their father's mother "passed" at age 101.

They attended Douglass school and high school. With a classmate, Louis Laird, they poured over an old school photo identifying students and teachers -- "Aunt" Susie Crockett and Mr. Thomas A. Moore -- "the most wonderful teacher anyone could have had."

Was Webster a good place to live?

"I'd say it was a good place for white people," Mrs. Brown said bluntly. "Oh it's better for Negroes now. People can go to school, to the Y, to picture shows. In our day it was, 'Stay on your own side of town.' You couldn't go to the swimming pool. Our taxes helped pay for it but we couldn't use it."

A classmate, Harold Esaw, interviewed by high school students for their history project book, "In Retrospect", published last year, expressed contentment with his relations with white people. Asked if there had been racial problems, he replied:

"Very seldom. Webster had been one of the nicest places. Some of the nicest Christian white people in the United States live right here in the city limits of Webster Groves and I think we've got along very nice."

A large percentage of those who grew up in what was known as "North Webster" have stayed there. The St. James family now have four houses, the most recent built by Land Clearance in 1961, on the land where they grew up. Across the street in front of Henry's house stands a gnarled pin oak, its trunk almost hollow but its branches still leafy and proud against the sky.

It was planted by Henry's boy (he retired as a U. S. Army major last year), one of the trees given school children on Arbor Day.

Its roots are deep, as are the roots of many of the families in north Webster.

Jenny Gray Williams, once a slave.

Sarah Williams Caldwell, when she attended Lincoln Institute.

The area where the St. James family lived was called "The Hill" by black families who lived in the "Old Community" around Rock Hill and Kirkham.

"And Kirkham was always Kirkham in our neighborhood, not Shady avenue," recalled Mrs. Sarah Caldwell.

Mrs. Caldwell and her older sister, Mrs. Bessie Bush, live in Kirkwood's Meacham Park but they would like to move back to "the old homestead," the two story white frame house which still stands at 438 W. Kirkham avenue. A young man named Bill Jenkins painted a watercolor of it around 1915; it hangs in their bedroom.

These two are one generation of slavery. Their parents, Jennie Gray and Jordan Williams took their names from the last families that owned them before Emancipation. There were eight children in the family. The father dug cisterns and died young. The mother worked for the Kauffmans on Rock Hill and other white families. "We had a hard way to go," says Mrs. Caldwell.

They went to Douglass school when it had three rooms and three teachers. Mrs. Caldwell went on to Lincoln Institute in Jefferson City. Mrs. Bush, like her mother, worked for families, for the Gores and the Helfensteins who still had all their bells to summon slaves hanging in the kitchen.

Mrs. Bush, born in 1880, is now 95 and hard of hearing, still brightens with laughter as she reminisces over the "old settlers" they remember — Romeo Burnett and Arnold, Mary and Eleanor Brown, the Sims, Inge, Morrison, Breedon and Elazer families. And Mrs. Bolden, old when they were young; they would stop on their way home from school and thread needles for her.

Street lights? They remember none. Public transportation? What was that? They walked: to school, to work, to town, up to Prehn's to buy a bucket of molasses for mama to cook with the beans.

What was it like, in that era from 1900 to 1910? Different for each child, each adult, in each neighborhood. But Ruth M. Owen gave a charming picture of what it was like for many, in a newspaper article, "Do You Remember Webster As It Was 35 Years Ago?"

"It was such a little town then," she wrote. "Wide, quiet, dusty roads, grassy plots in the middle and shaded on each side by huge, overhanging maples. Houses every once in a while, long spaces in between. Board walks with wide cracks between the boards and holes that unexpectedly let your foot slip through to the tall grasses underneath. Splinters lurking, long and sharp, that sprang up and attacked you every time you went barefoot.

"Little rustic bridges over every ravine of any depth, where sweethearts like to linger. . . leaning against the flimsy railings and almost hidden by the drooping maple foliage from above.

"The time of two telephone systems, you, of course, having a Kinloch when all of your friends had a Bell.   Those were the days when the annual football dance was held in the old Bristol building and the whole family went -- even grandma. My, but you thought the hall was beautiful, all decorated. . .in pennants and ribbons and flowers. And the girls were so stylish, too, in their high buttoned shoes, little stiff boned collars, long sweeping skirts and big pompadours. Little dumpy you sat there in your red woolen dress, black stockinged legs dangling over the edge of the seat, tight braids looped over each ear and finished off with big red bows, and just filled yourself with looking.

"The whole football team came on the stage and there was your brother Henry. . . Mr. Hixson, he was the principal of the high school, made a speech and so did Coach Roberts. . .and then Coach Roberts presented each one of the team with a big orange "W". The whole place

Remember what it was like. . . way back then?

cheered and yelled until you thought sure the roof would cave in. . .you couldn't help but think how smart Henry was going to feel after this and how he was going to think that he shouldn't have to clean out the chicken house at all any more."

Ruth Owen remembered the "old base burner" which heated the house where you could see red coals through the isinglass. . .the grocery man coming around on foot each morning to take your order. . .chocolate sodas at Mueller's drug store. . .boys swimming in an old abandoned quarry. . .

"Those were the days when the great tragedy of the spring was that it was always too cold at Easter to take off your long underwear. Mama always had to cut out the neck of one of your old suits and maybe the sleeves too, so that you could wear your new white dress without it showing. You had new long white ribbed stockings too and black patent leather slippers and a leghorn hat with blue forget-me-nots on it and you wouldn't have missed Sunday School for the world. You and Henry colored eggs the night before Easter but you never ate them because Mama thought the dye was poison."

There was a dance pavilion at the end of the Manchester car line called "Stump Hill" but you never went there because it was supposed to be

The Lockwood children perch above Lockwood pond.

tough and visited only by "kitchen mechanics." More permissible was the nickelodeon owned by Mr. Burton and operated by his son Earl, a couple of neighbor boys, the piano player and one operator. They showed great classics, like Mary Pickford in "To Save Her Soul."

And in the early spring, children would go into the woods and pick violets.

"The streams were up, water gushing, the ground was soft and squashy and the prettiest violets were always in a field with a fiery-eyed wicked looking cow and you and your red coat were afraid to venture near.

"In the fall it was nuts that drew you into the woods and persimmons and lovely lovely autumn leaves. While Henry was up in the tree knocking down the nuts and persimmons, you loved to pile the leaves together and make a house of many rooms. You were queen, a princess, a great lady with a vast domain which you presided over with such fairness and such great justice that your subjects or servants or friends bowed down to you. . .

"Life seemed so simple, so sweet and so satisfying.
"Do you remember?"

Chapter Twelve

City Hall —
Police —
Fire Departments

It wasn't all sweetness and light in the 1900 to 1910 period, and even in the glow of nostalgia, it is clear that the comforts of daily living left much to be desired by today's standards.

"We had cistern water, coal oil lamps and plumbing in the backyard," recalls Paul Strippgen, who lived, as he still does, in the Old Orchard section of town.

"Tuxedo was a mud road, Newport avenue was a mud road, and when it rained, it was like the old ranger used to say about the mountain roads, they weren't 'passable or jackassable.' "

In memory, Strippgen can walk, as he walked then, along Lockwood and remember each store -- Fred Kaenter's bakery, Pete Franke's tin shop, Hess's feed and grocery, Van Nort's drug store, Moreley's butcher shop, the two story hotel where National Food now stands, Busch's grocery and meat market, Fritz's cigar store. Beyond that was the Lockwood farm and the lake "where kids went fishin' and fightin' in summer and skatin' and fightin' in winter."

It was a time when you "went to the bakery and bought six loaves of bread for a quarter and the baker gave each kid a doughnut." Or you "went to the butcher where you'd get five pounds of pork chops for 15 cents and the butcher would give each kid a wiener."

Kids were expected to earn their keep, though. Strippgen's father worked on the construction of the St. Louis World's Fair in 1903-04. Children were prohibited from being on the grounds while work was in

Old Orchard Pond. . . fishin' and fightin'.

progress but their father would pile the kids in the wagon, and, as he approached the pass gate, toss a tarpaulin over them and "sneak" them in. For an outing?

"Heck, no, we worked," said Strippgen. "We were his source of cheap labor."

City Hall in the early days was as primitive as the rest of town. Official business was conducted in the Moody real estate office. Early city records are contained in big ledger books, written by hand in beautiful script. They are a continuing chronicle of improving streets, widening roads, providing better streets lights, and trying to control such health hazards as stagnant ponds and such nuisances as "keeping hogs on Gray avenue." It was the day when the River des Peres was still known for its inimitable fragrance as the River Despair.

Mrs. Mary Lou Paillou, city clerk, feels something of a proprietary interest in that first book of records. When she became clerk, she found book number one was missing and undertook an exhaustive search for it. One day, looking for something else in the properties room of the Police Department, she found it, high on a shelf, covered with dust, and returned it to its place of honor. On reading it, she came up with this observation:

"The first thing the early city fathers did was to provide a jail and license dogs and business men."

And it is true that the licensing of dogs (and merchants) takes up much

First City Hall, as painted by Marilynne Bradley.

space in the first book. There is also a stern ordinance to "restrain the running at large or pasturing in the streets and highways of certain domestic animals."

Health problems of all kinds were paramount. In February 1902 there was a small pox epidemic and the city required that all unvaccinated persons be vaccinated. An early book of records of births and deaths kept by Dr. Marshall Baker gives an idea of ills of the times. Among causes of death were bronchitis, scarlet fever, LaGrippe, cholera morbus, cancer, apoplexy, summer complaint, and, in the case of a three year old, "negligence."

After Mayor Fleming's term ended, Thomas C. Young, an architect, became mayor. Following Young in 1903 was E. S. Hart, printing executive who served until 1911.

By 1907, the handwritten ledger had given way to a typewritten record. The typewriter was rented from Fuller-Coult Company, $5 for three months.

"Granitoid" sidewalks were being built in many parts of the city. Livestock continued to be a problem. A new ordinance required that "chickens, geese, ducks, turkey and other fowl be kept within a wire netting fence sufficient to prevent their escape therefrom." For

Fowl on the loose.

violators, a stiff fine was imposed, $1 to $10.

Lighting varied from electric on the main streets to none at all in many parts of town. Paul Strippgen remembers carbide lights in Old Orchard and Captain Tom Gibson wrote of Fred Algoet, "The old lamplighter." The lamps he lighted were kerosene, oldtimers say. The records of July 1904 contain an ordinance which granted St. Louis County Gas Company power to "construct, maintain and operate gas works, lamp posts to light streets, avenues and alleys and other public places."

Some areas resisted the newfangled modern improvements. Captain Gibson in a chapter on the "bloody Fourth ward," the Tuxedo Park area, reminisced:

"We wanted to give them electric lights and water but they did not want them. I can see them now at night time, wandering up and down paths with lanterns in their hands. . . They would send children to the spring with buckets for the family water supply. . . We regulars of the city administration felt a missionary spirit to bring them into the fold so we could tax their belongings. . . .." James Bettis, he recalled, wrote a poem about those residents entitled, "We Don't Want No 'Lectric Light."

Water and lights prevailed but Sunday blue laws were maintained for many years. In May 1910, according to City Hall records, the Gem Moving Picture show requested permission to be open on Sundays. Petition denied.

Transportation was improving. In 1912, a request was sent to the United Railway Company to provide owl car service so that if one missed the midnight car from Broadway and Market, he would not have to wait for the first car to leave the barns at 4:34 a.m.

In 1914 the city was reclassified as a third class city. In 1918, the commission form of government was adopted. In 1932 the present City Hall was built. And in 1954, the charter form of government was adopted.

Mayors throughout the years have been:

1896 - W. Scott Fleming	1929 - E. F. Wilson
1901 - Thomas C. Young	1931 - John B. Chipman
1904 - E. S. Hart	1937 - Edwin F. Chapman
1911 - V. O. Saunders	1945 - Clarence Appel
1912 - W. F. Biederman	1953 - John Cassidy
1914 - C. W. Biederman	1954 - William Guffey
1915 - R. S. B. Tidd	1958 - Charles Graubner
1919 - Carl H. Holekamp	1960 - Gus Nations
1921 - M.B. Peterson	1964 - Jackson Adams
1923 - J. B. Chipman	1970 - John W. Cooper, Jr.

Named "Citizen of the Year" in Webster Groves in 1967, for two efforts, his work in developing the ice skating rink and the Webster Groves Historical Society, Mayor Cooper has a long record of achievements outside of Webster Groves as well.

He has been president of the St. Louis County Municipal League and president of the mayors of the large cities in St. Louis County. The 1972 Republican candidate for Congress in the second district, he is also a director of the East-West Gateway Coordinating Council, state commissioner of the Missouri American Revolution Bi-Centennial Commission for 1976, past president of the University of Missouri Alumni Association, director of the Human Development Corporation of Metropolitan St. Louis, member of the Legislative Affairs committee of the State Municipal League, and a member of the National Committee on Environmental Quality, National League of Cities, Washington, D.C. He is listed in a recent edition of "Outstanding Civic Leaders in America."

A part of Webster Groves City Hall leadership since 1960, Mayor Cooper has said that he felt Webster's one time image of a community interested primarily in its own activities, living "to itself" is changing to one of a community equally cooperative and concerned with the world around it.

Since 1954, city managers have been a part of Webster Groves government. The first was Harold C. McClintock followed by Richard L. Black, George L. Majoros and the present manager, Joseph B. Morrison.

Present Council Members are: Marshall M. Burton, Dorothy Anne Drinkhouse, Malcolm Holekamp, John S. McCarthy, Alexander B. McMillan, and William F. Symes. Interestingly, all but Symes are second generation residents of Webster Groves.

Police Force

From the days of Officer Nace, police protection grew with the town. In the early days there were bills for horseshoeing of police horses but by 1918 the chief was allowed $20 a month for auto maintenance.

They were called marshals at that time. Precise records are not available as to exact years of tenure, but the early heads of the Webster police department included Thomas Dunworth, Arthur Madden, Fred Knickman and John Donnelly. In 1924, Andrew McDonnell became Chief of Police, followed in 1948 by Ovid Yadon, who served until Fred Zinn took over in 1964. The present Chief of Police is Clyde Wallace.

Longest in point of time and one of the most colorful of police chiefs was Andy McDonnell, whose sister, Miss Mary C. McDonnell, was a practicing lawyer in Webster for 30 years.

Robert Hereford, writing about Webster Groves in the St. Louis Star-Times, reported that it was once said that "bums beating a ride on the boxcars, when caught, would say, 'Don't put me off in Andy McDonnell's town.' "

A kind of suburban Sherlock Holmes as another news story described him, McDonnell was the first law enforcement officer in the area to use police dogs. His were bloodhounds. Private individuals had donated money for them after a rash of house prowlers in Webster, and he kept a close accounting of what he spent on their maintenance. A firm believer in their efficacy, he once said:

"If there is one thing a criminal fears, it is a bloodhound." His first dogs, Buster and Jenny, came from Texas and were later sold to Georgia for use in convict camps there. They had helped solve a robbery on the Pevely farm of Daniel C. Kerckhoff among other achievements. The Chief's favorite dog was Webster Baby, an English

Webster Groves Police Department, 1928. Taken on lawn of Masonic Temple, Lockwood and Elm avenues. Left to right: Eugene Piper; Wm. Grey; Patrick Wheylan, Clarence Brooks; Edward Herron; Marshall Strassinger; Andrew McDonnell, Chief; Woodrow Teice; Fred Smith; Dad Carter; George Linze, Frank Lenz; Charles Niel.

Webster Groves Police, 1939. First row: A. Larson; O Yaden, Lt.; A. McDonald, Chief; P. Whelan, Captain; W. Smith. Second row: F. Smith, T. McCarthy; M. Houghton; M. Strassinger; G. Heggs. Third row: E. Heron; A Quante; C. Gray; C. Marshall; F. Lenz.

bloodhound who caught a murderer and a filling station embezzler. In the latter case, the dog kept returning to the car of the filling station manager who had reported the robbery; finally he admitted he'd invented the story and hidden the money.

In 1939, Chief McDonnell was the one policeman praised by a St. Louis County grand jury which blasted law enforcement in the county. He was known as a friend of boys. One of his innovations was a Saturday morning boys court run by the boys themselves to pass judgment on minor infractions.

On one occasion, Chief McDonnell caught a boy taking a sign from a merchant's place of business. In his defense, the boy said that everyone was doing it; it was a hobby, collecting signs. The chief made the rounds of schools giving a talk in which he said:

"When you take a sign from a merchant's store, you might as well be taking money from his cash register. Those signs cost money. I want all those signs returned. Why don't you fellas bring them down to the police station Saturday and we'll return them?"

On Saturday, the windows of the police station were totally obscured with a stack of 200 signs which were returned to the merchants of Webster Groves.

Lt. Col. Henry (Hank) Kuhlmann retired after 31 years on the police force, 1942 to 1973. He recalled that when he started out, there were 12 to 14 men on the force and no civilian employes. The present staff consists of 46 men and five civilian workers. Officers did their own typing then. There was one dispatcher and cars were equipped with one way reception radios.

"If we received a call, our dispatcher would call St. Louis and they would call us. The message was repeated twice but there was no way of checking up to find if we'd received it or not."

He recalled that two police men were killed on duty in his time. Their pictures are on the wall of the Police Department: Jacob Busch, shot in a holdup March 11, 1923, and Laine C. Braun, killed on a motorcycle, May 17, 1970.

Next to the day he was married, Fred Zinn considers June 1, 1948 the biggest day of his life. It was the day he became a member of the Webster Groves Police Department. He was 22 years old and thought he "had all the answers." He worked for Ovid Yadon whom he describes as "the kindest, gentlest, most patient man who ever lived." Zinn's first job was walking a beat in Old Orchard 10 hours a day and night, $165 a month. (Incidentally, Webster police still do a certain percentage of "walking" time although they operate from cars.)

Zinn remembers murders, suicides, sad and dramatic incidents but thinks the most important work he did had to do with juveniles. He believes in corrective work, starting early, at age 7 or 8 in a boy's life when he needs not permissiveness but firm direction.

Zinn became chief on March 1, 1964. He has the interesting

combination of FBI training and a college degree from Webster College and has long advocated the training of policemen in drama courses for better communication in crisis situations. In retirement, he works for a security firm in Clayton and still lives in Webster Groves, where he has lived for 42 years.

Clyde Wallace is the new chief of police, and his men continue to make the news. In 1974, Harold Jones posed as a hippie to catch marijuana pushers.

Fire Department

Little boys of all ages have delighted in following the firemen and there are many memories and much memorabilia about the Webster Groves Fire Department.

It all started with a hand-pulled hose reel and a group of volunteers in 1906. Two volunteer departments were formed, one at the Gore-Lockwood area and one for Old Orchard. A framed picture which hangs over the desk of Deputy Chief Joseph Beaver is dated 1908 and volunteers in the picture are identified as: Harry Rhodes, Fred Knickman, Howard Whitnack, Fred Hess, Ernest Hess, Joe Chamberlain, Matt Pollite, Adam Macrander, Tom Macrander, Ed Bartley, Theodore Wolfram, Harry Newel and George Bopp, chief.

Mrs. Louise Crieger, City Hall receptionist, has a gold badge presented to her father, A. M. Paullette, on August 13, 1908, honoring him as a volunteer with the Webster 2 company. Other early volunteers were named Gabelman, Zinn, McDonald, Holekamp, Henry, Schultz, Clamp, Freund, Crider and Zuroweste.

The first apparatus and teams of horses were purchased through subscriptions of businessmen and equipment was kept in the livery stables, Parker's in the Old Webster area and Hewlett's which was later Bopp's in Old Orchard. Old timers remember the white horses and the steam operated pumping apparatus.

Volunteers were called out by the ringing of the bell in the Presbyterian church and one in the Old Orchard Fire Tower. One old time resident, Paul Strippgen, recalls that "they'd have to go home and get their helmets," and that it was a familiar jibe that "our firemen never lost a foundation or a chimney."

Early volunteers of the Fire Department.

They battled against odds. Occasionally a horse would drop en route to a fire. Mrs. May Killian remembers when a house burned to the ground because the volunteers went up Frisco, a less passable street than Ridge, and horses and equipment were mired in the mud.

Everyone remembers the white horses.

Webster was the first county municipality to have a paid fire department. The first paid chief was Richard M. Odien who started in 1912 and stayed until 1917. Other chiefs have been Ralph Eddie, 1917-1950, James Yadon 1950-64, Harold Busch 1964-68 and the present chief, Fred Entrikin Jr.

The early fire houses were built, not from taxes but by the volunteers from money raised by holding picnics and carnivals. Long after it had a professional force of fire fighters, Webster had its dedicated volunteers. Mayor Clarence Appel shared with New York Mayor Fiorello LaGuardia the reputation of following the fires. As a youngster he had the job of keeping the horses covered in return for the privilege of riding on the truck, and his interest continued into adulthood.

Dr. Marshall Conrad, director of the St. Louis Fire Department medical program and a grandson of Dr. Marshall Baker of early Webster, is another fire buff who assembled data and pictures for the Historical Society. As a college boy, he worked summer vacations as an extra man at one engine house. He remembered that he didn't sleep the first five nights waiting for the bell to ring.

Another fire follower, Richard Holekamp, recalled a fire at the

Company No. 1's first truck.

Holekamp lumber yards when the temperature was 10 below zero and the fire hydrants were frozen and had to be thawed out. At the Holy Redeemer church fire in the 1940s, the hose froze to the plugs.

Annals of the fire department include records of fires great and small. A record book from 1934 lists a number of everyday routine calls, with cause of fire listed as "sparks from flue, shorts in wires, rubbish in basement, burning leaves." March 16, 1934 must have been a windy day, for there were 12 weed fires reported that afternoon. In 1951 there were 232 fires, in 1974, 650. But fewer house fires are serious today and most of them are quickly brought under control.

Chief Richard M. Odien in his Model T.

Chief Fred Entrikin names the biggest fire he can recall the 1953 Tretolite Chemical Company fire which firemen fought for 18 hours. Long time Websterites remember other spectacular fires -- the Jannopoulo house which burned just before Christmas in 1920, the Ambrose Mueller drug store fire of 1939, the Westborough Country Club fire, and the Presbyterian Church fire on New Year's Day 1958.

It was the Elizabeth Holloway Woods memorial chapel which burned. Once it had been the main church, then the Sunday School until 1938 when Woodson K. Woods had it remodeled in memory of his wife.

Crowds gathered as soon as the fire was spotted early in the afternoon and stayed until after dark by which time the chapel was, as a news story described it, "a blackened soggy shell." Members of the Presbyterian Church and members of other churches had tears in their eyes as they watched the ladder swing up and the top pane of the stained glass arch shatter. The handsome panelled doors with their big Christmas wreaths went down before the ax. And Webster neighbors sympathized and consoled and mourned the loss of a landmark because a landmark is an important thing in Webster.

To encourage interest in fire fighting, Fireman William L. Entrikin developed a program under Chief James P. Yadon in 1957 in which 60 boys, age 9 to 14, studied fire fighting techniques.

When the boundaries of the city were extended south from Glendale road to Highway 66, in the 1950s, Engine House No. 3 was built at

Fire at the Presbyterian Church, New Year's Day, 1958.

1300 South Elm avenue. The fine new engine house next to the City Hall was completed in March 1974. The former firehouse on Lockwood is now an architect's office and the one in Old Orchard was torn down for a supermarket parking lot.

The present day Fire Department has 35 paid people including the chief, deputy chief, fire marshal, eight captains, 15 senior firemen and nine firemen. The latest piece of equipment, an automatic pumper, is Diesel operated and cost $65,000.

"Our men not only fight fires and do preventive inspection work but much emergency medical work, too," Chief Entrikin said. "Almost all our men are E.M.T.s - emergency medical technicians.

"We've had some tremendous firemen in our history. The reason our department has gone up is that we had a good foundation to build on. Our salaries are good: one man remarked recently that he made more in one recent day of overtime than he'd made in 15 days 15 years ago.

"We have strict standards. The one question we ask of our firemen is, 'Are you willing to go out of your way to help somebody in trouble?' "

Answering yes to that question, today's firemen live up to the best traditions of the early volunteers.

Chapter Thirteen
1910-1920

"Webster Groves, from first to last, has a certain subtle air of distinction about it which continues with the beholder on closer acquaintance. It is seven years since the author first visited it on a quiet Sunday morning in the month of June, and the fine shade trees which gave it a prestige then seem only to have grown in beauty and enhanced its weird fascination by the passing of the years."

Today's reader may smile at the choice of words, but there is no mistaking the enthusiasm of the anonymous "author" who compiled the booklet entitled, "Picturesque Saint Louis With Some Of Its Distinguished Neighbors," published by the Finkenbiner-Reid Publishing Company in 1910.

Webster Groves, one of the "distinguished neighbors," was pictured as a "haven of rest and happiness" for the business man weary of the "busy mass of humanity."

Its population of 12,000 was "animated by the best of ambitions and aspirations to make their abiding place an example." The Mayor, Edward Hart, was "one of those servants of the people who have the highest conception of the responsibilities of the position." The Business Men's League was made up of "the progressive and go forward elements" of the city.

The Board of Aldermen was made up of "the best citizens, elected without opposition." Best of all, the evil saloon had been excluded and because of this, plus "intelligent and vigilant policing," crime was virtually unknown. "The municipal lock up remains almost continuously vacant. Ladies travel the streets, freely at night, unaccompanied and unmolested." Clearly, Webster Groves was maintaining the idyllic image of the "queen of the suburbs."

Councilman Louis Booth, in a paper dated 1911, gives a less flowery

Lockwood and Gore, 1910.

but equally favorable picture of Webster. Looking back:

"Twenty years ago," wrote Booth, "Webster boasted a population of one thousand. It had no limits, but extended as far from the Missouri Pacific and Frisco stations as anyone wished to say it did. It had a few board walks, a few rock roads, no street cars and no lights on the streets but the citizen's lantern and the moon. It was a delightful country home place. One big family socially and the only blot was one saloon. For years only an occasional new house was built and we just drifted.

"Then St. Louis people began to wake up. Real estate men opened subdivisions, street cars were talked of, our one saloon grew to five, a murder was committed, and we waked up to the fact that we were drifting backward. Men like Messrs Hart, Martin, Fleming, Blackmer, Sanders, Baker and others realized that our only hope was incorporation. This required a fight but it was accomplished. These men knew that incorporation meant taxes and burdensome taxes for a while but it was that or move away.

"We did not want saloon money, so closed them all up and our only revenue was derived from direct taxation of the property. Police, street lights, street repairs, etc. cost a great deal of money from a few but as we had included within our limits plenty of vacant ground for other good people to build houses we knew that a clean town morally and reasonable improvements would in a few years increase taxable values so much that excess taxation would pass. To illustrate: Vacant lots assessed in 1900 at $400 improved, including personal taxes, will average $4000 today or 10 times the revenue without additional cost of maintaining the streets, policing the town etc.

"Our water supply was from cisterns and the drought of 1901 forced a bond issue for the water system. That necessitated sewers and the sewer system necessitated septic tanks, not all in one year but in nine years. . .and the year 1911 will see them all paid for except a few bonds that will not be a burden to carry. Our population increased and still growing and our people are proud of our City."

One of the new residents was Captain John E. Massengale, founder of the St. Louis & Tennessee Packet Co. who bought a home at 537 Lee avenue in 1910. His daughter, Mrs. Rebecca Sievers, who moved into 546 Lee in 1913 after her marriage, recalls that, "Father wanted us where he could see us every day but none of us was to live together." Eventually her sister had the house next door, her brother across the street.

Mrs. Jane Stuessie, Mrs. Siever's niece, who also lives on Lee, remembers that the old house had a "home gasmaking plant" in the basement because the electric was inclined to go out. She also remembers the neighbors. Three sisters and a brother owned one large piece of property. They frequently had differences of opinion and one would move out and build a house. Eventually they had three houses.

She also remembers Robert Emmett Funsten who bought the "old Lee house" and had a greenhouse and the first automobile she ever rode in.

One of the facts of life difficult to realize is that an automobile was a rarity in the 1910-15 period, at least in the countryside. In the early part of this century, the livery stable, the feed store and the blacksmith shop were the equivalent of the auto dealer, the filling station and the car mechanic of today.

The first heated garage in Webster Groves was built in 1914 by Edward and George Bopp at 668 East Big Bend. Their automobile agency, general repair shop and gasoline station remained at this location for 32 years.

Not everyone mastered the intricacies of the "horseless carriage" at first. A favorite story told by Farrand Booth is of a Dr. Carter, who was one of the city's first automobile owners. He built a garage but while attempting to start his vehicle, drove it through a rear wall. To protect himself from a repetition of such a mishap, he had a second pair of doors placed in the rear wall and a driveway laid beyond them so he could move his car in either direction.

Livery stables gave way to progress.

Parker's Undertaking Home.

The coming of the automobile meant the end of some lines of business. Parker Bros. Livery and Boarding Stables began to put its second line, "Funeral Directors," in small print on its stationery. Its big business was the rental of carriages, surreys and horses and the care of horses for other people, but because horses and carriages were rented out for funerals, this business became their sideline.

Most burials were conducted from private homes in those days but as embalming practices were improved, the undertaker came into being. In 1913, fire destroyed the Parker building and shortly thereafter Mr. Parker died. His widow, Laura A. Parker, took over and moved this business in 1916 to the Ferguson home, its present site.

The St. Louis Republic of April 26, 1914 had a feature on "Webster Groves — Our Six-In-One Suburb" in which it showed a cartoon of "Ye happy Websterite in his favorite pose" — cutting the grass with a hand mower. The story, by Robertus Love, detailed the merits of Webster Groves, quoted Judge G. A Wurdeman as calling it "a second Cambridge" and W. F. Biederman, "the genial mayor," as saying, "If you want to LIVE, live in Webster Groves."

Two familiar family names in Webster history are the Salveters and the Claytons. When Mabel Salveter Clayton died in 1970, she had been a member of the Webster Groves Presbyterian Church for 84 of her 97 years, the all-time membership record, according to the Rev. Dr. George Sweazey, minister of Webster Presbyterian at that time.

"Mother and father's life was bound up in the church," her daughter, Helen Clayton recalled.

The family life of the Edward H. Clayton family was of a pattern followed by many a family in the 1910-20 period when Helen Clayton was growing up.

"We went to Sunday School every Sunday and always stayed for church," she said. "Sunday nights we went to Christian Endeavor meeting and then stayed for night services. On Wednesday night there was prayer meeting and you couldn't have a date on Wednesday night unless you went to prayer meeting first. Your date could meet you at church and could go out from there but prayer meeting came first."

Rigid as this might sound to a present day teen-ager, it did not inhibit the normal fun and high spirits of the teen-agers of the times. The high school class of 1917 (Helen Clayton's class) and others of the period had lots of parties, dances, wiener roasts in the woods and hayrides on moonlit autumn nights.

"In winter, one of the boys had a bobsled and another had a horse," she remembered, "and they'd hitch the bobsled to the horse and five or six couples would go for a ride. I always asked them to call for me last because I wasn't allowed to go out on school nights but if my father saw the rest of the crowd on the bobsled, he didn't have the heart to refuse me."

"Going steady" was not a feature of life in the 1912-16 Webster Groves scene, but there were plenty of couples and much pairing off, even though it was not as definitely defined as later.

"We had dance programs at parties in those days," Mrs. Clayton remembered. "There were two groups of high school boys that gave parties – the Foot Club, 'followers of Old Terpsichore' they called themselves, and the Dionysius Club. They met at the Monday Club or the Old Kirkwood Country Club on Gill avenue – it's all part of a subdivision now – not far from the lower line streetcar which ran along what we called Shady avenue, now Kirkham."

Dance lessons were given once a week by Jacob Mahler, the leading teacher of St. Louis, who came to Webster for the occasion. They danced to "Twelfth Street Rag," "By The Sea, By The Sea, By The Beautiful Sea," and (Mrs. Clayton recalled with a dreamy look in her eye) a song called "Nights of Gladness."

Besides dances, parties, hayrides, bobsledding, there was the nickelodeon and later on the airdome on Lockwood. Fourth of July was a tremendous occasion and a noisy one.

"How Father loved it," Mrs. Clayton said. "He'd be up at 6 o'clock in the morning and we'd have every kind of firecracker.Cannon crackers, snakes in the grass, and in the evening Roman candles, pinwheels, and, of course, sparklers. We'd get what we called 'caps' and put them on the streetcar tracks and when the car came along, they'd explode under the wheels, startling for the passengers, I'm sure, but great fun for us."

Their mother, Mabel Salveter Clayton, lived in "the old Salveter place" on Elm avenue, third house on the east side from Swon. When her family moved to Webster Groves in 1884, it was country, dirt roads and lanterns when you went out at night.

But by the 1910 period, it was a thriving, bustling place with all the "modern conveniences" and a booming commuter business. Helen Clayton walked with her father from their home, then 121 Plant avenue, to the Webster Park station each morning to watch him get on the businessmen's train. The family had lived in the house known as The Ark, later the Ozark theater site, when she was born but then bought property in the Plant and Cedar area and owned several houses from time to time.

There were three houses in the block when they first built, the Becks and the Goodloes and Claytons. The Prince house (Alfreda Prince Gale grew up there) backed up to theirs and that family had an "old

Southern mammy called Flora" who gave the children in the neighborhood cookies. Their uncle's home (he was Clarence Clayton) was the big frame building, later Red Cross headquarters, on Lockwood. Mrs. Mermod (of Mermod-Jaccard-King jeweler) lived nearby. Helen Clayton went from being Miss Clayton to Mrs. John Clayton, marrying a man of the same name. Her two sisters and brother and she all lived in Webster Groves most of their lives. Edward H. (Ted) Clayton still lives there. Helen and sister Mildred Clayton Chamberlin live in The Algonquin apartments, and another sister, Mary Clayton Tyler, recently moved from Webster to a retirement village outstate.

"I liked it here and wanted to come back to live," Helen Clayton explained. "When I graduated from the University of Wisconsin, I was offered a job in Chicago but my father wouldn't hear of my going to such a big city. I worked for the St. Louis Provident Association but it took so long to get to their north side office that I left and went to work for Dr. Irene Blanchard who had an office in Webster and examined school children here. She was a wonderful person. If she had a patient in the hospital and they had another doctor on their case, she'd tell me, 'Don't send them a bill if I make a hospital call. One doctor bill is enough for anyone to pay.'"

It was that kind of world in that kind of town.

Helen Clayton's class was the class of 1917. Louise McClelland was in the class of 1918, perhaps the most reunited class of Webster High. A newspaper story about the class's fortieth reunion in 1958 related that more than half the living classmates attended and 46 of the 75 lived in the area.

Perhaps they stayed together because of the nature of their graduating year. It was an austere wartime class. Some of the boys had already joined the Army or Navy and their parents walked down the aisle to get their diplomas. Some had left school to go into service and did not graduate; perhaps the most distinguished "drop-out" was Harris Armstrong who married Louise McClelland and became a distinguished internationally known architect despite his interrupted education.

The class of '18 was proud of having been the class to start The Echo, the school paper and yearbook, with their teacher, Ada Stapleton, when they were sophomores. The 1918 Echo had a service flag frontispiece and a class prophecy which in some ways hit the mark.

"The class of 1918 is composed chiefly of geniuses, some redheads and a few Irishmen and withal they have been the supreme outstanding and truly representative element of Webster High since the sunny September morn they entered its whitewashed halls," the prophecy began.

The class prediction that David Skilling would become a doctor came true. So did the one that Mabel Haizlip would marry football player Carl Stadelhofer.

Merritt (Pat) Williams did not become head of the Navy but a nationally known Episcopal clergyman.

Gene Kropp did not become a "manufacturer of musical soupspoons" but vice president of Union Electric Company. Ken Hageman was not a motion picture star but a stock broker. L. Farrand Booth was not a circus performer but an engineer.

Others of the class of '18 who attended the 40th reunion were George Massengale, class president and later an Olympics star, Alton Horton, Lloyd Koenig, Edith Gray, Inez Bacon, Kitty Beck, Helen Lacy, Isabel Wright, Virginia Smith, Aline Morton, Lee Honig, Grace Maybury, Clara Kooser, Teddy Hodgdon, Nellie Ridpath, Henry Buser, Irene Mueller, Dorothy Haizlip, Margaret Digby, Alvin Spencer, Shelby Lacey, Aristotle Jannopoulo, and Janet Stine, the unofficial class historian who had been largely responsible for keeping the reunions going.

A "What's My Line" game identified professions of many of the classmates although they all disqualified themselves for Mrs. Norman Carlsen, bridge expert who had taught most of the bridge players in town.

The Class of '18 rememberd that two noted orchestras, Gene Rodemich and Gus Haenschen, played for their dances, at what was then called Woodlawn Country Club, and they remembered most of the songs — "I'm Forever Blowing Bubbles,' 'For Me and My Gal,' 'Poor Butterfly,' 'Moonlight Bay' and 'Let the Rest of the World Go By.'

It was a time when many in the happy insulated and isolated suburb would have liked to have let the rest of the world go by but that was not possible. World War I came. Class member Richard Kopplin was killed in France. And for Webster Groves and the rest of the world, life was never ever again quite the same.

Chapter Fourteen

Letters from Our Brave Boys

They called them with unabashed, unashamed sentimentality, "Letters From Our Brave Soldier Boys." Under dates of 1917 and 1918 and datelines, mostly Somewhere in France, they were sent to fathers and mothers and wives and sweethearts and the Webster New-Times printed many of them. It is one of the regrettable facets of this history that the files of that newspaper were destroyed by fire, but fragments of the news clippings remain in the St. Louis Public Library, quite possibly placed in their now yellowed envelopes by indefatigable Webster historian-librarian Kate Moody. A special decoration for valor should go to all librarians who thus help to preserve history.

The clippings crumble and must be put together like a jigsaw puzzle but, assembled, they convey an indelible picture of World War I, of the tenor of the times and of family life in Webster Groves. You can almost hear George M. Cohan singing "Over There" as you read letters like the one from Arthur Click, Co. F., 138th Infantry, to his parents, Mr. and Mrs. F. Click, 428 Oak St.

Somewhere in France
July 25, 1918

Dear Dear Father:
Just a few lines to let you know I am well and hope you are the same. We were just relieved from the trenches about two weeks ago. We certainly were lucky while up there, only lost one man and three or four injured. Went over the top, captured prisoners and killed a few Germans.
It takes about one month for us to get mail and we have been traveling around so much we never get it on time. . . We have not been paid for two months but expect to make up for lost time. . . Gee, but the scenery is great, some hills or rather young mountains. I guess you read

about the big drive the French and Americans made the last three or
four day.

You have no idea the way the Germans act when the Americans
come over the top after them. They get down on their knees and cry
comrade, comrade, and start running.

This liquid fire is certainly fierce, you throw the bomb, it
explodes, sulphyr and fire comes out of it and wherever it gets on you,
it is impossible to rub it off — if you try you spread it and it burns
holes in your flesh or clothes and puts you in great pain.

What's the latest dope in St. Louis? Has mother received
my insurance policy and how about my allotments, are they coming?
Sometime in August, you will receive my Liberty Bond for $100.

Well, Dad I guess this is all I know this time but will write
more when I hear from you. Give my love to mother and yourself.

Your loving son
Arthur.

And from Fred J. Collins, Battery "D," 17th Field Art.

Somewhere in France

My dear Father:—

I received your most welcome letter today and was sure glad to
hear from you. Well Dad, I just got back from the front for a few days
rest. I was surprised to see that so many of the boys are in the service.
I heard today that we will be leaving in about ten days where we will
get to see some real fighting. They shelled our Battery all day yesterday
and they are still going to it this morning.

I guess you will be able to read this letter. We are down
in our dug-outs and shells bursting all around us so you know
it is not very pleasant to try and write while under fire. It's a wonder
they haven't sent us over some gas. We always have our mask in the alert
position. The first night they shelled our hut I was on guard. I think
I broke all records getting into the dugout. We haven't lost a man yet
and hope we never will for we sure have a fighting bunch of men in our
gun crews. They don't care if school keeps or not. . . The 17th is
going to make a name for itself. Air battles are a common thing, you
can see them any time you look.

I see that a few of the boys are over here. Mother was asking if
I saw Ted. I haven't up to this date. I sure would like to come across
the old boy! I see that Herman Knickman is in the machine gun company, well
he sure will get to see some real service, the machine guns and the French
75s sure do the work. Well dad I'll have to close hoping to hear from you
real soon.

Your Son

The letters are as varied as the personalities of the men who wrote
them. Devoutly religious in tone is the one written by B. C. Chase,
Battery F, 128th Field Artillery:

Lt. Carl Stadelhofer at camp.

My Own Precious Mother:

This is the first chance that I have had to write for more
than three weeks. We have been at the front in this last big drive and now
we are back of the lines. . .

You want to know whether I am O.K. or not? Yes, my Heavenly
Father has kept me from harm and has brought me through many narrow escapes
without even a scratch. Our battery came out with less casualties than
any of the others. There were many casualties in the other batteries and
in our Infantry there were 1400 left out of 3200. Many of my friends I
saw lying dead as we advance through the German trenches and dugouts. I
have tried to find Charles Montague but have not found anyone who has
seen him. His company was almost completely wiped out. . . we advanced
17 kilos and the morning we ran the Huns back their breakfast fires were
still burning. . Our Division was honored for bravery by Gen. Pershing.
The French said there had never been a Division that fought to the last
man like the 35th. We drove the Huns out of places which the French and
British said never could be taken.

I don't know how soon we will go back but if we do I know God
will be with me. I will tell you just one little experience of how he
watches over his children. The night before we left for the danger zone,
the chief mechanic and my tent mate and I had gone back 3 kilos to a little
village. We were eating supper when a squad of six Boche planes came over
and our anti air craft guns and machine guns fired on them but did not

get them. They fired down on us with machine guns and also dropped three bombs within 50 feet of us and none of them went off.

Well we knew we would be shelled that night so we went across the road and dug a little place in the ground about 4 feet deep, room enough for three of us to lie down in. We covered it over with timber, rocks and dirt and after dark we spread our blankets down and put a blanket over the opening, then lit a candle and proceeded to read our N.Y. Herald which told about the Bulgarian peace. Then I asked Smith if he would read the Bible. I gave him my Testament and asked him to read the 3rd chapter of St. John. Then we prayed and went to sleep and all slept from 9 o'clock until 5:30 next morning. They said the shells dropped around us almost all night but Our Father kept them from harming us.

I will close now. . . hope to hear from you soon. With all my love and God bless you. From your devoted son,

Carson

If the boys of World War II thought of mom's apple pie, at least one in World War I thought of a Webster mom's homemade bread. Wrote Lloyd A. Bartlett, Co., L. 138th Infantry:

Dear Mother:—

Received your letter while doing my first hitch in the trenches and believe me I surely enjoyed it. We are now way back of the line, resting. Our rest consists of drilling eight hours a day. Do you wonder at the scarcity of shoe leather in America?

Got a letter from Gus 'Bawling me out' for not writing. He was well and apparently enjoying France's hospitality but, believe me, when we get back and can take a flop in that nice soft bed of ours and get our teeth set into some of that good old homemade bread of yours, that's Thanksgiving Day for me. . ."

The Gus to whom he referred could have been Pvt. August R. Weber of the quartermaster corps who wrote:

"We went to Orleans and had a big parade. The French sure treated us royally. We had a swell dinner. It consisted of vegetable soup, fruit, salad, meat (beef roast), potatoes, a glass of champagne and a cigar. We are now in one of the largest cities in France. It is Tours. We have a canal running through the outskirts and my chum and I went fishing last night. . . had pretty good luck. Six small fish. . . we gave them to a poor French woman."

And again Pvt. Weber told his parents in no uncertain terms:

"If any of our friends there are against President Wilson, forget me to them. If they are not, remember me to them. I am for our PRESIDENT and those that are not I don't want to know."

The Ladies' Home Journal

VOLUME XXXV
NUMBER 5

THE FAMILY MAGAZINE OF AMERICA

PHILADELPHIA
MAY 1918

THE POWER OF MUSIC
From a Painting by Gilbert Gaul

Somewhere in France (Painting by Gilbert Gaul, 1918, Ladies Home Journal)

Most of the letters are from the trenches and from France. But there were men in Navy duty, too.

C. Brooke Todd Jr., recently 1st class signal quartermaster of the S. P. 119, now of the Naval Flying Squadron, wrote about the storm that beat against their ship on patrol duty. . .

"The storm increased in violence and the sea became heavier as wave after wave washed down our decks. Water was oozing in at every port hole yet our little craft kept her head to the storm as each turn of the propeller seemed to bury her deeper in the oncoming waves. Under the heavy strain, the engines stopped completely and we were left to the mercy of the storm. The strong ebb tide was carrying us out towards sea and we thought it best to use our large anchor. It was nightfall now and I was ordered to call Fortress Monroe or any ship passing for help. The Fort did not pick up our message, neither did a ship pass. About an hour must have gone by when we discovered we were adrift again but not towards the sea. The tide had turned to flood and we were being driven toward the southern shore.

"After ten-thirty, the signal was flashed from the Fort asking our whereabouts and if we were in trouble. . . help was on the way. However the winds and waves were so violent, no help could reach us before we were washed towards the beach and aground. Several of us went overboard and made fast to the shore and as each wave raised the ship, we hauled her in. . . Although it may have turned out disastrously, King Providence turned the tide in our favor and we were none the worse off for the few hours of thrill and danger."

Back home, the letters were interspersed with lists of the ever increasing Honor Roll. A July 20, 1917 clipping contains a story headlined, "Numbers Drawn For Webster," and relates that the draft began with J. E. Bennett, number 309. Each week a longer list was published.

There were women in service, too. One list had the names of Hazel Flint, Edith Mae Ferguson, Mrs. Laura Finney Paden, Florence Podmore, Lillian Buser, all Red Cross nurses; Jeanette A. Fischer, student army nurse, and Mrs. William Prehn, Junior Red Cross field secretary. Many years later, in 1968, a feature story told of Mrs. Harry B. Wells of Webster Groves, who had attended the golden anniversary of the women marines — the Marinettes of World War I — of which she was a member.

News stories told of casualties and decorations. One contained a letter from John Valle Janes, Dated October 3, 1917, in which he told his family:

"Maybe you will be surprised to hear that today, about an hour ago, I was decorated with the Croix de Guerre and got a silver star with it, which is the highest decoration an unwounded man in the ambulance service can obtain."

The news story continued with a quotation from a Paris newspaper which said that Janes "distinguished himself on September 5, 1917 by carrying out, absolutely heedless of danger, the evacuation of wounded from a village under a violent bombardment.

His letter asked his family not to spread the news for fear he would not "fit in" upon his return.

Another news items told of Dr. Goodrich of Webster Groves, reported to be in Goltsinger prison camp in Germany, where he was "allowed considerable freedom in camp" and was giving medical attention to British prisoners. . . "the Tommies worship him," said the story.

And another news story:

Lieut. John B. Cushing Wounded

In a recent letter to his parents, Lieut. John B. Cushing states that on October 7 while reconnoitering from a forward outpost position, he was severely wounded in the stomach and left leg by a German shell. He is recovering nicely in a Base Hospital south of Paris and anticipates no permanent ill effects from his wounds,

Back home, civilians were urged to conserve food and energy and to buy Liberty Bonds to support the war effort. Residents who were children at the time remember the troop trains vividly. Nora Savignac Phemister recalls that:

"As a 10 year old I saw the World War I troop trains go through. It was usually at night and all the shades were drawn but the long climb the Frisco made from St. Louis out to Kirkwood often meant stalled trains. When that happened, 'the big kids' called out and whistled until the shades went up and there they were — our soldiers."

And the letters continued to come.

Somewhere in France
Friday, Sept. 13, 1918

Dear Papa,
    Even if this is the 13th, we have nothing to complain of. You will have seen by the papers what we were doing about this time and see that we are lucky. This is a great game over here, and the only bad feature is that winter is apt to put a stop to active operations before

"Over There"

"Home Again"

134

we get tired. We have been going some for the past three days. . . three
nights and days without sleeping but am not tired. You ought to see us
work. Have gotten to where we can snipe with the 75m. The American army
is some army. . . Have not had time to write those semi-orphans of mine
yet but appreciate the gift and know they will. It is 11 p.m. now and guns
on both sides and to the rear are firing but we are quiet at present.
Everybody is itching to get at it again.

6:45 a.m. day after

Since I stopped last night have been firing almost continuously
and have been having a big time. . .

Have been in the top of a tree high as the big pine in the
back yard with a telephone and field glasses all day, directing fire,
ate dinner and supper there. Our infantry went over the top again at
5 p.m. and are progressing right along. They captured a train with 1600
Germans yesterday. That is going some when a train can't get away. It
looks like we are going to spend the winter in Germany or at least in
Lorraine. All of our Brigade were mentioned today, commending us for
getting into position and delivering the goods.

Something is going on again so will get this off.

With love,
Prentiss

Sergeant Charles Glader wrote to his mother:

I was just talking to some of the boys in the 138th and I was
informed that Lanie Chapman was not killed in action altho he was at the
spot where the big shell exploded. He was buried underneath a big pile of
mud and sand and during the search for wounded, he was dug out about five
hours, later, slightly wounded and he is doing fine and in good spirits. . .

I had to throw away all my clothes on account of mustard
gas and they sure gave us a plenty. We now have the news that Austria
has quit and we sure hope it is true.

Duke is a stranger to me now. Reg. Hqt. is about seven
miles from here. I last saw him two weeks ago and he looked fine
and healthy. McChesney is still at Officers Training School. . . I guess
he will be back here soon, as some of the others have come back.

Just now the Germans have started to send their good night
greetings over in the shape of a few big shells about 9 in. boys that
throw rocks and dirt for an hour after they explode. . . If there is
anything in the paper about our drive send them over as reading material
is very scarce. Plenty of 'Frog' papers but only two English papers. The
word 'Frog' is what we call the French on account of their mustaches;
every one of them wears one.

Well mother, I guess I will close for I have to go to the gun
position. So give my love to all the family. From your son

Charlie.

Some of the letters were fairly typical son to mother letters. For example, there was one from Pvt. Joe Biederman who told his mother not to send any more socks — he had plenty — couldn't wear them all out if the war lasted for years. His letter also contained this information:

"The Huns drop propaganda on us continually. One doesn't
know whether to laugh or cuss at their pamphlets. The latest one said
that we were responsible for the burning of French towns and the perishing
of women and children. . . On top of these pamphlets they sent over a spite
barrage consisting of mustard gas. . . but it's done little harm. . . Will
close with love
                                    Your loving son Joe.

Roy Russell wrote to his Dad,

"You cannot guess whom I saw the other day. The first fellow
I have seen from home since I left. Wilson Todd. I was in a camp where we
stopped over night. It fell to my lot to go after a few tardy fellows and
on the way back someone walked up, grabbed me by the arm and said, "Roy
Russell." Even then I did not recognize him until it gradually dawned upon
me who he was. He doesn't look like he used to. So different. But I guess
anyone would that has gone through what he has. . .
    "He has been in six big drives and come out without a scratch.
But he has been gassed and poisoned and was just out of the hospital on
his way to join his outfit. He says there are very few of the Webster boys
left. Duke Orbock is driving the Colonel's car now. Vorbes Trobridge was
all right last time he saw him. . . Wilson had his horse shot from under
him. . . a shell burst eight feet from him, threw shrapnel over his head
and killed a fellow twenty feet from him.
    "But the war is over now. . . it was on the hour that we came
into this place that we heard news that an armistice has been signed. Such
rejoicing you could not imagine. Everyone yelling and waving flags and
the whistles blowing and the airplanes overhead shooting sky rockets and
doing stunts — like a little kid turns somersaults. And that night! For
the first time since the war began this town was lighted. Some of the
officers dressed up to represent the Kaiser and put a rope around his
neck and led him about the town. And then the morning after!"

For some the war was over permanently. And life in Webster Groves, too. They recorded their names in gold:

Kenneth Malcolm Copley	Marshall Moore
Richard Kopllin Jr.	Elton Sampson
James A. Kowze	Edgar J. Schneeberger
J. Harry Lewis	Percy L. Watson
Calvin Mitchell	

Chapter Fifteen

Larson Park —
The Octagonal House —
and the 1920s

Webster Groves is made up of clusters of communities, each one a mini town in itself, each one with its special characters, special sights and sounds and special memories.

For instance, there was the area around what is now Larson Park. The Prehns lived there and the Bergs and the Comforts and the Becks and the George Brooks family and Mrs. Mamie Garrison and many others. What was it like years ago, say in the early 1920s?

Edna Carroll didn't live there; she lived in the city, but she came out to visit and she remembers it well.

"The beautiful apple trees, the plum trees, the peaches. Roses on a fence — Seven Sisters roses, pink and white. And phlox all over. When you'd come out in the spring on the Kirkwood-Ferguson streetcar line, you'd get to the Murphy stop (put there for just one house) and then the car would go through a shaded tunnel and you'd see those beautiful plum trees in bloom. You can't imagine the beauty of the place and the joy it was for the people who lived there."

The street car right of way was a thoroughfare for people, there being no other road between Shady (now Kirkham) and Lockwood. People from Berry road who wanted to get to "downtown" Webster walked along the right of way. They'd stop to visit with residents who lived alongside it as they waited for the streetcar and in summer, kids would set up their lemonade stands for the hot and thirsty people.

Edna began taking the streetcar ride when she was five years old

Roses grew where Larson Park stands today. (Mary Prehn Berg and Blanche Matthews Carroll)

John Prehn, early landowner of Larson Park.

because her father ran one of the Kirkwood-Ferguson cars and all the men who worked on the line knew her and knew she was going to visit her great aunts Lizzie Brooks and Mamie Garrison on Denver place.

Another area resident who still lives there, Mrs. Louise Berg Rutherford, remembers when Edna's father, Jack "Red" Carroll, was courting her mother, Blanche Matthews. In the interests of aiding and abetting romance, Louise would "snitch food" from her kitchen and bring Blanche a picnic lunch so "Red" could stop over for a visit while his car, on the last run of the evening, went to the loop and back.

Louise's paternal grandparents were the John Henry Bergs and her maternal grandfather was John Prehn, cousin of Henry Prehn who had the country store on Gore and Pacific. Prehn's Hill, scene of many a sled ride, extended from Pacific avenue down to Shady on Gore. Her Berg grandparents built first on Lee avenue and then at 155 Parsons. The home were she grew up is now part of the park; the pagoda stands where her father's barn stood. She lives in a 67 year old house built for Grandmother Berg on Clairmont.

Streetcar to Meramec Highlands.

Most of the houses in the area were built in the early 1900s. They were not too fancy and all had outdoor plumbing but the natural setting was beautiful.

"We went to Bristol School," Louise Rutherford recalls, "and walked the long way around, down to Kirkham and then up Gore because you couldn't walk on the streetcar trestle in icy weather. My sister Dorothy was more of a tomboy than I and she'd walk it. One day she fell off the Rock Hill bridge into the creek, through the ice and I had to take her back home; it was the only time I was ever late to school in my life. The railroad crossing at Rock Hill was dangerous; after several people were killed, they put up a crossing gate. There was a board walk and steps up over the crossing when we went to school."

Into the "old Woerner house" which had been "the old Stinson house" on Denver place, the David family moved with sons Russ and Joey.

On Saturdays, Louise's mother baked coffee cake -- "the most magnificent coffee cakes I've ever seen," Edna Carroll describes them. "The smell of cinnamon and sugar was mouth watering."

Russ David would straddle the porch railing and ride a make believe

139

horse until the post rattled. Louise's father would say mildly, "Russ, you can stay but that horse has got to go." Then Russ would be very good and quiet until the coffee cake was baked and he got to take a piece home, still warm from the oven, to have with milk.

"Most kids hate to practice piano lessons but Russ loved it," Louise recalls. "He'd run home from school and start playing as soon as he got in the house. Even as a kid, he was really good."

Russ David has been playing ever since, on radio and television for a generation of dancers and listeners in the St. Louis area and across the country. But the people from Larson Park remember when -- when he loved that cinnamon coffee cake.

In those days, the place to go to dance was Meramec Highlands, at the end of the Kirkwood-Ferguson car line. There were two dance floors there and it was "the" place to go in summertime, for swimming and canoeing and picnicking. The canoe was the convertible of its day; the boy who owned one was the envy of all others. But most of the young people went on the streetcar. Few automobiles were around.

"Denver place was so quiet all week long. Only one automobile would go by, that was the postman," reminisced Edna Carroll. "But on Sunday, there'd be cars. They'd come out for the baseball games at Larson Field. Such hot baseball games. The air would ring with applause and shouts of "Yea!"

"And interspersed with the sound would be the streetcar with the motorman bearing down on that ding-ding-ding as the cars bounced down the long hill from Berry road with everyone hollering and singing and waving flags out the windows.

> "Every Sunday afternoon all summer.
> "It was a happy time."

There are many more memories of this sylvan area. The creek which meandered through the valley, crossing under the Kirkwood-Ferguson tracks twice. Children went to the creek for "crawdaddy" fishing. There was the quarry where they'd slide down steep slopes on the snow. And another quarry near Meramec Highlands where they'd go for wiener roasts on moonlight nights. Comfort's grocery stood where Jansen's IGA is now.

Louise Rutherford remembers that Grandpa Prehn was a redhot Republican and that every election there'd be a big meeting and a torchlight parade that would start from his house.

The Octagonal House, 1904, the Jannopoulo residence.

And Edna Carroll remembers taking long long walks, with her great aunt Mamie all the way up to the end of Lee avenue at Berry road and standing there, awestruck, admiring the legendary Octagonal House where the Jannopoulo family lived.

One of the most colorful families to live in Webster Groves, the Jannopoulos have an entire book devoted to their fascinating lives - "The Octagonal Heart" by Ariadne Thompson, who was Ariadne Pasmezoglu as a child and later a writer under the name Paz Van Matre. It was her uncle Demetrius Jannopoulo, owner of the Missouri Tent and Awning Company and the Greek consul in St. Louis, who lived there with his wife, Elene, their children, Aphrodite, Achilles, Demosthenes and Aristotle, his wife's father, Panagiotis Phiambolis, a priest who founded the Greek Orthodox Church in St. Louis, and the children's governess, Thea.

The house was called Parnassus and stood in the midst of 30 acres of cultivated land about where Berry Road Park is today. It was octagonal in shape and a showplace.

Visiting there in the summertime and on other special occasions were

Hector and Penelope Pasmezoglu, who was the sister of Elene Jannopoulo, and their children, Ariadne, Artemis and Pericles, who were younger than the Jannopoulo children.

Ariadne Pasmezoglu Thompson wrote of those beautiful and innocent and somehow other-worldly days just before World War I and for a short time thereafter.

Like other visitors to Webster Groves, she, too, remembered coming by streetcar from the city and the first sight of the long driveway bordered by evergreens. Jogging along in the surrey that met them, they would crane their necks to catch a glimpse of the house, which, "rising elaborately and fancifully in the midst of so many trees and flowers, had a fairyland quality."

"The house is long since gone and in the place where it once stood, surrounded by landscaped lawns and fruitful orchards, by rolling pasture and fertile farmland, there now flourishes that new development indigenous to the American countryside known as the subdivision," she wrote. "In the place where violets grew beside a brook and cattails waded in the water, where chestnut trees covered the ground with their prickly burrs, and in all the cool, still dark places where we first discovered toadstools and lichen moss and angleworms, there now stand ranch houses. Against the sky where we used to watch to see Apollo's Flock -- the soft, white clouds that gather together in the sky before sundown -- television antennae now form their jagged patterns.

"The outbuildings are all gone, too: the laundry house with its black iron tubs of steamy water and the vats of thick boiled starch and the flatirons heating on the stove -- the huge barn with its sweet summer smell of new mown hay" and "Mercury, a beautiful sleigh, arched and curved like a lady's slipper, painted dark red and ornamented with the golden wings of the god of speed. . . all gone, along with the chicken house, the carriage house, the playhouse and the cowsheds lined with pails of warm, foamy milk. . .

"And the main house is gone, with its great octagonal entrance hall, an open well rising four stories to the cupola above, each floor surrounded by an interior balcony from which hung a bronze fringe, decorated with colored balls and golden acorns. . ."

This beautiful and legendary house and its beautiful inhabitants are remembered by many who lived in the northwest part of Webster Groves.

"We used to go up and play with the children. Our dog was always fighting with their dog, Hector," Mrs. Jane Stuessie of Lee avenue remembers.

"We never saw Mrs. Jannopoulo except in her carriage from afar," Mrs. Louise Rutherford adds her memory. "We thought of her as a queen, a Greek queen."

Those who knew the children in later life find prophecy in "The Octagonal Heart." Demosthenes, who as a boy was always inventing things, kept at it throughout his life. Aristotle, who played judge in the younger children's disputes, later became lawyer and judge. Aphrodite, who broke with Greek tradition to study medicine, broke still further with tradition to marry outside the Greek world. She and her husband, Dr. Armin Hofsommer, lived on Lee avenue for many years and Dr. Aphrodite Hofsommer was known as much as a grower of beautiful orchids as for her glamorous early life.

The Pasmezoglu family were at dinner in their home in the city one winter evening when the doorbell rang and Aunt Elene and Uncle Demetrius stood before them, smudged with soot and pale with shock.

They had returned to Webster Groves from a shopping trip to the city and when they alighted at the station, all eyes seemed to be on them. A stranger came up to them and said there had been a fire and he would take them home. As they approached Parnassus, the sky glowed pink, then red, and as they drove through the gates, both cried out as flames roared against the sky and only the black ragged silhouette of their once magnificent home stood out.

In a few hours, all was gone, but as Ariadne Thompson wrote many years later, the spell of the octagonal house remained -- its billiard room and wine room, the attic rooms crammed with trunks and toys and treasures and even the little girl in the paperweight on the parlor table, standing in her flurry of snowflakes -- all remained in those hearts shaped by its memories.

Like the plum trees in Larson Park and the roses rambling over the fences, the lemonade stands and the sled rides on Prehn's Hill and the clang-clang-clang of the trolley and the laughter and singing of the picnickers returning from Meramec Highlands, all the happy memories of a happy bygone day come alive whenever someone lovingly calls them back.

There's a group of women who meet regularly to call back memories of the late 1920s. First they called themselves the Contemporary Arts

The Memorial Day Parade was the big event.

Club and then it was the Dessert Club and then the Evening Club and now it's just The Club. It's been meeting for more than 40 years and while its members pursued careers and had babies, their club format changed from luncheons to sandwiches to "brown-bagging it," each bringing her own. Now they meet to sew and talk, especially to talk about Webster High and the classes of '27-'29.

"Tom Curtis was in my class," said Dorothy Daniel. "He argued so fluently, we all said Tom would be a great lawyer some day."

Tom became a much respected lawyer and a much reelected Congressman. Gordon Jenkins who dropped out of the class of '28 became a well known composer and musical director for theater and screen. A roster of the classes reads like a roster of successful business men and women of the area.

Those who meet in The Club to reminisce include Dorothy Daniel, now a Latin teacher at the high school, Helen Hawkins Pickel, Elisabeth Tenney, Dorothy Alley Doerr, Virginia Skinner Harris, Betty Clymonts O'Brien, Mary Harvey Yost, Mary Jane Richards Moise, and Harriet Schulz McMillan. Many of the original club have died -- Margaret McClure, Mary Kerruish, Marge Wirthlein and Sue Goodall Johnston. Some have moved away; Nancy McComb Wirtel's address is now Chiang Mai, Thailand. But the majority have stayed in the Webster-Glendale-Kirkwood area.

They, too, remember the streetcar on Kirkham -- it was called "the lower line" -- and the rides to Meramec Highlands. And they remember a place to go was Old Orchard Mineral Springs on Sunnyside and Summit where a German couple sold mineral water but always gave it to the children free.

They remember when telephone numbers were easy to remember, just three digits like 140 or 837. They remember Wick's Candy Store at the station. And the games children played at night like Fly, Sheep, Fly (Run, Sheep, Run some called it), and kick the can, and playing jacks and the sand stores you made with colored sand and sold for pins. And July 4 when they'd send up hot air balloons with little baskets that dropped off and how children would hunt for the baskets.

On Memorial Day, everyone would gather at Bristol School to decorate his car (a Maxwell, Moon, Dorris) and march with banners from Gray to Big Bend and Lockwood. When you reached eighth grade, if you were fortunate, you were selected to be one of the carriers of the tremendous Red Cross flag. A few Civil War veterans were still around to march in the parade.

Girls wore white middies and shirts and rayon bloomers. The name of the high school pep club was the Yellow Jackets and one year the girls decided to dye their stockings yellow but they came out all shades of orange.

Jim McMillan was a senior and a big man around school and people wondered why he dated a mere sophomore, Harriet Schulz. But when Harriet became a senior, she was the Echo queen with an important rating of her own.

The class of '26 at Webster High was still small enough that a photographer photographed the entire group in two segments. While he reloaded, some clowns ran around the back to pose with the other half and could be seen at both ends of the picture.

It was the big thing to be a "booster" for your home town in those days. A trip to Yellowstone National Park was like going to Europe today. The Webster-News-Times offered one as a contest prize one year, along with a Nash 6-cylinder car, a Graphonola and $50 in gold. Radio was getting popular, "talking pictures" came in during this time and the Ozark was one of the first houses to show them.

It was the roaring twenties and, even in Webster Groves, "flappers" and "sheiks" went "joyriding," which meant you took somebody's Ford (no keys needed in those days) and drove to Valley Park.

The younger kids had their escapades, too. There was an old house on Gray avenue; the owners had moved out and left their furnishings. One summer -- "in the days before planned recreational programs," as one of them describes it -- some of the youngsters decided the house was haunted, and bravely got up a party to go in and investigate. They pried open a window and tiptoed around. One girl sat at the piano and played the funeral march.

And then the police came.

"But they were so nice," one of the culprits recalls. "All they said was, 'You know you shouldn't be doing this -- now go home.' And we did."

Down on the corner of Gray and Lockwood was the Lockwood Gardens, an airdome in the summer, children 10 cents, adults 15 cents. There you might see Tom Mix in "For Big Stakes" in which the ad promised, "Tom Mix and his clever horse break up housekeeping for a bunch of bandits." Or May Murray in "Fascination." Plus a Max

A not-so-merry-moment in an Oldsmobile.

Sennett comedy and music by Miss Webb's orchestra.

Mrs. Mary Marshall remembers there was a lovely restaurant down the street from the movie theater and they'd go to Sunday dinner there. But you couldn't go to a movie on Sunday. Horrors, no!

Websterites in Old Orchard have their memories of the '20s too.

Instead of Prehn Hill, they went sledding down North Laclede Station road. And Mrs. J. G. Heap ("Ma" Heap to the kids) would put cinders on Tuxedo so sleds wouldn't go into the intersection. Then she'd fire up the furnace, roll up the rugs and make gallons of cocoa for the 100 boys and girls who'd go tramping through.

Mrs. Ellen Foley of Old Orchard remembers going to the Veiled Prophet parade on the Frisco trains -- "they were so loaded, people would be hanging on the sides."

Mrs. May Killian remembers the winter in the '20s when a big ice storm put the electricity out for days and they had to live by coal oil lamps. One of their neighbors had a death in the family. "As was the custom then, the wake was held in the house," she recalled. "There they were, in pitch dark with the coffin in the front room and friends coming to call. We loaned them the lantern we kept for the cows and they put it at the foot of the coffin."

Mrs. Cora Koenig, many years later a "Citizen of the Year," moved to Webster Groves in the 1920s when she had a baby and the rule of her

South St. Louis flat was "no pets and no children."

Her husband met a man on the train and was invited to the man's home, in Webster Groves. They walked by a house not yet finished and fell in love with it. Even though they'd already ordered their winter's load of coal for the flat, they moved.

The House was on Oakwood avenue. There were no such things as milk deliveries. She walked to Big Bend to get a pail of milk for the baby. People thought nothing of walking from Maplewood which was the end of the street car line at one time.

She remembers -- like so many others -- those car rides to Meramec Highlands. The open cars with the seats back to back and the men wearing their straw hats with a string around the neck in case the hats blew off. And getting the first watermelon of the season and putting it in the river to get cold while you went swimming.

You did a lot of walking in those days.

"But it was beautiful walking down the street. Oakwood had a long lane of arching elms that touched."

Cora Koenig looks out the window of her apartment in Old Orchard's Colonial Village. The elms are long gone but she can still see them.

"It was beautiful, just beautiful.

"Webster Groves in the 1920s."

Chapter Sixteen

The Monday Club — and Many Others

It was a quiet but powerful force for good, in the 1920s and before then and since then. The Monday Club of Webster Groves in its clubhouse on the corner of Maple and Cedar avenues.

Sophisticates -- in the 1920s and before then and since then -- might poke fun at "the girls" and their hats and teas and lectures, but out of the Monday Club came the Webster Groves Red Cross and the Webster Groves Public Library -- and many an educated, happily liberated woman long before the days of women's lib.

It was founded at the home of Mrs. James F. Allen in 1887. When the club had its 25th anniversary in 1912, she wrote of those days:

"The early life of the Monday Club was intermittent," she recalled, "not from lack of interest on the part of its members but often from bad roads and absence of sidewalks."

In 1892, each member was provided with a program written in longhand. In 1894 the first printed calendar appeared. At that time, there were 17 members.

"Surrounded as we are at this time by such glorious opportunities for learning and culture," wrote Mrs. Allen in 1912, "we can hardly realize what the club meant to the pioneers in its work. Webster Groves was a small community. . .social life was confined to the village. . .meetings were society events to be planned for and anticipated. . . Tradition tells us that the club was a sober-minded serious body and its members attacked with perfect assurance the most difficult problems in the realms of science and art. . ." She concluded her history: "It has always stood for the right and been an important factor in the civic growth as well as the social and intellectual life of the town."

Interior of the Monday Club.

An early pageant scene at the Monday Club.

The same could be said all these many years later.

In 1896, the club became a charter member of the Missouri Federation of Women's Clubs and the following year affiliated with the General Federation. By 1904, it had more than 100 members and became a departmental club with four sections, art, current topics, history-literature, and science-education.

Its efforts toward establishing a public library for the city led Mr. and Mrs. William C. Yaeger to offer to donate a lot on the corner of Maple and Cedar avenues for a club building, if, in return, the public library would be housed and staffed by the club for two afternoons and evenings a week. The new clubhouse was dedicated on October 9, 1911. The provision concerning the library was carried out until 1929 when the library moved into quarters furnished by the high school on Selma avenue.

The original club building had dining room, kitchen, assembly hall, the walls of which were lined with bookcases. The brown tinted walls were stenciled by club members with a design of pine cones. It was one of three women's clubs in Missouri to own its own building, the others being the Wednesday Club of St. Louis and the Athenaeum in Kansas City.

The club worked for such causes as establishing a lunchroom at the high school, civil service reform, pure food laws. It sponsored writing contests and the first community Christmas tree and carol singing in Webster Groves. It has given funds to international and foreign student funds, to day care nurseries, girls town, meals on wheels, and organized a senior citizens club.

It figures in the fondest memories of many Websterites. Miss Adele Stine, for instance, remembers that when she would come home and find her mother away she would know it was meeting day for the Monday Club and would go there. And if she were a good little girl, "they would let me pass the cakes."

Miss Stine remembers, too, that the expansion of the Monday Club (in 1929) was designed by a young architect, Harris Armstrong, and that he made marvelous use of the small area to add resources to the club's activities. And though she does not mention it, Miss Stine won the New York Herald Tribune competition as press chairman in 1938.

At the start of World War I, the American Red Cross made a plea for more chapters and Webster Groves was the first community west of the Mississippi to respond. Its nucleus was the group of women who had been working at the Monday Club. Mrs. George Adams was executive secretary of the chapter which was first known as the welfare office, its location 105 W. Lockwood. It was the only agency to care for the local needy.

Mrs. Vivian Harris headed the Red Cross for six years in the 1920s while it had rooms in the Gorelock building, and Mrs. Minnie Anderson Roop was in charge from 1926-46. Its work was largely volunteer and in tune with the times -- Thanksgiving and Christmas baskets for local families, a steady flow of sewing and knitting for veterans at Jefferson Barracks.

The next move of the Red Cross was to 19 E. Lockwood to a private home but by World War II more room was needed so it moved to 212 E. Lockwood. Mrs. Margaret Prescott, Mrs. Mary Virginia Goldman and Mrs. William D. Bowie managed the chapter until Thomas W. Irving was appointed executive secretary, followed by Marvin Teeter.

Now known as the South County Region of the American Red Cross, with its administrator Mrs. Dwight Donnan, in a building of its own at the 212 E. Lockwood location, the organization has come a long way from the days of the ladies rolling bandages at the Monday Club.

Similarly, the Webster Groves Public Library in its beautiful classic building on the corner of Lockwood and Orchard avenue is a very different place from that first reading room.

Mrs. Nora Phemister of Sun City, Arizona, wrote her recollections of the Monday Club library.

"What a dear person Mrs. Morrison, the librarian, was, all prim and proper in her dark dresses with lace collars, a velvet ribbon set with a cameo around her throat. She watched what books we selected and didn't hesitate to refuse issuing some she considered 'too old' for you. I was sure she was addicted to those little candies we called 'red hots' and I was quite grown up before I learned it was library paste which was the true source of that delectable cinnamon-cloves odor."

"She's Bossing $230,000 Building Job" was the title of the feature story about Mrs. Charles B. Kenamore in May 1951. As president of the board of the Webster Groves library, Etta Kenamore was supervising the building of the library's new home, which would move it from the high school where crowded conditions made it necessary for the Board of Education to take over its space.

Along with Mrs. A. C. Lishen, Mrs. Kenamore had served on Webster Groves Post War Planning committee and was instrumental in the passage of a bond issue for $150,000. By the time a site was purchased and an architect selected, prices had advanced so much this was not enough and citizens voted to raise another $80,000.

The library was carried to successful completion, a triumph for Mrs. Kenamore. It was only one of many building projects in which she had a hand. She had been co-chairman of the Monday Club addition, on the committee to build the new City Hall, and she and her husband, a

Webster Groves Library built in 1951.

Post-Dispatch executive, had remodeled 14 houses in Webster Groves, moving from one to another but always staying in the community they loved.

The library itself has had a distinguished line of librarians including Miss Mildred Allen, Mrs. Eleanor B. Manning, Mrs. Sofia Jackson, Mrs. Marguerite Norville and Miss Helen Mardorf.

Ask any former residents what they miss most about Webster Groves. High on the list will be the library.

Ask any gardener and she will be hard put to say if she misses the room of garden books which is a specialty of the library or the garden clubs, another of the features which make Webster a very special place.

They began in the '20s, January 28, 1926 to be exact, when Mrs. J. P. Larson, then of 414 Selma avenue, invited a few friends to her home to form a neighborhood garden club. Its purpose was "to advance themselves in the art of gardening and thus enhance the beauty of their homes, exchange information regarding flowers and their culture, with this particular January date as the club's own day."

From this small beginning, there were 14 groups organized by 1942, each one starting out in Mrs. Larson's home. In that year, on February 4, the Men's Garden Club was also organized at the Larson home.

Flower shows, conservation causes and civic beautification have been part of the garden clubs' programs. From time to time, the Association has honored some of its own outstanding members. One was Marguerite Krueger, whose interests extended from reforestation to the restoration

Left to right, Mr. Lishen, Mrs. John Caughlan, Mrs. Albert C. Lishen, Mrs. J. Marshall Magner, planting trees donated by the Lishens in the Lockwood Parkway, 1969.

of the Henry Shaw home. There was Mrs. Albert C. Lishen, made a national life member by her clubs for her contributions to the parks and recreational life of Webster Groves. And Janet Harper Stine, described in a ceremony honoring her as one who "took her membership seriously."

Webster Groves homeowners take their gardening seriously. It is not a mere accident that streets are bordered by green and there are more flowering trees on the lawns than you can find in the woodlands in spring. To select any garden or gardens for comment is a very sticky wicket, but there was one gardener who once received a letter simply addressed to "The Beautiful Garden on Sherwood."

The azalea garden of Mrs. Donald Wright.

The garden was that of the Donald Wrights. Wright was editor of the Waterways Journal, a student of river lore and a health enthusiast who frequently bicycled all the way downtown. Mrs. Wright was a lover of azaleas who increased the magnificent display around her home for many years. The azalea at one time was thought unsuitable for the St. Louis climate but a Websterite, the late Clarence Barbre, did much to improve and popularize it.

The men's club, now headed by A. H. Roche, has had its list of notables with showplace gardens, among them Ed Minard, Walter Berkemeyer, Dean McCoy, Dr. Henry Allen.

One chestnut of a garden story is part of Webster lore. As Kate Moody related, two early residents, J. P. Dawson, ardent gardener, and a friend, Judge Henry Sutton, were walking in Dawson's garden while Dawson meticulously described each plant with its correct Latin name. Finally, the Judge, a little bored with it all, spotted a tall gaunt walnut tree and cried, "There's a Walnutus, dead as Hellicus."

The park named for gardener Jasper Blackburn, the Plant Memorial Bird Sanctuary, and plantings of many kinds testify to nature awareness. Many specialists have banded together, the Marguerite Krueger Conservation Club, the Herb Society of Webster Groves, the Four Seasons Garden Club, and four African violet societies. One Webster violet grower, Mrs. Neva Anderson, was national president of the African Violet Society.

The Webster Groves Nature Study Society observed its 50th anniversary in 1970. It was formed in 1920 by a group of people who simply gathered together to study nature. As their printed history described, "They took walks into the fields and woods, down pleasant shady streets, across vacant lots and even along the railroad tracks.

Organized by Alfred F. Satterthwait, who was in charge of the United States Entomological Station, the group began with 85 adults and 30 children. It soon had a lodge on the Ranken estate on Antire road, an area which became Beaumont Boy Scout Camp and Tyson Park. Its members were among the first participants in the National Audubon Society's annual Christmas census; its membership has included many authorities in scientific fields -- Edgar Anderson, Julian Steyermark, Stuart O'Byrne, Dr. Ralph Swain, the Marshall Magners, Albert and Dorothy Heinze, Dr. Edwin P. Meiners, J. Earl Comfort and many others have been on its distinguished rolls.

Club memberships often intertwine. Janet Stine, garden club leader, was a leading DAR. And Francis McMath, rose grower, did much to nurture the early Boy Scout movement.

Someone once wrote that if Webster Groves ever decided to change its name, it could be called Scout City. It has the record of a higher percentage of available boys in Scouting than any place else in the nation. At present, there are 13 active groups of Boy Scouts in the area. It was in 1908 that Dr. David Skilling returned from Canada to interest men and boys in the Webster area in Baden-Powell's book, "Scouting for Boys." The movement then taking hold in England began in Webster Groves two years before the Boy Scout National Council began.

Owen Thompson, George Adams, Wallace Rinehart, Hubert Lacey, and McMath were among the early active leaders. McMath recalls that in

1911 business men of Webster built a Scout cabin on the west side of Elm between Swon and Jackson. Like many another parent, he became more involved when his son joined. Later he and his son received Eagle badges at the same time in Troop 304.

Girl Scouting began in Webster in 1920 when Miss Jennie Belding organized a troop. Miss Dorothy Peterson was the next leader. The first Brownie troop was organized in 1934 by Miss Leah Caldwell. Early Girl Scouts had activities ranging from building their own crystal radio sets to help war-torn countries by collecting clothing.

Also youth oriented and very much a part of Webster Groves is the Young Men's Christian Association and its sub-organization, Indian Guides. The Y operated at first in one room quarters on Lockwood and Plant until the mid-40s when its quarters were enlarged. In 1960, expanded facilities and a swimming pool were provided by subscriptions from citizens. Not only have many Webster residents participated in local Y affairs but a large number have been active in the metropolitan Y planning.

The YWCA has no facilities in Webster Groves but operated a teahouse in 1918 in the old Robinson house known as The Ark, which later was torn down for the building of the Ozark theater.

Older than any other organizations, even the Monday Club, is Webster Groves Lodge No. 84, A. F. & A. M. Free Masonry first came to Webster Groves in 1868 when a charter was granted to Grove Lodge No. 296. After six years, the lodge disbanded. Twenty-three years later, Webster Groves Lodge U. D. was instituted, with Worshipful Brother Joseph H. Trembley as its first Master, with 22 charter members. The meeting place was the first floor of Brannon Hall on North Gore.

Later it was given the number of 84 and moved to the new Bristol Building and still later to the Empire Building at 23 N. Gore. Its present location on Lockwood consisting of a frame building and tract of land was purchased in 1914. The new brick addition was dedicated on May 20, 1961 with Worshipful Brother Forrest Donnell as speaker.

On one occasion, in 1956, the Lodge honored three members who had been Masons for 50 years — Leo Vogt, Robert Grable, and James Gentles, Gentles having been a Past Master for 50 years as well. Webster Groves Lodge has been honored by having Grand Lodge appointments of four members, Earnest M. Rosevear, Fay Fulkerson, John Alverson, Edward McMurray. In 1970, William H. Chapman was elected Grand Master of the Grand Lodge.

Organizations which meet in the Webster Temple include Webster Groves Lodge No. 84 A. F. & A. M., Rabboni Chapter Royal Arch Masons No. 131, Jeremiah Council, Select Masters No. 48, Webster Groves chapter Order of the Eastern Star No. 64, Judea White Shrine of Jerusalem No. 14, Rabboni DeMolay, Job's Daughters Bethel No. 6, Daughters of America and Reema Club.

The charter of the Webster Groves Council No. 2119 of the Knights of Columbus is dated April 20, 1920. The man often referred to as "The Father of the Webster Groves Council" of the Knights of Columbus was the late William V. O'Donnell, who first brought together the charter members, many of whom were already members of other councils but liked the idea of having a headquarters close at hand. The second basic purpose in founding the new council was to provide recreational facilities for the youth in the area.

The Council's first important step was to purchase the eight and one-half acre Gallagher Estate on Big Bend road in Old Orchard. Part of this ground has been sold from time to time and proceeds used to benefit the Council Home. The present meeting hall serves many purposes — meetings, ceremonies, Communion Sunday breakfasts, parties and wedding receptions. In the rear of the Home is a field for baseball, softball, soccer and football. The Council sponsors a softball team, bowling league and golfers and has won many trophies.

In 1924, under Grand Knight Christopher A. Lang, the Council sponsored a troop of Boy Scouts, the first troop under Knights of Columbus sponsorship in the United States. In 1931 a Cub pack was added. In 1933 under Grand Knight Fred S. Henderson, the Father Dooley Circle No. 104 of Columbia Squires, junior organization, was started. Later Art Gidionsen, Dr. A. L. Nickson and Joe Teipel organized the Sea Scouts. The Explorer Scout Post was the first Catholic post west of the Mississippi.

Many of the Grand Knights have been men prominent in the Webster community and others. Father Wally Ellinger of Springfield (Mo.) was one; so was Martin Dooling, executive producer, CBS in Los Angeles, and Police Chief Andy McDonnell. The present Grand Knight is E. G. Reifsteck. Mrs. Delores Hampel is Auxiliary president.

The Daughters of the American Revolution began in 1912 with a discussion of the possibilities of a chapter by Mrs. William Glegg, Mrs. William C. Rumsey and Mrs. William Greenhalgh. An organizational meeting was held at the home of Mrs. Charles M. Skinner and the chapter charter granted in March 1913.

The Webster Groves DAR is now headed by Mrs. Francis Deane. Another DAR chapter, Fort San Carlos, also has a Webster Groves regent, Mrs. David Ferrenbach. A former Webster chapter regent, Mrs. Charles C. Barnett Jr., served as state regent and national vice president. The DAR, conscious that many think of it as a group of old ladies, likes to emphasize that, in Missouri, more than one-third of the members are under age 35. Conservation and citizenship as well as the promotion of patriotism are their interests.

The civic organizations found in most towns are active in Webster Groves, too – the Rotary club, Optimists and Opti-Mrs., the Kiwanis and Sinawiks, and several chapters of P.E.O. The Rotary Club was the first in St. Louis County, organized early in 1917, with 17 charter members. Carl Holekamp, William A. Straub, E. F. Wilson and C. E. King were its first officers.

The Kiwanis Club of Webster Groves was chartered June 7, 1939. Its motto is "We Build" and the Webster Groves club has been dedicated to the improvement of boys and girls in the community, especially the underprivileged. Through its fund raising "Kiwanis Kapers" it has provided scholarships, contributed to children's homes, providing free swimming for youth, furnished football, basketball and baseball teams with equipment, and trained teams in league play.

Presidents of the civic organizations in Webster Groves at present are: John E. Cerny, Rotary; Herb Weber, Kiwanis; and Lawrence D. Taylor, Lions.

All of the organizations are listed in a yearbook put out by the Webster Groves Lions Club, which is only one of its many contributions to the community. The Lions Club, which celebrated its 50th anniversary in 1975, was founded by W. Vincent Brennan; its first two presidents were Herbert Barthel and Fred Holekamp. Dr. John H. Steinmeyer, optometrist, is the only living charter member of the Lions Club; he was president of the Lions Council of Greater St. Louis in 1949 and welfare chairman of the Webster Lions for 35 years. The Lions annually sponsor the carnival which is a part of Webster Days over the July 4 holiday. In its 50 years of existence, it has donated more than $300,000 to charitable and community needs.

Another 50 year organization is the League of Women Voters of Webster Groves which counts its birthday from a treasurer's payment to the League of Women Voters by the old Suffrage League in October 1919 before the actual adoption of the Nineteenth Amendment. One of the first actions of the new group was to send Mrs. E. Cushing to Joplin as a delegate to the League of Women Voters of Missouri.

Through the years, it has participated in the public education work of the League nationally and state-wide. One of its special Webster projects is the recent publication of the second edition of "Know Your City," a handbook of local government, first researched and written by the late Mrs. John R. Stockham in 1960. Revised editions have been made possible by those who knew Dorothy Radford Stockham and desired that her contribution to the people of Webster Groves be a living memorial. The 32 page guide has information about Webster's history, form of government and city services, and a directory of organizations.

This history owes a great deal to the Lions Club and the League of Women Voters informative booklets.

They tell about Webster Groves. But their very existence and the existence of so many public spirited, civic minded, humanitarian groups, clubs, and organizations tell a great deal, too.

Chapter Seventeen

Business

Webster Groves was primarily a community of commuters but there were, from the first, those who chose to have their business as well as their home there. The first ones were in Old Webster close to the railroad station. Here Augustus Moody had his store as did Henry Prehn. This business center ended at the Bristol Building on Lockwood and Gore where Will Straub began his grocery business and Ambrose Mueller first dispensed drugs.

Mueller's later moved to the Gorelock building across the street and then to his own building a little north on Gore, later occupied by the Kaegel Drug Store. When Mr. Straub moved into a new store opposite the Presbyterian Church, the First National Bank occupied the first floor of the Bristol Building until it failed during the depression.

Contemporary with these two was the feed and grain business owned by Henry Schulz, now the site of Rolling Ridge Nursery operated by his daughter and son-in-law, Harriet and Jim McMillan. The Schulz business began in 1893 and at one time its joint businesses — moving and storage as well as feed and grain — were of such proportions that the Missouri Pacific Railway built a spur to accommodate his needs.

"He was an institution in himself," his daughter says fondly. "His large office safe was a place of security for valuable papers of his friends who trusted Hank more than they did the bank."

So loved was he in the community that when his wife died in 1916, all the stores in the area closed on the day of her funeral. A man of many interests, he was a bank director and also an avid sportsman and fisherman, who always wore a silk top hat when he went fishing with his friend, Hans Lemcke, high school band director.

A garden enthusiast, he once tended a bed of zinnias on the corner of Gore and Lockwood in front of the bank of which he was one of the

Henry Schulz Feed Store.

Schulz (top hap) fishing with buddy Hans Lemcke.

directors.

He lost his right arm in an automobile accident in 1926 but switched to his left and kept on with his hobbies of horseshoes, quoits and pinochle. As a story teller, he was supreme.

A favorite game among oldtimers is recalling "what was where" in the lineup of places of business. A bright and chipper oldtimer, Otto Zinke, born on College avenue in 1894 (his father was custodian at the Protestant Orphanage, his mother a nurse-midwife), can go right down the line and name them as if it were only yesterday instead of 1908-10 that he worked after school at Conklin-Wehmeyer grocery, salary $4 a week.

Starting at Lockwood and coming down the east side of North Gore, there was a vacant lot where the Webster Groves Trust Co. stands; then at that passageway between buildings, Fred and Henry Thattenhorst had their tin shop. Next was Dawson's restaurant, Martin Smith's barber shop and, on the corner of Moody and Gore, Curtis grocery. Across the street but on the same side of Gore, Mr. Woodson, a black man, had a barber shop and Mr. Farrington a dry goods store. ("Don't ask me first names," says Zinke, "to us kids, they were all Mister in those days.") Then Williams drug store, and between there and the depot, Dr. Armstrong had his office and Mr. Duffy his saddle shop. Later Fred Clamp the plumber was there. (That's where Marshall Mitchell started out.)

On Marshall and Gore was Brockman's blacksmith shop, then Schulz feed store, then some private homes down to Kirkham.

Across the street where Red LaMore is now was a fenced in lagoon. Next to that, Mrs. Young had a hotel. Then, in order, Thiebe's notions, Miss Kipp's shoe store (where Jones, locksmith, is now), Yaeger's market and Prehn's grocery store.

The Webster Groves Bank and Trust Co. had its first offices on the southeast corner of Pacific and Gore, later Jones Market, now The Artichoke. Moving up toward Lockwood was Mrs. Benson's restaurant, Claude Lang's hardware store, the Post Office once stood in the place where Reed's Audio-Visual store is now and the jail was in the basement. Next to that was Charles Conklin's and Henry Wehmeyer's grocery (where Zinke worked), then a building known at that time as the Empire Building, Parker's Livery and Undertaking (where Rudolph's is now), Pitts shoe shop, Satchell's and Jack Donovan, tinner.

Blacksmith shop on Marshall and Gore.

Interior of Yaeger store.

The story was told that one day Joe McDowell who worked for Donovan was firing up the old cannonball stove when boom, he thought a cannonball had hit him. It turned out Jim Satchell next door had been fooling with a gun. It went off, penetrated the Satchell wall, and Donovan's wall and struck McDowell. He recovered, but Zinke is of the opinion that McDowell still has the bullet in him.

Near the corner was Mr. Bates, the harness maker, and on the corner where Glaser's is now, Moody's Real Estate Co. and then a vacant lot until the Gorelock building was put up.

Other oldtimers can remind you that not too many years ago the 5 and 10 cent store (where you could really buy things for 5 and 10 cents) had two entries, the one on Lockwood and one onto Gore, where a card shop is now. Some women recall that the first hairdresser in the area was Miss Tierney who lived in the Gorelock building, gave shampoos and hair drying and then said, "Now put it up with good grace," as the customer completed the procedure. You took your own lemon for a rinse.

Next to the Bristol Building and Dr. Bristol's office, across Lockwood on the south side of the street, Zinke saw his first movie (around 1900, he believes that was) on a sheet on the wall of the building. Schwartzenbach, the cobbler, was in that block and Peterson's ice and coal company. Where the Reliable Insurance Co. has its building on the south side of Lockwood was Laclede Gas Co.

Alongside was an express company where perishables for merchants and other freight were brought in by freight car daily and then distributed throughout the town. Holekamp's Lumber Co. had the space occupied by the Shell station now, and then came a sinkhole into which was at a very early day a structure known jocularly as The Little Red Onion. That was the jail, the clink, its bars painted red. It preceded the basement jail on Gore. Between it and the Gorelock building site, then vacant, was a frame house where a Mr. English, city engineer, lived and operated an ice cream business on Sundays. Appropriately enough, this is in the vicinity of the present Velvet Freeze.

Somewhere in that block of Lockwood at one time in the past was the Polar Wave Ice House. A forerunner of Gorelock Hardware, operated for 50 years by Al Miller with Otis Hopkins, his longtime assistant, was the McCurdy Hardware store.

Websterites for the past 40 years or so remember Lammert's Department Store as the chief occupant of the Bristol Building and

Big Bend and Old Orchard in 1920.

Webster's only "big store." Started by C. W. Lowry, it was originally at 638 Big Bend, and took its name from an early partner, Ed Lammert. But most people remember Ward Lowry, a genial gentleman always on hand to okay checks and dispense information. Blonde LaNita Kuerz was store manager. The store carried name brands such as Nelly Don, Tom Sawyer, Red Goose and Prince Gardner and, at its height, had 25 employees.

As close to perennial as any business in Webster is the Old Orchard Pharmacy at 640 E. Big Bend. The story is told that Richard Hassall went into the small store in 1918 to buy a cigar. Casually, he asked how business was. Told it was poor, he asked what the owner would take for the business, got out his checkbook and bought the store along with the cigar.

Hassall was not a pharmacist so he took in Albert Lishen as a partner. Twelve years later, the ownership changed to Lishen, Ben Gnaegy and L. C. Taylor. Taylor is now the owner.

Remodeled with new fixtures in 1925, the store is basically unchanged since that day, maintaining much of the old hometown drug store atmosphere, including the ice cream counter, ceiling fans and metal ceiling. Gone is the little ice cream table and chairs which May Killian remembers from the days of the nearby airdome and gone, too, is the

Opening day of the ice cream department of Old Orchard Pharmacy. Early 1930's. Ben Gnaegy 2nd from left, Al Lishen and Lawrence Taylor.

branch post office which once was part of the store.

During the depression, unable to obtain ice cream at a reasonable price from dairies, the owners decided to make their own. The project included door to door canvassing by four women for a week to publicize the venture. A pint of ice cream was given free with each 50 cent purchase and everyone entering the store received a free ice cream cone. The kids kept coming back so much they had to be marked with an indelible marker but then the bright ones discovered they could go to the nearby filling station and have the mark removed. Old Orchard gave up free sampling but kept making their own ice cream for 14 years.

And speaking of ice cream. . .further out Big Bend road was another landmark, Pevely's, with its outdoor garden and fountain with colored lights, so popular a place on summer nights that people drove from all parts of St. Louis for cool breezes and cooling refreshments. It's now Louis IX, still dispensing ice cream but from airconditioned quarters now.

One business many women shoppers recall was Mrs. Levy's drygoods store. Webster Groves, as sociologists and critics have noted, was and is a community conspicuous for its absence of Jewish merchants and residents but if Mr. and Mrs. Al Levy felt out of place, it didn't show.

Their store, on Big Bend where the Paint Pot now stands, was their domain and, as another Old Orchard resident says, "a store and a half."

"If it was in the drygoods line, Mrs. Levy had it," said May Killian, widow of veterinarian Dr. Gilbert Killian, proprietor of Happi Gifts and official Old Orchard historian. "Mr. Levy would buy remnants from the downtown houses and my mother always went there to get dress material for us. Sometimes Mr. Levy would cut a price and sometimes Mrs. Levy would give you a better one but there was nothing like their bargains.

"She had a big box of buttons — later, I think, it was a barrel, and if you needed a button to match one you had, you dug down and found it. If you were lucky, you might come up with four matching ones. When Mr. Levy died, Mrs. Levy's brother, who had Gutman's store in Clayton, helped her run the business."

There is a story told by oldtimers that in the earliest days of Levy's, Mrs. Levy put her own wedding presents on the shelves to increase the apparent size of their stock. Another widespread story concerns the Old Orchard bank failure during the depression. It was Mr. Levy, they tell, who saved many a small depositor with his own funds. The story isn't confirmed but those who know the Levys believe it's true. Mrs. Levy, now 93 years old, still lives in the Old Orchard area but the store is only a memory.

Another Old Orchard fixture which is no more was Schattgen's Bake Shop, a family business started June 1, 1933, and continued for a quarter of a century. On busy days, there would be 12 men working in the bake shop and 10 women in the store. Their decorated birthday cakes were traditional.

A family business also started in 1933 and still going strong is Wichman's Flower Shop, operated now by Ernest "Bud" Wichman. Displaced by I-44, it moved to a handsome new shop at 564 Gray avenue. Mrs. Wichman and Mrs. Robert Reed (of the Audio-Visual business) are sisters and this may be as good a place as any to note that in Webster, it often seems to the newcomer, everyone is related to everyone.

Trembley-Wilson real estate company was a related-by-marriage firm, Adele Trembley having married Edward Wilson, who later became mayor.

The Velma Benner history of Webster Groves made note of the fact that manufacturing and industry are not apparent in the landscape and do not exist, according to the average Webster citizen. This is because most of them are not of manufacturing proportions nor the major means of livelihood for inhabitants, she explained. Their locations are off main traffic arteries and the community gives the illusion of there being no heavy business.

But for many years, there have been sheet and metal works, chemical and other light businesses. One manufacturing plant of size is the Tretolite plant formed by W. S. Barnickle, who moved to Marshall avenue in 1920.

In the 1920s and '30s there was a thriving Business Men's Association. Early photos show rows of smiling men at picnics and other gatherings, a large and lively group. Later, the Webster Groves Merchants Association was incorporated in May 1937 as the present Webster Groves Chamber of Commerce, which now has a membership of 202.

Its membership list compiled by Mary Batz, executive secretary, shows many "old settlers." The Arcade Shoe Repair Co. is a 38-year resident. Belcher Typewriter started 28 years ago, Blanner Electric Co. in 1913, Cerny Floral Shop in 1925, Holekamp Lumber in 1907, Mac Hardware in 1928. Other longtime members include Anderson Plumbing, Graubner Printing, Porter Paint, Roberts Boys Shop, and the dean of doctors, Dr. H. A. Goodrich.

Established in recent years in the Webster area have been the Reliable Insurance Co., Farm and Home Savings and Loan, the Big Bend bank, and Clayton Federal Savings and Loan, all with new buildings which changed the landscape.

One of the most attractive building renovations was that of the Webster Book Shop on Lockwood and S. Gore started by Julie Robinson and Natalie Sheetz in 1965, now a popular cultural asset to the city.

Some businesses have had changes in name; Schnucks, for example, replaced Bettendorf's in the Big Bend-Elm area. It now is the center of one of Webster's five cores of business, they being the Old Webster Store Town, Old Orchard, Big Bend-Elm, Yorkshire Shopping Center near the city's southeast border, and the Marshall avenue area.

The character of business has changed with the character of the times. Antiques have become popular leading to Harris House, The Finer Things and others. In 1971 William Stroud wrote:

"Gore avenue in Webster Groves is becoming a fashionable street of small shops where conversation is blended with commerce and

Big Bend and Old Orchard today.

craftsmanship is prized." His story told how once vacant buildings were being renovated by Shirley Brown's Global Village, The Station, The Ark and The Artichoke, as Old Webster Store Town came into being.

In Old Orchard, near Webster College and its lively liberal student body, shops are more "mod" in type, a change deplored or applauded depending on the viewer. One wonders what an early settler would make of "Saturday's Child," the "costumes" of the '20s, bluejeans and patchwork skirts, the folk music shop, Leonard's where young men rent their evening attire and ruffled shirts, Indian jewelry shops, health foods, pizza, Kentucky Fried Chicken and One Hour Martinizing.

Once it was Augustus Moody's general store. Now there is the ETC. shop. It's a changing world, with something for everyone, especially in the business community of Webster Groves.

Chapter Eighteen
The 1930s

Louis Farrand Booth brought his bride-to-be, Helen, to visit Webster Groves in the spring of 1930 just before their marriage. As she later recalled, they chugged out Manchester road in his 1928 car and turned left at Rock Hill road. The bridegroom at this point apologized for bringing her into Webster Groves by the "back way." Most people at that time approached Webster via Lockwood and on the Rock Hill approach, one went through a wooded wilderness before touching the northern city boundary at Bismark avenue. Two blocks beyond the city line, they turned up Lee avenue, where Booth's grandparents, the Lees, had built their first home in the 1850s.

"The immediate impression which I had, being a city girl who loved the great outdoors, was one of unalloyed delight," said Helen Booth, in a talk on Webster history many years later. "In the East, around New York and Newark, the suburbs had already taken on the aspect of the city, and although I had a vague foreboding that the midwest would suffer the identical fate, it was a joy on that day to know that here the suburbs were in truth SUB-urban, where footpaths crossed vacant lots, and streets had the look of roads — without curbing and often without sidewalks. . . in the 30s, it was a relief to come into an area where open space still abounded."

Webster Groves in the 1930s still had the natural wildness of the country, but it was also moving ahead progressively. One of the big evidences of its progress was the new City Hall. Its completion, in 1932, ushered in "a new era of its history. . .

"Its glorious record of accomplishments in the past justifies faith in the splendor of its future."

These proud and brave words concluded the history to date of Webster Groves as recorded in the Dedicatory Program of the new City Hall. The world — and Webster Groves — was sliding into an economic

Mo-Pac watchtower at Gore. (Painting by Webster Groves artist Leonard Schultz)

depression. "Brother, Can You Spare A Dime?" was to become the theme song of the next few years, replacing the 1920s theme, "Ain't We Got Fun?" But the spirit of the city fathers was that of John Ruskin, quoted on the program cover:

"When we build, let us think that we build forever. Let it not be for

The new City Hall.

present delight, nor for present use alone, let it be such work as our descendants will thank us for, and let us think, as we lay stone on stone, that a time is to come when those stones will be held sacred because our hands have touched them, and that men will say as they look upon the labor and wrought substance of them, 'SEE! this our fathers did for us.' "

It was a handsome building, as its architect Hugo K. Graf described it and it represented, as he hoped it would, "the civic pride of its citizens." In the dedication ceremony, the Rev. George M. Gibson gave the invocation, the Rev. Father P. J. Dooley the benediction, and, in between, C. A. Reichardt, chairman of the Citizens Building Committee, presented the keys of the new City Hall, Mayor John B. Chipman accepted them, and an address was given by Forrest C. Donnell, described as "former city attorney of Webster Groves."

The dedication was the culmination of a decade of hard work on the part of officials and citizens. The Plan Commission had first come into being in September 1923 when a meeting was held at First Congregational Church with George W. Adams presiding. At this meeting, it was resolved that Harland Bartholomew, engineer for the St. Louis City Plan Commission, would be retained as an expert adviser for future building.

The announced purpose of the commission was to do the "greatest good for the largest number of citizens, doing at the same time, the least possible injury to those unbenefited." Some of the problems they hoped to meet were those of playgrounds, wider streets, grade crossing elimination, better drainage and sewers, an improved water supply, adequate fire protection, parks and modern street lights.

A $465,000 bond issue proposed in the spring of 1926 failed to pass. The commission went on to carry out many of the proposals just the same. Members of that first commission were George W. Adams, chairman, Carl G. Haizlip, vice chairman, C. R. Comfort, T. G. Woolsey, C. A. Reichardt, J. B. Chipman, William Stoecker, E. M. Rosevear, Henry Schulz, E. G. Curtis and Herbert Rountree.

With slight changes of membership and chairmen, the Plan Commission continued its work. In 1932, P. O. Viall was chairman; members included H. O. Brinkmeyer, D. Donnelly, F. W. Holekamp, Henry Schulz, J. B. Chipman, B. Forester, T. H. Heath, J. B. Clayton Jr.

In 1928 a Board of Adjustment was set up, its purpose to hear appeals from aggrieved persons or anyone affected by decisions of the building commissioner. It was composed of five members with G. W. Stephens, chairman, Carl Holekamp, L. O. Honig, G. B. Perkins, and M. E. Coggeshall.

The new City Hall, triumph in optimism that it seems, was only the first of many signs of progress in the 1930s.

On March 24, 1939, the Webster News-Times published what it called its Golden-Silver anniversary, golden because it was the golden wedding day of the publisher, G. W. Kriegesman, silver because it was the newspaper's silver anniversary. It was also its Achievement Edition. Its front page headlined, "10 Years of Progress in Webster Groves."

"The very same years many of us have been prone to picture with gloom have brought along their share of good things," the news story stated. "It is very heartening to sit down and take stock.

"Heading the list is nearly $5,000,000 building permits issued in that time. Over $3,000,000 of that was for single family residences... Nearly $1,000,000 was given Webster in WPA projects. Estimated receipts to be received from PWA for lateral sewers. . .$230,000.

Almost half a million dollars in school improvements were made."

Two columns of type were taken up to list the improvements made under the big bold heading of **PROGRESS**. These included:

New $100,000 City Hall
2 New Post Office Buildings
$60,000 Addition to Bank Bldg.
2 Beautiful New Churches
3 Handsome Church Additions
Utilities Headq't'rs Improvements
684 Acre Addition to City
$823,417 WPA Projects
Modern Drug Store and Grocery
$4,456,645 Building Permits
City Lighting Improvements
$350,000 School Improvements

Big New Recreation Center
New Peak in School Enrollment
Sanitary Sewer System
New Fountain on West Big Bend
Modern Florist Headquarters
Modern Upholstery Building
Plant Park and Bird Sanctuary
Webster College Dormitory
Nerinx Hall Addition
6 New Filling Stations
PWA Projects

The very mention of WPA and PWA indicates that artificial priming of the economy was still very necessary. ("Who's Afraid of The Big Bad Wolf?" and "Happy Days Are Here Again" were the pop tunes.) But the record of 1929-39 was indeed something to which citizens could point with pride.

Another special edition, this one of the Watchman-Advocate, St. Louis County paper printed in Clayton, highlighted Webster history and achievements on September 23, 1938. One of its news stories told of better and brighter street lights designed to provide three times the existing light in Webster Groves. Also shown was a picture of the new Post Office on Lockwood and Maple. There were still sub-stations at 14 N. Gore and 640 E. Big Bend.

You can tell as much about an era from its advertisements as from anything. Benne's on Marshall avenue was advertising a "complete food store." The term "supermarket" had not yet come into use. The Brentwood Fuel and Material Co. advertised coal and coke for heating, although the St. Louis County Gas Co. was proud to advertise that the new city hall was being heated with gas, a new and revolutionary development.

In The Blue Book of Webster Groves, compiled to welcome new residents to the community, Brennan's grocery advertised free delivery, the Columbian recreational center on Lockwood and Big Bend invited you to bowl, and Lammert's Department Store announced that it had Shirley Temple and Deanna Durbin dresses for girls, and "smart dresses" for "particular women" at $1 and up. Mac Hardware had Philco radios ("No stoop — no squat — no squint" was their slogan) and

Warren Kendrick had Norge refrigerators. Mrs. Ebert made tea cakes to order, Elizabeth Goodall specialized in millinery and Mary Rasmussen in dressmaking, St. Louis Dairy had a Vitamin Shop and fountain service, Busy Bee had a sweet shop and automobile and service station advertisers pictured the latest in "snazzy" cars at their curbstones.

There was a picture of the Florence Dress Shop's elegant salon-like showroom and a picture of Mary Blackwell Stevenson's elegant pianoschool living room. Auto Supply Kit advertised model airplanes, a new fad of the times, and L. A. Perrin not only did upholstering and bedding renovation but had antiques, something different in that day. Duren's Cigar and News Store had a rental library (3 cents a day) and Theo. Johnson's dry goods store had Jantzen Swim Suits. Suburban Cleaning and Dyeing Co. did storing, mothproofing, repairing and relining. People still weren't throwing their clothes away when they got old.

The beauty shops showed sketches of the newest in hair-dos, a swept-up look with pincurls and little corkscrew ringlets on top of the head. This look was reflected in the 1938 Echo yearbook.

The Echo that year had a distinguished staff. Hal Knight was editor in chief, Jane Taussig associate editor, Bill Copeland was circulation manager and Carl Holekamp advertising manager.

Wallace Williams, who was in that class and later photographed many a senior class for the Echo, has the yearbook on a shelf in his studio. It was a loyal class, he recalls; at its twentieth reunion, 95 percent of the students still alive were there. Marjorie Johanning was Echo queen for that class and Betty Pentland was May queen. The joke pages did a lot of kidding about candid cameras which were new and Superintendent Goslin began his message with a challenge: "I challenge you to make friends. . ."

Telephone numbers were still four digits with an exchange, REpublic or WEbster. There was an active Peace Council, an aftermath of the war years, an annual Milk Fund benefit, a depression outgrowth, and the News-Times cooperated with real estate firms like Coggeshalls by picturing a home of the week for sale on its front page.

Young people still had fun. Just as in the early years they rode streetcars and went joyriding in the '20s, in the '30s. It was a great daring thing to drive cars to Kirkwood and race up and down the hills on Geyer road.

"I drive over Geyer now," said Barbara McKay Stephens, who was one

The old Ozark and the Airdome, now the Webster Cinema.

of the 1930s teen-agers, "and wonder whatever happened to those hilly humps in the road. Maybe we wore them down."

There were car radios but no television, and airconditioning had not made much of an impression on suburban civilization. The Ozark Theater still had an airdome as well as its winter picture house and everyone rushed to see Dolores Del Rio in "Flying Down to Rio" or the latest Bing Crosby film. Clark Gable was big, too, and women everywhere agreed he should be Rhett Butler in that best seller of the late '30s, "Gone With The Wind."

In 1935, Sunday movies were voted down again in Webster.

But then, on April 4, 1937, it happened. Sunday movies were legalized — "repealing a 28 year old blue law," said the news story.

It was a sign of progress which was reported on that long proud list in the Webster News-Times, but it did something to change the pattern of life in the city. Ask any child who has queued up in the long lines outside the Ozark on Sunday afternoon or any parent who lined up with the car pool chauffeurs.

One of four honor rolls displayed on front of Webster Groves City Hall showing the names of men who served during World War II. Those who were killed in action are engraved in gold.

Chapter Nineteen
The 1940s

A telephone repair man, walking through the backyard of the house at 55 Joy avenue in Webster Groves, spotted a four leaf clover, picked it and brought it in to the lady of the house.

"Put it in a glass of water — for good luck," he said.

The day was the first Tuesday in November, 1940, but it was not until several days later that the lady of the house, Mrs. Forrest C. Donnell, realized that luck had indeed been good to them. What had looked like a victory for the Democratic candidate in the race for governor of the state of Missouri had taken a dramatic turn, and Forrest Donnell, Republican and underdog, had been elected.

"I'm glad we were home when it happened," Mrs. Donnell said. "Every important thing that has ever happened to us has happened when we were home to enjoy it."

The Donnells moved to the governor's manse in Jefferson City and, in retirement, to a city apartment but for many years Webster Groves was "home" and collective chests in Webster swelled with pride when Donnell became governor and later United States Senator.

In recent years, the political persuasion of Webster residents has become more equalized but in its early days, it was predominantly Republican, going all the way back to the torchlight parades from the Prehn home. A Republican native son, Thomas B. Curtis, whose great grandfather lived in a house on Gray avenue in 1890, was Congressman for 18 years with the enthusiastic help and support of his Webster neighbors.

Officeholders from the Webster Groves area have included Judge Amandus Brackman, state representatives Robert Copeland, Richard Marshall, Corley Thompson, and state senator E. Gary Davidson,

Forrest Donnell greeting well-wishers on the occasion of his election as Governor, 1940.

Republicans all. Bruce Alger of Dallas, one of the first Republican Congressmen elected from Texas, was originally from Webster.

Of course, there was Circuit Judge Douglas Jones, elected on the Democratic ticket, but everyone explained away that lapse from the faith. He came from a lovely family — and from Webster Groves, which meant he was qualified in any political party.

As Forrest Donnell took office, a popular song came out with the optimistic promise, "Goodbye dear, I'll be back in a year, I'm in the Army now." Within the next five years, more than 2500 Webster men and women were in the Army, Navy, Marines, Air Force, Coast Guards, and many of them did not come back alive.

Tom Curtis, Second District Congressman for many years.

But the class of 1940 didn't talk too much about the imminence of war, as one of its members, Sally Kaufman Hennies, remembers it.

Sally (her mother named her for Mrs. Straub at the grocery store) has memories of growing up in the South Old Orchard, Laclede Station road area of Webster which are not too different from the happy, halcyon memories of Websterites in the 1900-10 period. They still cut through the pasture to walk to school, hurrying to avoid the fearful bull. There was a grove of persimmons and beautiful blue violets, and a pond where Blackburn Park is now where the boys would skinnydip and girls coming upon them would cover their eyes with their hands.

Their homes didn't have gas until 1940; they used a wood burning cookstove until then. Cars for teenagers were rare; even bicycles weren't too common and you walked everywhere, from Laclede Station road to Highway 66 and on to Gravois, and thought nothing of it.

There was still a 9 o'clock curfew. Kids in their neighborhood hurried home after school to help with the chores, especially in vegetable gardening season. The more social set at high school went to Carpenter's ice cream parlor located on Lockwood and Plant where Harris House is now. Fred and Gertrude Hertwick catered big dinners for men's clubs, Neef grocery was on Glendale and Elm (once it was Berry's), the Ozark *still* had an airdome, and there were streetcars. It was 1950 when the tracks were taken up on Summit and those on Lockwood were covered over.

"Pop" Hixson was still principal of the high school, girls wore sweaters and bobbysocks, got new hats for Easter and did jitterbug dancing.

A senior poll listed Glenn Miller as the favorite orchestra with Kay Kyser, Tommy Dorsey and Benny Goodman runners-up. "Wind and the Rain in your Hair" was a favorite song and so was "Tuxedo Junction." Bob Hope, Jack Benny, Charlie McCarthy and Rochester were favorite radio personalities, Bette Davis was a favorite actress, hamburger the favorite food, and most girls listed as their future occupation, 1. marriage, 2. nurse. Bob Gates was the "most gentlemanly" senior and Barbara Martin the "most attractive." Jean Langley was Echo queen and Virginia Mattox was May queen and their dresses had fitted waistlines and full skirts and little puffed sleeves. The yearbook was dedicated to "a true Democracy. . .because in these days of unrest, Democracy stands above all else as a true standard of living." On the cover, the Statue of Liberty held high her torch.

It was an idealistic age and audiences stood up to applaud the Municipal Opera's first production of the summer, "The American Way."

Changes came fast, for the class of '40 and '41 and those that followed.

"I am on Okinawa, doing the usual 'you know what' after participating in the beachhead landing on Tsugen Jima," wrote Pfc. James B. Jennings 37408670.

"I am in Northern Burma on the Ledo road with a signal outfit. Saw Jack Stadelhofer at my debarkation port," wrote Pvt. W. H. Ellstrom.

"Our division ran wild over Germany, hit the Rhine, turned north and met the First Army," wrote S/Sgt. Lawrence Brown 37182807.

"We have been doing our bit to knock out Jerry and have sixteen sorties to our credit now. Our pilot is very religious, which makes things better, and I know what a prayer can do for a person." S/Sgt. George W. Schneider 37633037.

A chance to sing was always welcomed by the service man off duty, and this opportunity was offered every Sunday afternoon at the Webster Groves YMCA-USO Center. Pleasant surroundings and pretty girls helped too. (Reproduced from the Webster News-Times.)

"I am using the German that I got from Herman Gaul, and wish that I could thank him personally." T-4 Robert L. Harter 37181807.

"Would give my right arm to be in Webster instead of running around the Pacific on a Destroyer Escort." James E. Garner, Jr. USN.

From Mr. Verby's office: "To you, our Webster High boys and girls in the Armed Services, we proudly dedicate another issue of the Webster Hi-Lites."

The issue of May 1945 had news from all over the world. Science teacher Hugh McDonald had been awarded a purple heart. So did First Lt. Martin Kelly, class of '29, Pfc. Robert Bird, class of '43, and Marine Pfc. William Mylet, class of '34.

Robert McKelvey, a staff sergeant in the Southwest Pacific had 1238 hours of flying time, 505 combat hours, and had been awarded the

DFC. Bill Bartz was with Patton's Third Army. And Second Lt. Paul Claus, Flying Fortress pilot who was held prisoner after being shot down over Germany early in 1944, had been awarded the Air Medal with two oak leaf clusters.

There was a long list headed "In Memoriam." Even today, the reader's eyes blur over as you read that Lt. William H. Sherrill Jr. was honored in a memorial service by parishioners of Kirby Bedon Church, Norwich, England, who placed in their sanctuary a marble tablet "To the memory of four gallant airmen. . ." and with it the words of Abraham Lincoln, "Let us have faith that right makes right and in that faith let us, to the end, dare to do our duty."

It was an idealistic age and a proud time and the churches were packed on the night that V-E Day was declared. By this time, there were 42 gold stars on the flag in the high school auditorium.

But most came back and soon, instead of the sad songs like "Miss You" and "I'll Be Seeing You," the bands were playing, "Kiss me once and kiss me twice and kiss me once again, it's been a long, long time."

It hadn't been such a long time in history, only five years. But it seemed longer for those involved.

It hadn't been such a long time in Webster's history as a city, just 50 years, but in 1946, its 20,000 residents celebrated. On October 29, 1946, at a dinner, Mayor Clarence H. Appel said that Webster Groves could be truly proud of its record of half a century and its reputation as a home community. Its slogan, he said, was a most appropriate one: "If you want to live – live in Webster."

Two big bond issues had been voted for public improvements in Webster Groves, an $800,000 one for school improvements in December, 1944, an $800,000 one for civic improvements in October 1945. In a radio talk in 1947, Mayor Appel reported that $2 million worth of improvements were taking place. The most ambitious one was the $180,000 for Memorial Field, to be located on a 40-acre tract at Elm and Glendale. "Forty Acres" became a geographical designation to Websterites and soon meant the new swimming pool, athletic facilities and stadium.

These improvements had come about through a great deal of work on the part of a great many people. In September 1945, a pamphlet entitled, "Webster Groves Post-War Program" was published by the "Citizens Committee," and the proposed projects were described. General Chairman was Edwin F. Chapman. Committees were headed by

Mrs. Jane Holman and David H. Tompkins, parks and recreation; Hugo K. Graf, buildings; John G. Niemeyer, streets and sidewalks; J. E. Jewett, storm and sanitary sewers; Mrs. F. K. Habenicht, health; Alfred Lee Booth, transportation; Arthur H. Gidionsen, finance; and Ray W. Behymer, publicity.

Eight separate propositions were on the bond issue proposal and the tax rate was discussed frankly.

"If you have an average $3000 assessed value on your property, you now pay $18.60 a year on the 62 cents tax," the pamphlet outlined. "With passage of this bond issue, you will pay $24.00 a year on the 80 cents rate — an increase of $5.40 a year for your share in $800,000 worth of community progress and development. . . Many citizens feel that the future of Webster Groves is dependent upon the extent to which facilities comparable to that of neighboring suburbs are made available."

The programs would be carried out by a Citizens Advisory Committee and Memorial Field and the city park would be administered by a Citizens Board serving without pay.

Webster Groves was bigger in its geographical area, another change brought about in the 1940s. The city limits had been extended to include acreage south of Big Bend, along Rock Hill road to U. S. Highway 66, and east to Laclede Station road. There was a jog in the dotted line outlines to avoid Grant School, which would have caused a confusion on school districts. The new area quickly was developed into some of the prettiest homes and gardens in the city — Webster Gardens, Webster Acres, Webster Knolls in what came to be called "South Webster."

In all, 486 acres were added to the city in the annexations of 1940 and 1944.

Included in the plans for civic improvements was the $150,000 for the new Public Library, which was later augmented, as described in a previous chapter. The sum of $65,000 was voted for a city park of 37½ acres, on Edgar and Jackson roads.

On August 28, 1949, this park was named for Jasper Blackburn, a gift of $25,000 for a picnic and recreation area having been donated by his widow. Both Blackburns had been well known gardeners and civic workers. Mrs. James Weaver, his daughter, wrote the lines which are on the bronze plaque dedicated to him:

Children's laughter, bright flowers, tall trees
How dear to his heart were all of these.

While war and peace and civic improvements made the big headlines in the 1940s, a lot of ordinary living and small changes in lifestyle went on. A few news stories taken at random from the News-Times remind us that:

In 1940, it was big news that "those spiderwebby stockings made basically from coal, water and air — duPont's nylon — about which there has been so much talk during the past year — will reach the retail stores soon." Prospective customers were warned not to expect them to wear forever, as they were rumored to do.

In May 1940, a flag week committee announced its goal was to put a flag in every home in Webster Groves.

Square dancing had a big revival in the '40s with summer groups dancing at Forty Acres.

The U.S. Weather bureau established a cooperative station in Webster in 1945.

Men weren't the only ones in uniform. The August 10, 1944 paper had a picture of a bride in uniform, Ruth Ann Moir, lieutenant in the Marine Corps Womens Reserve who married another Marine, Capt. Arthur N. Nehf Jr.

The big German cannon captured in World War I was moved from its place on Big Bend and given to the scrap drive.

Almost everyone had a Victory garden, raising vegetables.

In the mid-40s, Charles E. Garner, assistant superintendent of schools, did a survey on Webster Groves youth and came up with some reassuring facts which he brought out in a summary titled, What Is Right With the Youth of Webster Groves. According to his study, Webster youth had good study and sleep habits, took responsibility for work around home, were active in Scouts, Hi Y, sports and music, and thought two nights a week out for fun were sufficient.

It was about this time, too, that Look magazine named Webster Groves among the 29 city schools on their honor roll of American public schools. No one in Webster was the least surprised.

The Red Cross and USO were busy in Webster as elsewhere in war years. In a May 1945 News-Times, Alvin Busse was listed as chairman of

The World War I cannon went for WW II scrap.

the Webster Y, Mrs. R. Walston Chubb, a Webster woman, was reported as state president of the League of Women Voters, and 10 churches announced they would have vacation Bible school.

In the postwar years, there was activity among the American Legion, VFW and the new organization, Amvets. A VFW post was named for Robert E. Field. The Legion had its first father-son team of commanders, Carl Stadelhofer, a second lieutenant in the tank corps in World War I and Dick Stadelhofer, a Marine Pfc. in World War II.

There was a clean restaurant bill passed in Webster in 1945. And one restaurant, Toll House, made news by ejecting some of its teenage clientele that same year. This led to the formation of the Club 17 at the YMCA and was viewed as a blessing in disguise.

Trains were still running to Webster Groves: wartime traffic had been heavy but in postwar years there were still six a day.

All of these facts, great and small, were duly reported in the Webster News-Times, which made news itself as an award winning publication in that time. Guy McElwain's Webster Times had merged with George

Father and son commanders, Carl Stadelhofer and son Dick.

Kriegesman's News in 1914, and from 1939 to 1948 the News-Times was published by Ray Behymer, who was the son of F. A. Behymer, well known Post-Dispatch writer, and a man with a great dedication to Webster Groves and good journalism.

The newspaper was sold to Glenn Thomas in 1948 and on December 14, 1949 was struck by disaster. A fire of undetermined origin swept through the press room of the building at 336 Selma avenue, killing pressman George Reichwein and doing vast damage to the building and its contents. The Behymers, who still owned the building, were asleep in their apartment upstairs when the fire was discovered and Mr. "Bee", who had just returned from the hospital, had to be carried to safety.

Thomas renovated the building and continued to print the paper, finally selling it in 1957 to the Brentwood Scope.

Its publisher apologized in the December 15, 1949 issue. It was to have been his biggest issue to date, he wrote, but instead they were lucky to have gotten it out at all, and at that, some of the pages were perfumed with smoke and others bore water stains. Even so, the paper printed the news vital to Webster Groves — students home from college, the March of Dimes campaign, a memorial to a high school student who had died, teas and weddings and garden club meetings and the announcement of the A Capella choir's vesper services.

In 1950, the News-Times printed a big issue, its special historical issue, which many a Webster Groves citizen still has in files of very important papers.

The 1964 celebration of Webster's 50th anniversary as a city had been a modest one, perhaps because most people felt it was not a true anniversary of the community which had started out so long before its formal incorporation.

But in 1950, the city celebrated in grand style, giving its salute to "150 Years of Progressive Growth." A show entitled "Webster Cavalcade," was directed by Harry C. Gibbs, from a manuscript written by Roberta Seibert. Its program had two pages of credits to the committees which labored long and hard to bring it about. The choral group was made up of young people from four preceding a capella highschool choirs. Names of its sponsors filled another page.

In song and story, the Cavalcade traced the history of the area from the western frontiers and the Indian settlers through the Sarpy grant and state organization, the first homes in Webster, the Civil War, the establishment of churches, schools, the city's incorporation and progress. There were scenes portrayed by the Inglis Players, The Theatre Guild, a scene of men in uniform honoring the war dead. There were horseless carriages, barbershop quartets, garden scenes, a wedding, and the Monday Club.

It was a big show.

The special issue of the News-Times reprinted many of the chapters from Velma Benner's history of Webster Groves, which was published at this time. In addition, it filled six sections with stories of the history of churches, schools, organizations, institutions and nostalgic recollections of Webster.

For the Webster of the day and its population (23,289), it provided a long, fond look back and a hopeful look ahead.

Much of the material for the special edition was furnished by Miss Kate

Kate Moody, whose saving nature preserved many historical items for future Websterites.

Twining Moody, and she herself was the subject of one of its stories.

She described herself as a "natural born hoarder" and for many years she had collected facts, names, pictures and data about Webster Groves. For more than 50 years, she had been a librarian at the St. Louis Public Library, so that her job and her hobby were intertwined.

One of her fellow librarians has memories of her, sitting behind a desk which almost completely obscured her from view, piled high as it was with magazines, newspapers and envelopes of clippings. In those days, the library remained open until 10:30 at night at which time a watchman rang a bell and ceremoniously locked the big iron gates.

Occasionally Miss Moody, the story goes, would doze at her desk and wake up after hours. She would then come padding down the steps and wait patiently at the big gate until the watchman would make his rounds and let her out, at which time she would climb aboard the streetcar and go home to Webster Groves.

Hoarding history proved beneficial to the St. Louis community on one occasion when Secretary of the Interior Ickes had turned down a St. Louis request that the Old Courthouse be included in the Memorial; his reason — it did not have enough historic interest. Miss Moody checked her files, found several documents, among them a poster announcing Carl Schurz as speaker at a Courthouse event, and sent them to Mr. Ickes who changed his mind and included the Courthouse.

When she died, Miss Moody left her files to the Missouri Historical Society at Jefferson Memorial. Webster Groves is greatly indebted to her for "saving history" for so many years.

Chapter Twenty

A Church Going Community

There are Chinese characters on the signboard in front of one of the churches in Webster Groves. A board of elders headed by Shing Chu, seminary student and mechanical engineer, purchased the building at 644 Bompart, built in 1908 for the Webster Groves Christian Church and occupied after that by the Church of the Lutheran Confession. The Rev. Peter Lai took over from the Rev. Fred Cheung and in June 1969 a new chapter in church history in Webster Groves was under way.

The 1975 Lions Club yearbook lists 28 churches in the city of Webster Groves, but lists the Baha'i Faith under organizations since this group does not have a building or scheduled meetings. It is a little difficult to take a church count in Webster as each year sees a new one come into being. In April 1975, for example, The First Assembly of God church purchased the former Washington Park school building and became the Washinton Park Fellowship, under the Rev. Gaylon Vinson.

A church going community, Webster Groves had four churches organized in 1866, seven more by the turn of the century. The rest have come into being since 1913.

It was on March 18, 1913 that a meeting was called to discuss the building of a Baptist church, the results of the efforts of Mrs. J. F. Lockett and Mrs. F. U. Whitis who had visited every Baptist known to them. Twenty-three attended the meeting and it was decided to start work as a Mission Sunday School, which would meet on Sunday afternoons, in the Suburban School of Music building. Officers were L. E. Stark, J. R. Black, Everett Pettingill and Mrs. Dora Whitis. In June 1913, the council of St. Louis Baptist churches met with the Webster Groves group to advise in organizing a church. Its constituent

Chinese Gospel Church

Old Community Baptist Church

membership at this time was 39. The Rev. Joseph Sskwor, a senior at William Jewell College, became its summer pastor. When he returned to school, the Rev. Harold I. Reader took over.

On September 7, 1914, ground was broken for a new building at Summit and Oakwood; the church was dedicated on February 7, 1915. The Rev. Dr. Reader left to be a chaplain in World War I and the ministry was under the Rev. Mr. Geistweit and the Rev. Mr. Carson. A Sunday School building and remodeled church were dedicated June 17, 1923.

The depression delayed a proposed building fund but by 1938 a financial campaign got under way and a new building was dedicated on February 2, 1941. The Rev. Mr. Reader who concluded 31 years of service in 1944 was succeeded by the Rev. Robert J. White. The present minister is the Rev. R. Joe Breshears, with Alan Stevens minister of music and youth.

Another church of the Baptist denomination, the Sherwood Baptist Church, was an outgrowth of the Maplewood Baptist Church which voted on December 5, 1956 to purchase property at 470 W. Big Bend as a mission site. The Rev. Ted Cox was its first minister, William K. Leek its first Sunday School superintendent and Grover Smallwood, the head of the missions committee which spent much time organizing the new church.

It remained Sherwood Chapel until July 1958, when it became a church. Ground breaking ceremonies for the present auditorium were held on May 3, 1959. The Rev. Ted Cox accepted a call from the foreign missions board to Japan and the Rev. Robert B. Wallace became the new minister. When he left in 1967, the Rev. Bill Affolter served as interim pastor until the Rev. Vern E. Baird was called on June 18, 1967.

A small but growing church, Sherwood Baptist has, at present, 280 members. It has ordained four preachers and has two busses which bring children to Sunday School.

Old Community Baptist Church on Kirkham road, is not a new church but is a part of First Baptist Church which chose to remain in the "old community" when the rest of the congregation moved.

A growth of Christian Science in the area led the members of First Church of Christ Scientist in Kirkwood to decide to establish a church in Webster Groves in 1915. The first session was held at the Monday Club auditorium on September 19 that year. Later space was leased in the Gorelock building for a reading room.

Bethany Lutheran Church

Sherwood Baptist Church

The Christian Science church has no ministers but Bible and Christian Science textbooks are used. Sermons are comprised of scriptural texts and correlative passages from Science and Health with Key to the Scriptures by Mary Baker Eddy. Lessons are uniform for all churches throughout the world and in each congregation, two readers, chosen from the membership, preside. Wednesday evening meetings include testimonials of healing of human problems as well as sickness and disease through Christian Science principles.

On May 14, 1919, it was voted to buy a lot to build a church. This building was constructed at 17 Selma avenue and first services were held September 27, 1922. Christian Science churches are not dedicated until free from debt. This one was dedicated June 5, 1927.

A reading room was established at 48 W. Lockwood in 1942. This is open, except for Sundays and holidays, from 10:30 a.m. to 4:30 p.m. daily and on Friday nights, 7:30-9:30.

In 1920, a man went around Webster Groves, making a survey of unchurched persons, and proposed to the Board of Religious Education of the Evangelical Synod that a church be established. The man was the Rev. August C. Ernest, field secretary of the board, and this was the origin of the Evangelical and Reformed Church, now a member of the United Church of Christ, at Plant and Lockwood avenues.

First services were held, as many early church services were, at the music hall on Summit and Lockwood. Then, Rev. Mr. Ernest collected $2000 and bought a frame building on Plant and Lockwood, which members helped remodel.

Among early members were the Ed Moeller and Henry Ruhe families, the George Lauermanns, William Pehles, J. O. Doemelts, Louise and Marie Kuhlman, Mrs. Caroline Yaeger, Edward Kolb, and John and Edward Brockmann.

The congregation thrived and expanded. In 1928, the Rev. H. P. Vieth became interim minister, followed by the Reverends Titus Lehmann, H. H. Lohans, J. J. Braun, Thomas R. Marshall, Otis Young, and, at present, the Rev. Dr. Walter W. Grueninger.

In 1937 its sanctuary was built, and in 1955, an attached two-story educational facility was added. In 1967, both buildings were renovated at a cost of $210,000. With merger of the Evangelical and Reformed and Congregational denominations, it became the Evangelical United Church of Christ.

Mary Queen of Peace Church

Webster Hills Methodist Church

One of the church's community contributions is its pre-school facilities for the Eden Laboratory School held there.

Mary, Queen of Peace

Mary, Queen of Peace parish was formally established on Sunday, September 25, 1921, upon the authority of his excellency, the Most Rev. John Joseph Glennon, archbishop of St. Louis. The first pastor was the Rev. Michael Daniel Collins.

World War I was just past and the hope was for peace. Father Collins said that this was the first church in the world dedicated with the specific title, Mary, Queen of Peace.

The first Mass said in the parish was at the home of Mr. and Mrs. Fred Sackbauer, 3 Elm avenue, Glendale. A few weeks later, Fr. Collins set up a parish house at 2 Elm avenue in the home of his cousin, Mrs. Clara Jane Murphy.

Fifteen families formed the nucleus of the parish; its building committee members were Thomas J. O'Meara, Andrew H. Kley, John Murray, Charles Guenther and Edward Meyers.

A site was selected in 1922 on Beverly avenue (later Glendale terrace) and a temporary frame structure was erected. In October 1933, the frame church, hall and contents were destroyed by fire, believed to have been caused by an ether bomb. A building committee was set up again and on September 23, 1934, the cornerstone of the new church was laid on Lockwood near Berry. The following June 16, Archbishop Glennon dedicated the completed church.

After the death of Fr. Collins in an automobile accident, the Rev. Marion F. Forst served as interim pastor followed by the Rev. Sylvester I. Tucker, the Rev. Peter J. Dooley and then the present priest, the Rev. Joseph M. O'Toole who began in 1945. His assistants have included the Rev. Albert L. Stamm, the Rev. Joseph Eilers and now are the Reverends Hubert Creason and Robert P. Javanovic. The new school building for Mary, Queen of Peace was completed in 1948.

Webster Hills Methodist

Webster Hills Methodist Church on the corner of Lockwood and Berry, adjacent to Mary, Queen of Peace, stands where a farm house once stood. The field was the last unoccupied undeveloped tract of land in that area when, in 1929, the Rev. Dr. Franklin Lewis, district

Church of the Open Door   Old Orchard Chapel

superintendent of the Methodist Episcopal Church, met with John Higginbotham of the Cyrus Crane Wilmore office to consider it for a church site.

The first minister, the Rev. Edward Potts, was literally appointed to a vacant lot, with no semblance of organization except for a board of trustees. He spent his first year calling on people in the community to find interested prospective members.

At the close of the year, the church was organized at the home of Mrs. S. S. Scott, Cornelia and Berry road. The new church had financial problems in its early depression years. One of those who helped it repeatedly was Forrest Donnell, later Governor.

A depression project provided its first building. Wesley House, east of Grand avenue, was tearing down one of its facilities, which had been the Niedringhaus mansion. Dr. Lewis secured permission to dismantle it and with help from 25 men sent by the Provident Assn., the building was taken down and its materials moved, through the generosity of a trucking firm, to Webster Groves where it was rebuilt.

Ministers who have served this church since the Rev. Mr. Potts are the Reverends Ben M. Ridpath, Rev. Drs. Ralph H. Hicks, Walter D. Niles, T. Cecil Swackhamer, Charles B. Hart, Joseph B. Dickerson Sr., James McKelvey and the present staff, the Rev. Dr. Kenneth C. Johnston and the Rev. Jerrol M. Boehmer.

The present church building was dedicated by Bishop Ivan Lee Holt and the Rev. Mr. Swackhamer in September 1956. One hundred new members were received that day and the 750 capacity sanctuary had standing room only. An educational building was added in 1963.

Lutheran Church of Webster Gardens

On September 30, 1947, 19 people under the auspices of Concordia congregation in Kirkwood, met at the home of Dr. and Mrs. Theodore M. Hanser to start a mission which became the Lutheran Church of Webster Gardens. On April 11, 1948, they gathered for their first service in the auditorium of Grant school on Grant and Rock Hill. Charter members included the Hansers, Mr. and Mrs. George Krumm, Mr. and Mrs. Henry Gross, Mrs. Ruth Sweeten, Mrs. George Bekebrede and Mrs. Melba Oliver. A seminarian, Marvin Renner, served the congregation, and then another seminarian, Edward L. Schneider, became its first resident pastor in June 1949.

Webster Gardens, in the Missouri Synod tradition, placed emphasis on education and established a day school in September 1952. Continued growth of the congregation made it necessary to expand so land was purchased from Mr. and Mrs. Joseph Treybal in 1954, and in April 1959 the house of worship at 8749 Watson road was dedicated.

In 1965, a new education and youth building was added. A special part of youth education has been special classes for retarded children, started in Sunday School by Mrs. Ruth Meyer in 1965 and included in the day school under Lutheran Special Education in 1970.

After 20 years of existence, the school combined with three other parishes to form Christ Community Lutheran School. School principals have included Herman Wentzel, Paul Nickel, and Ervin Henkelman, pastors of recent years, the Rev. Victor Constien and the present pastor, the Rev. Martin W. Brauer, with the Rev. Rudolph Prange as assistant.

The Wesleyan Church

The Wesleyan Church, Elm and St. George's place, began in 1941 as

The Weslayen Church

The Church of the Annunciation

Pilgrim Holiness Church until 1968 when it merged with the Wesleyan Methodist Church. Charter members included the Rev. Frederick Lyon who became its first pastor, Mrs. Lyon, Mrs. Lester Haley, Mrs. Esther Sebastian, Betty Sebastian, Mrs. Margaret DuBuque, Julia Dorothy, and Rose Marie DuBuque, Dolores Asher, Bessie Storie, Olive Harris and Fannie Walker.

The first two years, worship was held in a residence, then a store building at 13 West Big Bend and a building at Chestnut and Elm. In 1944, the Rev. Ellis G. Maness became pastor. He was succeeded by Pastors Floyd Smith, Harold Bland, Darrel Hansen, Oren Atkinson and the present minister, Harold McGill.

In 1946, ground was purchased at Elm and St. George but the new church was not built until 1958. In November 1958, services were held in the new building. In 1973 the church purchased a parsonage at 131 East Rose.

Old Orchard Chapel

Old Orchard Chapel is an independent Bible church, having no affiliation with any denomination. It was founded by 17 believers, with William Henry Brookes as first church moderator and chairman of the board of Trustees, Mrs. V. H. Gerline, secretary and R. Glen Holland, treasurer. First worship services were on May 8, 1949. On May 9, 1951, William H. Brookes, William L. White and William R. White were elected as elders having been ordained in the Presbyterian Church in the U.S.A.

Early ministers included Dr. F. William May, Dr. Arthur Forrest Wells, Roger J. Andrus, William A. Bishop, Norman R. Linhart, George R. Kennedy and Lester D. Peck. Their house of worship is the building at Amelia and Fairlawn once occupied by the Old Orchard Congregational Church. The church maintains a conservative doctrinal stand patterned after the tenets of traditional sixteenth century Calvinistic Protestantism with strong missionary emphasis. Its members, 100 in number, are committed to full time Christian service.

Annunciation

In July 1950, the Reverend Arthur J. Ryan, pastor of St. Anthony's church, Sullivan, Missouri, was appointed to take over the new parish of the Annunciation in South Webster, which replaced the Annunciation parish of downtown St. Louis.

Father Ryan arrived in Webster Groves with a stole and a few surplices and looked for a temporary home for his parish. The Sisters of Mercy, then on South Laclede Station road, came to the aid of Fr. Ryan and he stayed in their chaplain quarters, holding church services in their auditorium at St. Joseph's Convent of Mercy.

Men from the parish gave time and labor to bring appointments from the old church. On Sunday, September 10, 1950, at 6:30 a.m. the first Mass was celebrated with 13 persons in attendance.

Ground for the parish site at Glendale road and Elm avenue was purchased and groundbreaking ceremonies held January 13, 1952, with the first spadeful of dirt removed by the Most. Rev. John P. Cody. The church building was designed by Carroll and Dean, architects. A school, opened on October 13, 1952, was under the direction of the Sisters of Mercy. The new church was completed and first Masses said on May 13, 1953. In 1955, a new rectory was built.

Now 25 years old, Annunciation has as its present pastor, the Very Rev. Msgr. Bernard E. Granich, who is also Vice Chancellor of the Archdiocesan Chancery Office.

Church of the Open Door

The Church of the Open Door was formed by the City Missionary Society (Congregational) of St. Louis and the Board of Home Missions, New York, to serve Protestant needs of southwest Webster Groves. A lot at Grant road and Big Bend was purchased, a parsonage erected and in January 1949, The Rev. and Mrs. Eugene W. Meyer came to create a new Christian fellowship.

First services were held Palm Sunday 1949 and the church was formally organized December 5, 1949. By the time of its first anniversary it had grown to 100 members, with 100 in church school. A contemporary building was later built and has been the scene of many innovative church services involving both music and dance.

Other recent churches of Webster include: Webster Groves Church of the Nazarene, 7717 Big Bend, Rev. Herbert Rogers; Church of Christ, 112 Oak Tree Drive; Church of God, 9018 Big Bend, Rev. John L. Walker; South Webster Presbyterian Church, 921 Edgar Road, Rev. Lindy Cannon; Webster Groves United Methodist Church, 627 Cornell, Rev. M. Errol G. Grant; Faith United Church of Christ, 210 Chestnut Avenue, The Rev. Anthony R. Lister.

Chapter Twenty-One

The 1950s

You say 1950 and it seems like a long time ago or a short time, depending on your own age. The teen-ager, even the young adult, thinks of it as the olden days, having heard stories of how the neighbors gathered around to gaze at the miracle of the age, the black-and-white television set with its 11-inch screen.

The older person thinks of it as "only yesterday," with fond nostalgia. It was a solid time, a comfortable time, in comparison with what came later. The big war was over; Korea with its loss of the lives of young men and inflation at home was a bad time; but then came peace and prosperity and a certainty of what would happen.

In retrospect, however, it was also a time of growing pains and a time of change, even for those who never want change.

One big and controversial issue of the times was the integration of blacks and whites in schools, restaurants and public places. Such as the new Webster Groves swimming pool.

The controversy raged heatedly throughout 1950 and the spring of 1951 with the result that for the summer of 1951 the pool was closed to everyone. The following year saw more debate, discussion and the concerted efforts of 13 ministers in the area to achieve integration, from the standpoint of justice and the moral issue of brotherly love. The following summer the swimming pool was opened. For everyone.

Also in the 1950s, although not given equal space in headlines, schools of Webster Groves integrated quietly, without incident.

A happy interracial story was that of the Nellie Salmon Day Care Center on Kirkham road in North Webster.

Mrs. Nellie G. Salmon taught school for 60 years, 30 of them in the Douglass school. Like most school teachers, she did not accumulate a

Nellie Salmon far right in the first row.

grand estate but when she died in March 1950, she willed her home, a modest red frame building on a hillside at 151 East Kirkham road, to the Webster Groves chapter of the American Red Cross with the stipulation that the building be used in some way to promote understanding between black and white races and improve social and racial relationships.

It was a small bequest for a large goal and it has had its effect through the years, perhaps not in the way Mrs. Salmon had envisioned but in a way that has helped achieve what she was seeking, dignity and true friendship between people of different color.

A board of directors was set up to determine a purpose and decided that the need of the community was for a day nursery for children of working mothers. It was a blue ribbon group of volunteers who got together in October 1950 — Tom Curtis, Robert S. Turner, insurance broker, Marvin Teeter, Red Cross executive, the Rev. W. D. Thompson and Walter E. Rusan, who was president of the Inter Racial Council and lived in the North Webster neighborhood.

They and others, 20 amateur ditch diggers in all, labored all one day to install a sewer connection. When they struck rock, they borrowed a pneumatic drill from the City and continued to work until midnight under floodlights to finish the job.

The day nursery which opened four months later was one of the first interracial ones with 18 to 22 children enrolled each year. It was staffed for the most part by volunteers. Some of its early ones were Mrs. H. A. Pflug, Mrs. Ervine P. Inglis, Mrs. John E. Gibson, Mrs. Alfreda Gale, Dr. and Mrs. Philip Gale, MacLean Johnson, Glenn Moller, Mrs. Joseph P. Logan, Mrs. John Stockham, Mrs. Robert Lasch, Mrs. Elsie K. Miller, Thomas J. Carroll, Edgar Roberts, Mrs. Marie Meyer, Mrs. E. Dorsey Ruth, Mrs. Hallie Ewing, William Wyatt, Miss Anna Morrison, Mrs. John A. Semmelmeyer, Jr., Mr. and Mrs. Thomas W. Kirk, Joseph Banks, Mrs. Walter Ambrose. Some were from other suburbs but the vast majority are names well known to Webster Groves as active church and civic workers.

There were always plenty of workers; a doctor or a lawyer would show up to mow the lawn or hang the screen door. Young people from church groups did clean up, paint up operations. Housewives and working mothers would leave their own frantic pre-Christmas preparations to help man the Christmas tree lot, an annual fund raising project.

But financially, the nursery was always on shaky ground, and eventually state regulations, necessary ones which raised the standards of day nurseries, proved to be the last straw. Funds could not be stretched to provide fire prevention equipment and other safeguards and the nursery closed in 1957.

Vandalism took its toll of the building and the board voted to sell the property. It was not the end of Nellie Salmon's dream, however. Proceeds were invested so that financial aid could be given each year to a deserving Webster Groves student to attend college. The Nellie Salmon scholarship has been given to black students and white and has provided the opening impetus for many a college boy and girl.

This has been the tangible result of Nellie Salmon's bequest. The intangible one has been many friendships across the invisible line between "Webster" and "North Webster."

This was a boundary line which was also to give way during the 1950s.

The area called North Webster was partly within the city limits and partly in an unincorporated area between Webster Groves and Rock Hill.

For city services and control of sanitary problems, there was little or no government in this unincorporated area, which came under the jurisdiction of the County Court. Conditions in North Webster became the concern of women in the First Congregational Church. Laura Inglis, wife of the minister, Mrs. Alfreda Gale and others were also active members of the League of Women Voters and were instrumental in getting the League to adopt as a study item the exploration of problems with the possible suggestion of a vote of annexation.

Studies had been made by Harland Bartholomew for the City Plan Commission and by the Social Planning Council of Greater St. Louis and these had been evaluated by Dr. Stuart Queen of Washington University. The City Council reviewed the reports and recommended that the city not consider annexation as it would be too costly and that the population annexed would not be homogeneous. Dr. Queen recommended annexation, saying that the alternative "would be continued neglect of property and deprivation to the inhabitants."

In 1953, the League of Women Voters was busy working for a Home Rule Charter for Webster, which was adopted at a special election on March 23, 1954. Annexation was not on the ballot for several reasons: it might necessitate a bond issue and raise in taxes, the community was still upset by the swimming pool closing, and it was thought sanitation problems might be solved by the newly established Metropolitan Sewer District, and housing problems by the new Land Clearance for Redevelopment (popularly known as Urban Renewal) program.

Citizens voted by an overwhelming majority to establish a Land Clearance for Redevelopment authority in April 1958, a project designated as MO-R 15, which meant it was fifteenth in the state. This program continued through 1971 with a total expenditure of more than $2 million in the area, federal money contributing two-thirds, the City of Webster Groves one-third.

Annexation finally came about in 1960 by a vote of citizens, not including those in the area to be annexed. Thirteen residents in the annexed area took the matter to court but the St. Louis Court of Appeals ruled that the area had been properly annexed.

Within the area affected, land clearance too caused disenchantment, and in subsequent years an organization called the North Webster

Community Improvement Association, made up of 350 members with black leaders like Dan Witt, decided it did not want urban renewal with its relocation and replacement but preferred to work out its own problems. But that was many years later, in the late 1960s and early 1970s. The most recent development in redevelopment has been The North Webster Redevelopment Corporation, assisted and guided by the City Council and the Plan Commission. One half of federal funds allocated to Webster Groves under the Housing and Community Development Act of 1974 are being used to assist North Webster.

Change has come. For those who wanted it and those who did not.

Between the all black area of North Webster and the all white neighborhoods south of Lockwood avenue was another district, almost a buffer state, which came to be known as Northwest Webster. It was in the late '50s and early '60s that residents of this neighborhood came to life and had the time of their lives in an organization called the Northwest Webster Improvement Association.

It started early 1957 at a coffee held to discuss a pending school bond issue. Ted Sperling outlined to others his idea of a neighborhood group that might be able to bring about improvements collectively that they could not do individually. A few weeks later, 15 or 20 persons gathered at his home, an open letter to residents was drawn up and officers elected. They were: Ted Sperling, George and Shirley Brown, N. E. Hansen, Don Cairns and Mrs. MacDonald Logie. The association was incorporated and its boundaries set to include 575 persons. Membership grew in the first year from 75 to 240. A long range planning committee was set up which went through the questionnaires filled out by members. A lot at Kirkham and Gore was named public eyesore number one. The area, owned by three persons, had been up for sale for a long time, was periodically flooded, covered with unsightly brush and trash around an unoccupied building partly burned.

Permission was obtained from the owners, who also contributed money, and a blitz crew was organized. Mrs. Virgil Patterson lined up volunteers for 700 man and woman hours. Members contributed shrubs and Mrs. Mary Jane Gaal did the landscaping. A blitz crew (later they called themselves the IMPS) went to work.

Later they were to learn that they had been instrumental in bringing one new family to the area. A couple had been looking at a house but were reluctant to buy because of the corner eyesore. When they saw the blitz crew at work on a subsequent visit, they told the real estate company they wanted to live around people who were that interested in improving their surroundings.

The IMPS didn't stop at Kirkham-Gore but also planted an area at Tyler and Harper, cleaned up the proposed Larson Field area and raised $600 to purchase an "unbuildable" lot for a playground.

It wasn't all work. There was a lot of fun, too, in those days. County Fairs were given for several years, the first a modest one at the homes of L. F. Booth Jr. and Ted Rimbach; later these became organized ambitious affairs with art exhibits, snowcone machine, a country store with a facade assembled for each fair, and competitions among home canners, preservers and seamstresses.

In the winter, there were shows and parties. An annual Open House at Christmas in half a dozen homes. Costume balls, amateur skits. A few of the highlights recalled by a participant were: A mock Veiled Prophet Ball with Clyde Gudermuth as queen. The retiring queen, Dee Eckrich, put her hair up in curlers and retired. One maid was introduced as holding "the record for pushing a loaded grocery cart through Jansen's supermarket. . . she feels this develops poise. "Another was the great-granddaughter of "Old Colonel Crosseyes who was responsible for laying out the first streets of Webster Groves."

Cleopatra on the Barge, a show and float party on the Mississippi river. Mrs. George (Dee) Helfrich was Cleopatra to Chip Eckrich's Mark Antony. The hit song: "Ptolemy, why not take Ptolemy?"

A Wild West show and party. Its memorable moments, Marilyn Kerwin as Annie Oakley and Penny Lee Addison as the girl in pink tights reclining in an ornate gold picture frame over the bar.

Everyone worked in the Northwest Webster area from Mayor Charles Graubner, who lived there too and led the band, to the children at Edgewood who made paper daisies to decorate the fairground.

It was a good time, it was the best time, it was a short time but such a good time.

There are other mementos in the scrapbook of the 1950s. A program for "Oklahoma!" covered with signatures of Webster residents who had paid a dollar as "sponsors" of the show given at Webster High in March 1955 with Margrit Schuhay as Laurey, Dave Cooper as Curley, Nancy Pennell, Ronnie Thompson, Marjorie Morse, Glen St. Pierre, Marion Placke, Dick Black and Bruce Pemberton in other roles.

This show was repeated at the St. Louis Theater on June 14, 1955, as a

Preparing for High School Graduation Party.

benefit performance for the Webster Groves Red Cross. The students involved spent the first five days of summer vacation rehearsing for it.

A high school tradition began, also in the 1950s. In 1952, a Webster Groves mother read a magazine article about a town in New York state which sponsored an all night party for its high school graduating class, the idea being to keep the young people off the highways and provide a memorable fun party for their big night.

Webster parents started out with a Family Fun Night, a carnival to raise funds. It grew in proportions to a gigantic project which now runs like clockwork, the wheels of its machinery oiled by years of elbow grease and experience. Mothers Club chairmen in 10th grade, 11th grade and 12th grade hold fund raising events to provide funds for the party.

During their child's senior year, the mothers, hundreds of them, work on committees planning the celebration, which takes place after the graduation ceremonies and includes a dance, midnight supper, 2 a.m. swim and a breakfast.

As a newspaper story described it, "It is essentially the same from year to year. Only the decorations change and, like the desserts of the women's bridge clubs, each succeeding group of hostesses tries to outdo the previous ones."

The gymnasium of Hixson Junior High School, where the party is held, has been transformed into a turn-of-the-century riverboat with a Showboat entrance and levee scenes, into a rose garden, A Mexican fiesta and even into outer space.

Fathers come into the picture as construction crews and many families work all night the night of the party. A strict code is enforced. Each graduate turns in a ticket, has his palm stamped for identification and must remain at the party. Any student leaving must sign out and may not return. At one average party, 500 students checked in and only 14 signed out, which parents took to be the mark of a successful evening.

Not only the Mothers Clubs of high school but the Parent Teachers Associations of all schools have long been a mainstay of Webster Groves with parent participation in school activities almost a requirement of residency. Numerous schools have had their own unique traditions — Lockwood's annual PTA show, for example, but a September Open House is common to all and the unofficial opening of the school year.

Amid all the changes in the social fabric of the 1950s, still another one took place although it remained inactive in that decade. An ordinance permitting liquor by the drink was passed in 1950. Its provisions were so strict, involving a 10:30 p.m. closing hour, a $450 license, and the refusal of a permit for a place within 300 feet of a church, school or library (which eliminated just about all of Webster), that no one took advantage of it. In June 1966, the ordinance was amended to be less stringent but still provided that it apply only to restaurants where 60 percent of the business was in food sales. Sir Ben (Bernard H. Kannis), whose restaurant replaced the A & P store and preceded Clayton Savings and Loan at the Elm and Lockwood location, was the first to receive a license in 1968.

But that was in the '60s, after the '50s. That long-ago era or only yesterday, depending on how you look at it.

Chapter Twenty-Two

Webster Groves Institutions — Their Character — and Characters

"Any history of Webster Groves should have a chapter on its institutions — Webster College, Eden Seminary and O. Walter Wagner."

The remark was made facetiously, but, like many a jest, has its basis in fact. The Rev. Dr. O. Walter Wagner — Walter to his fellow ministers, "Occie" to long time friends — belongs in any account of Catholic and Protestant organizations, perhaps as a bridge, an ecumenical bridge.

He, along with many other prominent religious leaders, form a part of Webster's church history, a history that is more than that of the individual churches.

Webster College

Approaching this facet of religious history chronologically, one finds that Webster College was first, in fact, the first Catholic women's college west of the Mississippi, founded in 1915 through the efforts of Mother Prasedes Carty, superintendent general of the Sisters of Loretto.

Originally it became part of Loretto Academy, an outgrowth of Loretto Seminary, a grade and high school started in Webster in the last part of the nineteenth century, on land given them by B. F. Webster. For some years, college and academy continued under the same roof on the site of the present college. But in 1922, the Sisters purchased the Lockwood estate which provided space for the high school, named Nerinx Hall after the founder of the Sisters of Loretto, the Rev. Father

Sister Jacqueline,
President of Webster College.

Charles Nerinckx. The college was named for Benjamin Franklin
Webster, the Sisters' early benefactor.

For many years, Webster College was a "girls' school," of high academic
standards and conventional patterns.

Then came Sister Jacqueline Grennan who became the school's
president on June 1, 1965. Wrote William F. Woo, in a Post-Dispatch
story at that time, "Webster College. . . is 50 years old this year, and it
is hardly an exaggeration to say that in the six years that Sister
Jacqueline, or Sister J. as she likes to be called, has been associated with
it, the institution has undergone more basic changes than in any
comparable period of its history.

"For one thing, Webster is developing something of a national
reputation as an intellectually freewheeling place of learning. . . Just
recently, for example, at Sister Jacqueline's suggestion the faculty
voted to abolish all required courses outside of major fields. What this

means is that while certain courses may be required for completion of a major, there will be no other rigid requirements — such as two years of foreign language or 15 hours of English — for graduation.

"Sister Jacqueline herself, a slender woman with big intense gray eyes and a mind that works something like a combination of an IBM computer and a fox terrier, has become a national figure in education. She is the only woman — and only Roman Catholic — on the President's Advisory Panel on Research and Development in Education. Only recently she was appointed to Sargent Shriver's committee for Project Headstart to help preschool children from impoverished areas.

"The Joan of Arc of Education. . . there is little question but that Sister Jacqueline gets people to do what she wants, from leaving prestigious schools for teaching posts at Webster to giving $1,500,000 — as Conrad Hilton did — to build a school theater."

Woo went on to relate that Sister Jacqueline would succeed Sister Francetta Barberis who was taking a position with the Job Corps.

Her new office, he wrote, was small, modest and furnished in contemporary furniture with a phonograph and low coffee table.

"On one wall," he wrote, "is a photograph of President John F. Kennedy with this inscription: 'To Sister Mary Jacqueline — From one frontiersman to another.' On another wall is a crucifix."

There was no doubt in Sister Jacqueline's mind that one could serve the Lord and the world, and that if the trappings of religion got in the way of doing a job for humanity, the formalities had to give. Although there were many of her most ardent partisans who felt she was more beautiful in the starched headband and flowing black robes of the Sister, she soon "kicked the habit", as one writer described it, and changed to contemporary dress and a short haircut. (Privately, she confessed later, that she'd had no idea what a bore it was having to go to the hairdresser regularly.)

A woman of humor and intelligence, she liked to quote Harvey Cox who had said, "Modern Christianity ought to be like a floating crap game — you go where the action is."

In an endeavor to follow the action, Webster College opened a summer school for the Upward Bound program for inner city youth.

"We wondered how Webster Groves. . . merchants in nearby Old Orchard would take to our bringing so many Negroes into the

Webster College on East Lockwood.

community," she said. She found the students courteously received and commented, "It's a credit to the college and a credit to the community, too."

Under Sister Jacqueline, Webster College severed its church connections and became a lay college early in 1967 and she herself left the order. She expressed the hope that the college would retain a religious background but an ecumenical one.

"By ecumenical, we meant not the lowest common denominator which would offend no one," she said, "but a commitment to the best in all religion."

Frequently asked, in this period of her life, if she planned to marry, Sister Jacqueline laughed off the queries. But in 1969 she was married to Paul J. Wexler, a Jewish widower, became president of Hunter College in New York, and closed a colorful and dynamic chapter of Webster history — Webster College and Webster Groves.

Dr. Leigh Gerdine assumed the presidency in 1970. Under his creative leadership, the College has continued to make great progress in developing innovative education.

Eden Seminary Library.

Eden Seminary

At Eden Seminary, at the time when Sister Jacqueline was changing the face of her college, one student seminarian was working on the "strip" in Las Vegas, another was a part of an inner city mission in New York city, a third worked for an institution for the handicapped in Germany and a fourth was helping a Boy Scout troop in north St. Louis.

"Probably the greatest difference in the training of a minister today is recognition of the fact that a great deal of learning takes place out of the classroom," said the Rev. Dr. Robert T. Fauth, Eden president and an Eden graduate, class of 1940.

Once a small denominational college for German-born students of Evangelical faith, Eden in the '60s had become a school supported by the United Church of Christ (a merger denomination formed from the Evangelical and Reformed and Congregational churches) with half its student body from other denominations including the Roman Catholic and Jewish faiths.

Eden has made its home in Webster Groves since 1924 when the campus on Lockwood and Bompart was bought and developed. Before that its location had been near Wellston, on what is now the Normandy High School site, and before that it traced its beginnings back to Marthasville, Missouri, 54 miles from St. Louis. When the seminary was started, it was accessible only by oxcart, horseback or foot.

A favorite and classic story of Eden concerns the day in June 1850 when two oxcarts of students set out to collect food from townspeople for their empty larders. As they left, Pastor J. A. Rieger called back one of the young theologians, tied a rope around his waist and said, "So now you may go."

"But Pastor Rieger," the student protested, "people will wonder why I am wearing this rope around my waist."

"Exactly," replied the pastor, "and when someone asks you, tell him, 'Pastor Rieger tied this rope around my waist just in case someone should be found willing to donate a cow to the seminary.' "

Before sundown, the young man came back with a cow and calf.

The name Eden was taken from a small Wabash railway station near Marthasville and not from any Biblical reference. Because Eden's graduates have gone far and wide, there are many Eden churches and hospitals and, in St. Louis, a publishing house. In 1885, the seminary moved to the St. Louis area, in 1924 to Webster and by 1950, it had an administration building, chapel, library and dormitories.

For many years, its classic Gothic towers were a part of the "skyline" and many were sad when its new library obscured the tower, but the handsome library dedicated in 1968 has been an addition to its facilities and to the community.

Eden has had many distinguished graduates, perhaps the best known Reinhold Niebuhr and his brother, Richard Niebuhr, once dean at Eden. Others are Hartland Helmich, Mark Bailey, Bishop Joseph Gomez and Bishop Gurbachan Singh (United Church of North India.) The Rev. Dr. L. W. Goebel of Webster Groves, who was president of the Evangelical and Reformed church, was an Eden graduate as were many many Webster ministers, among them the Rev. Dr. Raymond McCallister. Distinguished faculty members include the Rev. Drs. Carl Schneider, H. A. Pflug, Allen Miller, Allen Wehrli, Elmer Arndt and John Biegeleisen.

And Eden is especially proud of the fact that the merger of the Evangelical and Reformed and the Congregational churches had its beginnings in conversations between the Rev. Dr. Samuel D. Press, then president of Eden, and the Rev. Dr. Truman Douglas of Pilgrim Congregational Church in St. Louis. They laid the groundwork for more formalized meetings leading to the United Church of Christ. Eden has long been ecumenical in its outlook.

Ecumenical — the word was not heard much before the 1950s. It was in July 1950 that the Rev. Dr. O. Walter Wagner became executive director, or ecumenical minister as he preferred to call it, of the Metropolitan Church Federation of Greater St. Louis. Under his leadership, as many as 650 local area churches at one time were active in cooperative Christianity. The Federation board was made up of clergy and lay leaders who were leaders in the community and their concern, too, was "where the action was," in hospitals, inner city and suburbs with a great deal of political action which made headlines. Toward the end of his work, Dr. Wagner moved out of the Protestant domain into dialogue with Catholic and Jewish leaders too.

He retired in 1969 and has traveled extensively throughout the world as well as serving interim pastorates in the St. Louis area. But home to him is the house built-by-Joy on Greeley avenue in Webster Groves and rebuilt with joy by him and his wife, Dorothy, after the best traditions of Webster do-it-yourselfers. His favorite story concerning his rapport with his neighborhood is the one about the small boys who showed up at the door one day and asked his wife, "When can Dr. Wagner come out to play?"

The ecumenical minister has many accolades for his adopted home town and only a few complaints. One of these is that the number of Jews living in Webster Groves is "inadequate."

"As the oldest ecumenical minister in the community," he said, "I think I'll suggest to the St. Louis Rabbinical Association that they name me their resident rabbi! Maybe I could start a little synagogue in the abandoned Nazarene chapel."

Miriam School

There is some Jewish representation in Webster Groves institutions in the Miriam School at 524 Bismark. A private day school for children with learning problems or emotional problems, it is supported in large part by Miriam Lodge No. 17 United Order of True Sisters. Funds also come from the Switching Post in Clayton, a shop selling antiques, and the Miriam Shop, Skinker and Delmar.

The building and 35 acres were donated to the Miriam Lodge in 1913

Epworth School for Girls, 110 North Elm.

by the Bry family. The facility was first a convalescent home, which later became part of the Miriam Rosa Bry department of rehabilitation and long term care at Jewish Hospital. The ground was then used for a summer camp which was taken over by the Jewish Community Centers Association. It became a school for the mentally retarded in 1956 but this program was concluded with the advent of the Special School District. In 1962, classes began for children of normal potential who had learning and emotional disabilities. Miriam Diagnostic Preschool for younger children began in 1964. Over 50 women and young people serve as volunteers here.

Epworth School for Girls

The establishment of the first juvenile court in St. Louis in 1909 created a need for the care of teen-age girls. Two deaconesses from the Methodist Deaconess home took three girls into their homes, and before long the need increased so that the Epworth Emergency Home was started, at 3410 Morgan street. When this facility was no longer adequate, property at 4310 Morganford was acquired and the Epworth School for Girls began in 1913.

By 1922, more room was needed in buildings and grounds. Ways and

New classroom addition at Edgewood Children's Center, 330 North Gore.

means were found to buy a beautiful 13-acre estate at 110 N. Elm in Webster Groves. The Simmons Hardware Company had bought the grounds, originally the Dawson home, as a recreation spot for its employees but found it was "too far out of the city."

The only improvements on the premises were the residence, a cottage, carriage house and a swimming pool. Two residence halls were built in 1930 at a cost of $50,000 each. Mrs. Scott DeKins was secretary of the board and entered into much correspondence to persuade the national organization to give the support needed. A schoolhouse costing $60,000 was built and dedicated in 1948; it was named the Ann Schrader Building for Mrs. E. P. Schrader who had served the board as treasurer for 20 years. In the 1960s more modern dormitory facilities were added.

Eden's girls range in age from 12 to 18. Caseworkers work with the girls and with their parents in the hope that eventually the girls can return home to live with their families.

Edgewood Children's Center

Webster's oldest institutional building now fills a new need. The Rock

Lutheran Convalescent Home at 723 S. Laclede Station.

House at 330 N. Gore, which was once Webster College and later the St. Louis Protestant Orphans Asylum, merged with Forest Park Children's Center in 1956 to become Edgewood Children's Center. The Center now serves children with emotional problems and learning disabilities, 32 in resident treatment, others in day and foster care. New buildings have been added to the old throughout the years.

Lutheran Convalescent Home

The Lutheran Convalescent Home, 723 S. Laclede Station road, is Webster's newest institution, although it is housed in familiar quarters, which were, until three years ago, those of the St. Joseph's Convent of Mercy on a beautifully wooded area. The change might be looked on as yet another evidence of ecumenical cooperation, which has been a part of life in Webster Groves since its beginning

Chapter Twenty-Three

A Lively Interest
in the Arts

When Conrad Hilton made his generous million dollar gift to Webster College, it added an important cultural asset to the community which has always been noted for its support of theater, art, music and literature.

Its opening in May 1966 was a colorful event; Mr. Hilton was among the guests of importance who applauded the beautiful Loretto-Hilton Center for the Performing Arts. Richard Jones of the Post-Dispatch described it as "one of the most versatile flexible theaters ever built." In addition to its main theater, it had lecture halls, a ballet training hall, rehearsal theater, classrooms and offices.

In its first season, its program included such diverse selections as "Twelfth Night" and "Waiting for Godot." Sister Marita Michenfelder of Webster College worked with a staff of professionals and students. Since then, in its 10 years of existence, the Loretto-Hilton has become a popular place for night and matinee going theater lovers with many other attractions such as art shows, concerts, puppet festivals and manifestations of the "performing arts."

In 1966, another asset was acquired, the new Webster Groves Community Orchestra, which was under the direction of Gerald Fischbach of Webster College at that time, and is under the direction of Allen Larson now.

"It is a true community orchestra," Larson described it. "We have 65-70 musicians, who are high school and college students, people from the Webster community and other communities."

A member of the American Symphony orchestra league and supported in part by the Missouri State Council on the Arts, the orchestra gives

Exterior of the Loretto Hilton Center.

Lobby of the Loretto Hilton.

The Arion Club of the early 1900's.

four concerts a year at the Loretto-Hilton. A similar blend of college and community is the Choral Union, which is directed by Peter Tkach.

Concerts were a pattern of Webster Groves back in its earliest days. When Webster was a village, the Misses Mary and Carolyn Allen had a music studio in their home on Lockwood. Miss Mary was a piano teacher, Miss Carolyn an organist who was one of two women invited to play at the Louisiana Purchase Exposition of 1904.

In 1907 Mary Blackwell Stevenson came to Webster Groves and became a leading teacher of piano and an institution in herself. At one time, her school kept six pianos and eight teachers busy at her home at 238 South Elm street. Her recitals were elaborate affairs with symphony musicians such as Max Steindel accompanying and conducting. Ensemble piano work was her specialty; sometimes 33 students, three to a piano, 11 pianos, played simultaneously. Kay Thompson, Russ David and Gordon Jenkins were among her pupils. Her daughter, Gladys, became a concert musician.

An early 1900s men's singing group was the Arion Club, with Charles S. Blood as its president. Under Glenn Woods and Rodney Taylor, they gave concerts each winter in Bristol Hall. Audiences wore formal attire and the concerts were gay social events.

The ladies formed the Chaminade Choral Club in 1912 and they, too, gave concerts. Both faded out of existence with World War I but interested singers in each group got together in the Jessie Gaynor Club, named for the composer of children's songs who had worked with them. They, too, presented concerts; Leo C. Miller and William Parsons were among their directors, Helen Traubel one of their soloists. Other recitalists of the period were Mrs. Gaynor's daughter, Dorothy Gaynor Blake, and Dorothy Dring Smutz. Other musicians have included Ruth Harris Porteous, Ruth Salveter Cushing and Laura Parker.

When William A. (Pop) Gore became superintendent of schools in 1924, he announced that he was a music lover and intended having musical opportunities for Webster students. He began a program of teaching music in the grades with Mrs. Jessie Ruth Aull and Mrs. Frances Bolsterli, and started a music program at the high school with Hans J. Lemcke and William Heyne (later of the Bach Society) and brought Miss Esther Replogle to direct choral music.

Hans Lemcke, and later his son, Henry Lemcke, and Miss "Rep" stayed to become a part of Webster history.

"They Sing for Teacher Even On Holiday," was the headline of a feature story in the 1950s telling how Miss Rep's students came to rehearse at 8:30 on a holiday morning in order to work on songs for a special performance before the National Music Educators.

Tiny but dynamic, Miss Rep frequently kicked off her size 4 shoes and directed in her stocking feet, both when directing her high school choir and the First Congregational Church choir. One year, Mrs. Dorothy Gearhart who made an annual elaborate gingerbread scene took as her inspiration a Sunday in church, with pews, church members, ministers, primary choristers (looking this way and that) and Miss Rep and her tiny shoes, all in gingerbread.

A stern taskmistress, Miss Rep demanded standards of excellence rarely achieved in high school groups or by church choirs. On Memorial Sunday when her church choir sang"The Battle Hymn of the Republic," there was hardly a dry eye in the house. The high school singers' annual Christmas vespers service was a traditional high event with packed houses in awed silence.

For all of her no-nonsense approach, Miss Rep made lifetime fans of her students. When she retired, after 28 years of teaching, members of her choirs throughout the years gathered at her home to serenade her. Gordon Jenkins and Wilson Stone were among her students who "made good" professionally, as was Mead Metcalf who writes and produces shows at his Crystal Palace in Aspen, Colorado.

Hans Lemcke, who had played with John Philip Sousa's band, liked to

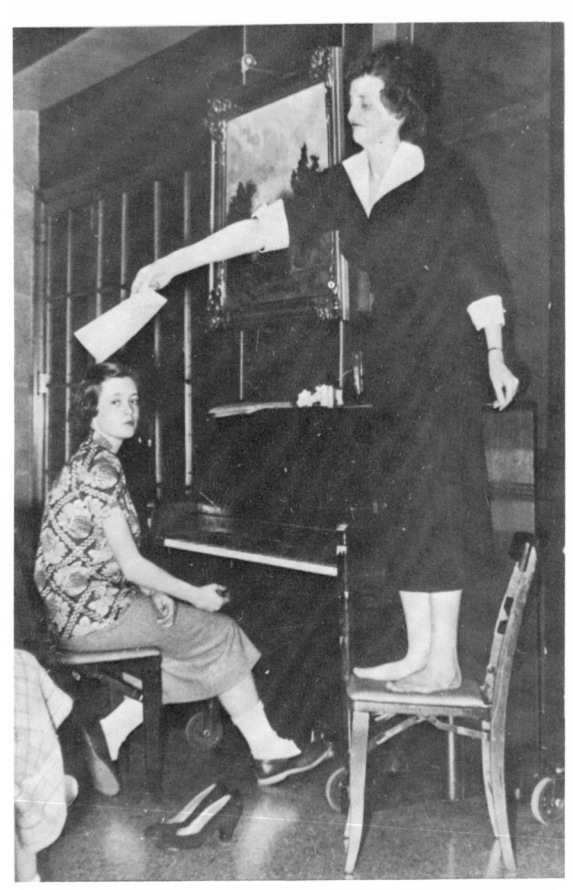
Miss Rep in a familiar pose.

tell how Webster was the first high school in the area to have a band. Among students who played in his band were piccolo player Tom Curtis who later became a Congressman, Gordon Jenkins, Russ David, and Al Hoemann, Kirkwood jeweler who has directed bands in that community for many years.

In the 1930s, the Webster band began having free summer concerts with high school students playing side by side with adult musicians, many women and men in other professions like Dr. William G. Klingberg) who played for the pleasure of playing. By the 1950s, the concerts were large affairs given under the stars at Memorial Field with name radio and television performers as announcers and an audience ranging from those in baby carriages to those in wheelchairs.

Hans Lemcke was succeeded in his work by his son Henry who became band director in 1953 and remained until his untimely death. In 1963,

Tony Carosello became music supervisor and H. Edward Carson became conductor in 1969.

The Webster Theatre Guild had its beginnings in 1927 and was well established when its members took the plunge and acquired its own building in 1952. The house which they bought for $8000 was appraised at $57,000 a year later, the difference accounted for by many man and woman hours and generous contributions by Webster merchants. Among its founders and early active members were the Russell Sharps and the Allen Richardsons. One of its early play writing contest winners was a Washington University student, Tom Williams, later known as Tennessee Williams.

"We always say we didn't choose Webster Groves, it chose us," says Dolly (Mrs. Sam) Sutton, "and one of our reasons for living here was the Theatre Guild and the wonderful friends we made there."

Many of the actors from the Theatre Guild also participated in the Inglis Players, theater group at First Congregational Church.

Another entertaining Webster Groves institution was Mrs. Carrie George, who, for more than 25 years, gave the Carrie George Book Reviews to aid good causes throughout the community.

Through Mrs. George, the Webster Groves Foreign Student Fund, which annually brings a foreign student to study at Eden Seminary, was inaugurated and supported. Mrs. George once estimated she had reviewed 175 books from "A Man Called Peter" to "The Man In the Gray Flannel Suit." In her spare time, she reviewed books for the blind. One of her regular listeners once said of her:

"Carrie George could review the telephone book and keep you hanging on every word."

The art of dancing has been taught for more than 25 years by LaVergne Blisner, in Webster. Other dancers, from young ballerinas to middle aged couples, go to the Virginia School of the Dance operated by Virginia Ulrich, on Lockwood.

A tradition now gone but fondly remembered was Mrs. Janet Condon's dancing school and Fortnightly for young people, described as "the last outpost of civilization." A delightful sight, reminiscent of dancing school scenes in "Penrod and Sam," was that of boys bowing and girls curtseying in Mrs. Condon's Monday Club studio, and occasionally (it happened at least once) a small boy escaping through the window. But for every rebel, there were many many young men and girls who wore their first formal clothes and enjoyed their first ballroom experience at Fortnightly.

Writers, artists, television and radio performers have made Webster Groves their home in large numbers, drawn no doubt by the esthetic attractiveness, by the intellectual atmosphere and by a certain amount of freedom which enables them to live as private citizens who can drop their public image at home.

One of these was Mrs. Sherwood Diller, better known by her first name Phyllis, who lived in Webster Groves with her husband and five children for several years. They had moved there because Diller ("Fang") had a sister who was an osteopathic physician in Old Orchard and a brother who was minister at Church of the Open Door.

For the time they lived here, they engaged in gardening, furnished their home in "early Goodwill," like many another Websterite, and sent their children to Webster schools. They had wanted, Diller said, "a nice old area with trees and birds" and found it.

Another Websterite who left for greater opportunity was Pat Fontaine, once Channel 4 Weather Girl, later of the "Today" show on NBC, but for a while just one of the mothers going to conference at Bristol School.

Familiar faces and familiar names on television and in Webster homes are Harry Gibbs (who was Texas Bruce, the delight of little boys), Clif and Nancy St. James and their daughter, Patti, professional singer, Chris and Clare Condon, Charlotte Peters and Russ Carter.

Webster writers of books would include the late Ruth Philpott Collins, prolific author of children's stories, Nicolete Stack, Chaille Robinson and Carolyn Ward. Among writers whose names and by-lines have appeared in newspapers who live or once lived in Webster Groves are: John Archibald, Vernon Black, Lucyann Mueller Boston, George Cooper, Jim Dutson, Jean Ehmsen, Eunice Farmer, Mary King, Wayne Leeman, Marguerite Martyn, Robert Morrison, Allen Merritt, Clarence Olson, R. Fullerton Place, Frank Peters, Keehn Spear, Sam Shelton, Caralee Stanard (Sylvia Stiles), Myles Standish, Clarissa Start, George Stroud, Bill Tucker and Tom Yarbrough.

When the St. Louis Artist Guild bought the old residence at 227 East Lockwood for its headquarters, in a long planned move from the city, it was like coming home to many of its members. The Guild traces its origin to the St. Louis Sketch Club whose members gathered around a cast iron stove in the early 1880s. In 1886 a new organization was formed, in order to admit women, and from this grew the St. Louis Artist Guild.

Many of these artists live or have lived in Webster. A list furnished by one of the Guild members includes:

Sylvester Annan, Metzy Appel, William Bauer, Edward Boccia, Genevieve Brackman, Marilynne Bradley, Mary Breyer, Fred Green Carpenter, Mildred Bailey Carpenter, Yoshiko Carpenter, Vivian Chevillon, Phil Conrath, Fred Conway, Leone Cooper, Eda Cushing, Margaret Ford, Lorraine Gerceceff, Hugo and Horace Graf, Dick Godwin, Mary Harford, Fred Henze, Eugene Hoy, Betty Jehle, Steve Kinsella, Robert Kissack, Nancy Knight, Cindy Knock, Helen Longmire, Viola Miller Longmire, Ed Luchtemeyer, Patricia Maull, Montrose McCardle, Richard E. Miller, Miriam O'Malley, Arthur Osver, Ernestine Osver, Martha Pattengale, Edith Phillips, Ruth Porteous, Charles and Dorothy Quest, Jessie Rickley, Nancy Ruhoff, Eugene Sappington, Barry Schactman, George Leonard Schultz, Stanley Tasker, Frances Tandy, Rudy Torrini, Beulah Warner, Heinz Warnecke.

Community art fairs, street shows and events such as Webster Arts Kaleidoscope in May, 1974 and 1975 have focused attention on many manifestations of art.

Crafts have enjoyed an upsurge of interest in the past few years. At L'Essayons studio on Big Bend, managed by Pauly Goetz, wife of landscape architect Robert Goetz, students of pottery, macrame and many art forms gather to improve their skills.

Going from the sublime to the frivolous, Webster's youngest citizens have, from time to time, been bitten by the desire to be performers. Take, for example, a group on Lee avenue a few years ago who, in their small way, contributed to the traditions of that area. To quote from a column in the Post-Dispatch, August 4, 1960:

"Standing in line at the ticket office, I saw a Standish but it was the wrong one.

" 'Are you covering this event in place of your husband, the distinguished drama critic? I asked Mrs. Myles Standish.

" 'Heavens no,' Marge said, 'I just brought the kids.'

"Since no drama critic had been assigned to cover the theatrical event which had brought both of us to the William B. Curtins' lawn, I assigned myself. The event was a presentation by a new company, the

Webster Groves Lee avenue 'Puny Opera' players who were to put on 'Cinderella,' benefit of the Red Cross, admission 10 cents.

"My neighbor and I and the four little boys we'd brought found good seats, third row center, joined the 50-some other spectators and laid in a supply of popcorn, cookies and Kool-Aid, also available for 10 cents. Promptly at 7 the curtains parted.

"The curtains would have been unique even at the Muny Opera – living curtains, two little girls, Lucy Rosenthal and Laura Jean Drake, in frou-frou tutus, ran back and forth across the grassy stage to indicate the lapse of time.

"The story followed the classic plot. The king told Prince Charming (Tommy Curtin) he must find a wife. End of scene one. Cinderella (Clair Curtin) was found cleaning the fireplace, running errands, cringing from the tempers of her cruel stepmother and stepsisters. End of scene two. "The fairy godmother appeared, along with a beagle hound who had to be chased from the scene. Cinderella was told of the transformation to come, and announcer Barbara Drake told us there would be a two-minute intermission which resulted in a rush for the refreshment stand.

"Music from 'Sleeping Beauty,' a bit faint as the record was played indoors, set the stage for the ball scene. . . " 'You dance beautifully,' Prince Charming told Cinderella, and so did he for a little boy in bedroom slippers. A series of gongs signified midnight and Cinderella cried that she must go before her coach turned into a pumpkin. Someone turned into a dog as an offstage yowl was heard. There was a 10-minute intermission and the Kool-Aid flowed.

"An adult couple arrived late and apologized.

" 'I'll fill you in,' a neighbor said. 'She's just lost her slipper.'

"With only one more intermission, the show wound to its glorious conclusion with Cinderella the only one who could fit into the golden slipper (possibly because the others were wearing tennis shoes.) The finale was followed by wild applause.

"Since Myles Standish was not there, I will say that stellar performances were turned in by the aforementioned and also by Gene and Mike Fleming, Carolyn and Betsy Wright, Lyle Callahan, Dean Manetzke and Tom Drake. Great credit goes to the producer-director, 12-year-old Molly Howat of California who was visiting the Curtins and unfortunately had to return home before opening night.

" 'She rehearsed the kids every day for two weeks,' said one mother. 'It was a Godsend to us.'

"It was good for the Red Cross, too. Proceeds $20 — $8 from tickets, $12 from refreshments."

The next summer saw an even more successful Puny Opera season. This time it was covered by Clarence Olson of the Pictures staff of the Post-Dispatch (who just happened to live on Lee avenue.) He noted that a simple factor governed the casting of "Snow White and the Seven Dwarfs" — "The tallest boy was drafted to play Prince Charming and the tallest girl became Snow White. She had to be taller than the dwarfs."

Chip Magner was Prince Charming, Carol Wright was Snow White and others of the Rimbach, Magner and the same families as before performed. This time, a larger sum, $38, went to the Red Cross.

Eventually the Puny Opera, like the early singing societies, went out of existence. Small as it was and far removed from the Loretto-Hilton (being all the way across town), it was still proof that in Webster Groves, residents old and very young take a lively interest in the arts.

Chapter Twenty-Four

Sixteen in —Where?

Webster Groves was flattered, pleased but not really surprised. The town had been chosen by the Columbia Broadcasting System to provide the background for a television documentary to be called "Sixteen in Webster Groves," a study of the sixteen-year-old high school student, his/her interests, problems, personality.

Why Webster Groves? Well, every true son and daughter knew the answer to that. Because Webster Groves was a Very Special Place. Even in CBS headquarters in far off New York, they must have heard of the large number of national merit scholars produced by Webster High, of the incredibly large percentage who went on to college, of Webster's cultural advantages, its outstanding a capella choir directed by Miss Rep, its 27 churches. Why Webster? Because it is outstanding.

The CBS reasons given officially were a little less flattering. They had chosen Webster, spokesmen explained, because of its central geographic location, because its income was average among incomes of American suburbs ($8500 annually), and – on a more laudatory note – because "it symbolizes the finest traditions of American history and pioneer values," and "it has a lovely name."

Needless to say, the producers, cameramen and crew were welcomed to Webster Groves in the fall of 1965 with enthusiasm, open arms and hospitable homes. Frontrunners of the group were Arthur Barron and Mrs. Paula Kaplan who spent September and October doing preliminary research for the show.

A newspaper story detailed Barron's qualifications. A native of Boston, graduate of Tulane, Ph.D. from the Russian Institute, Columbia U., he had worked with Eric Sevareid. In an interview, he expressed the hope his documentary would demolish the image of the teen-ager as delinquent and empty-headed.

He was astounded, he said, at the "openness and generosity" of the community, "started to cry" when the choir presented him with a decorated cake the last day of shooting. His reaction to the community was, "What a great place to raise kids!" He envied them.

The television coverage was thorough — George Brucker's math class, Dorothy Weirich's speech group, Miss Rep's singers, the Turkey Day bonfire, family groups, the Monday Club, churches. Hours of filming from November 1 to December 1, 1965.

Occasionally there was a dissenting voice, rumors that they had filmed drag racing on Lockwood. Nonsense, Barron said. He expressed himself as being tremendously impressed by the students. Like that beautiful girl who wanted to join the Peace Corps and "help humanity." He'd even gone off the Webster High campus to film Sister Jacqueline, who was making national news at the time; he considered hers "probably the best TV interview" he'd ever heard.

In retrospect, people wondered if they'd been too cooperative.

"Let's go through it one more time. Only look sadder this time. Like you're gonna cry. Come on, try again.

"YA WANNA BE ON NETWORK TELEVISION, DONCHA?"

"Pile a few more in that car. Don't be chicken. You won't lose your license. "YA WANNA BE ON NETWORK TELEVISION, DONCHA?"

"C'mon parents, lets see you dance like the kids do. Be good sports. YA WANNA BE ON NETWORK TELEVISION, DONCHA?"

Everyone did. They'd told grandparents in Tucson and Nantucket and aunts and uncles in Sioux City and Seattle to look for it.

First the film had to be cut to size. Everyone understood that. CBS had recorded 22 hours of it which they would reduce to one. Scheduled for early in February, the show was canceled, rescheduled for Friday, February 25, 1966. All over Webster Groves, TV sets went on. You could have heard a pin drop a minute before 8.

You could have heard a pin drop at 30 minutes past 9, a half hour after the show ended. Most of Webster was still sitting in stunned silence. They just couldn't believe what had happened.

The show began with an impressive scene, a flag raising and a crowd shot of solemn faced, somber eyed teen-agers. These were the 16-year-olds in Webster Groves, the audience was told. They were "children of privilege, of affluence." Why then did they look so sad? Was something missing?

Something was. A classmate who had died. The students were holding a memorial service for him, presenting a flag in his honor.

The flag was waved later. When Miss Rep's choir was singing that stirring patriotic "This Is My Country." Only a quick fade-in, fade-out of the clear young voices because they were just brief background for a black girl telling how she felt the lash of discrimination. Barron had said

he was having trouble finding a black student who would complain about discrimination. They all wanted to tell him about the black campus king and the yearbook queen candidate. But finally he had found one.

As the "documentary" unfolded, it was clear that its theme was to show that life in a typical suburb (which Webster Groves was described to be) produced young men materialistic in their aspirations, snobbish in their views, interested in decadence such as sterling silver.

The beautiful girl who wanted to help humanity ended up on the cutting room floor. So did most of the beautiful young people. So did Sister Jacqueline and the "best TV interview" Barron had ever heard. The 27 churches? One shot of a very elderly lady leaving one. A discussion group of parents who had expressed concern over the lack of "true integration" and school friendships between black and white was nowhere to be seen. Parents were shown, a pretty lively group of them. One Sunday School teacher took a lot of kidding from friends who didn't know she "could dance like that." She had to explain she couldn't. The camera had flashed her face on the body of the go-go dancer brought in by CBS for their entertainment.

The lengthy filming of the football rally was cut to the pompom girls incessantly shrilling, "We're from Webster, couldn't be prouder, if you can't hear us now, we'll yell a little louder. . ." The irony was obvious

Appalled was a professional actress, who'd been thrilled to be on network TV but hadn't realized she'd sound like a shrew on the prepared family fight script.

Most stunned were student performers who found their words used out of context, sometimes an answer used in reply to a question which had not been asked. Sample: A football player was asked what he did to prepare for the big game. "I go down in the basement and lift weights," he said. On the documentary, the question was about his reaction to the pressures from parents to excel. What did he do when pushed to his limits — "go down in the basement and lift weights."

Most disappointing in its omission was the town. The camera crew had filmed the beautiful autumn foliage in color, the rambling frame houses, wide lawns, tree lined streets. Only one house was shown. Where could it be, that pillared mansion, everyone asked.

"It's our house," one woman admitted unhappily. "It doesn't look like it. That's because the cameraman lay on his back and shot upward so our one story porch columns would look like pillars."

A column in the Post-Dispatch, written by the author of this history, called it "A Hoked-Up View of Webster Groves."

The column was a well read one and often elicited fan letters, sometimes as many as 20 or 30 on a controversial issue. This particular column drew more than 1000, all but a handful in total agreement. ("Thank you, thank you, thank you, thank you. . ." began a typical one.) Fewer than five disagreed. ("You snobs in Webster had it coming," one anonymous writer said. "You failed to mention there are no synagogues in Webster," wrote another.)

Letters continued to come in for a month or more, letters from former Websterites in Europe and Asia and Africa. A follow-up was written; the Post-Dispatch offered reprints of the two columns and filled 1800 orders.

Some of the letters came from college students who related in loving detail their recollections of a happy youth:

"I find it hard to communicate with other students my feelings about my home town," wrote a girl in Michigan. "They don't rush to visit teachers on their first day of Christmas vacation."

One of the high school teachers wrote:

"I didn't recognize my kids. When I think of the hundreds of hours they put in as Candy Stripers, at Operation Head Start and retarded children's camp, I seethe."

Others were philosophical:

"What should we expect from a licensed peeping Tom?"

"Maybe they're right. As I look around at my 40-year-old house, my aging car, battered piano and fine idealistic teen-agers, I realize we are affluent. But not in a way Madison avenue would understand."

Pat Corrigan, a student at Webster High (and later a professional journalist), conducted her own poll, an exhaustive collection of 147 written opinions by students. Typical responses were:

"I didn't like the program at all. It was definitely not a true picture of the teenagers in this town. CBS made us sound like a bunch of social climbers who all had two cars and a fine house. This isn't true and the people who do have those luxuries probably worked hard to get them."

"It should have been named, 'How a Typical American Suburban Town Can Make A Complete Mockery of Itself.' It shows what people will do and say to be on television."

"I feel it is unfortunate when a news special is produced by a group that arrives with a set of ideas and collects material solely to support these preconceived notions. From the picture presented, I couldn't recognize my home town."

"To me CBS made Webster High look like a rat race where you couldn't make it unless you had a lot of cheese."

"The CBS special portrayed many things. It portrayed a city full of wealth and snobs. It portrayed a horrid racial situation. It portrayed a better-than-thou attitude... It portrayed frenzied grade conscious kids... The one thing it didn't portray was being '16 in Webster Groves.' "

"On Friday the nation watched Webster Groves from the windows of a CBS helicopter," one student interpreted. "The Webster that these people saw was viewed from an angle I have never previously witnessed... the pilot had to tilt his machine... nevertheless the passengers felt they had received a true picture... It's too bad the helicopter never really came down to earth."

An interesting sidelight was that many out of town viewers believed the slanted picture but didn't think what it showed was bad.

"Last week CBS News went to an American community that is prosperous and happy and seemed alarmed to find that its young people like it there," wrote one newspaper columnist in another city.

And Terence O'Flaherty of the San Francisco chronicle quoted moderator Charles Kuralt's remark, "Webster Groves is six square miles of American dream but something is missing." Added the columnist, "I can't imagine what it is except discontent."

Those closer to home or familiar with Webster were loud in their outcries. "CBS Misfires" headlined St. Louis Magazine, which had done its own Webster "in depth" analysis a short time before. Some critics professed to see a Communist plot in television programming. Many an angry letter went off to CBS but none was acknowledged. Instead, CBS planned a return filmed visit. Most of those who had been on the original show recoiled as if asked to have a return cuddle with a cobra.

"Sixteen in Webster Groves" received nation-wide attention and was made available to church and youth groups for some time thereafter, apparently as a horrible example of what a stuffy, prejudiced community was like. Occasionally, a former resident would write in anguish, asking how to refute the picture.

An English teacher found the show an excellent opportunity for teaching her classes.

"We can talk about slant by selection and bias by quoting out of context, but we could never have gotten the idea across to the kids the way this program has."

In time we laughed at ourselves. How smug we'd been, the small town beauty asked for a date and then "stood up." Pride goeth before a fall. We had expected to be admired and found ourselves ridiculed. A delightful satire was written by Odie Dickens, titled:

A Visit From the Giant With One Eye — A Modern Fairy Tale

"Once upon a time, not so very long ago," it began, "there was a little village nestled snugly between two sets of railroad tracks. It was, in all honesty, a shabby, fuddy-duddy little place, which begrudged money squandered on such frills as street repair but constantly voted staggering tax rates for their schools. A very unsophisticated collection of people whose main extravagance was their children. . ."

"For the most part," she continued," the children turned out well. . . although there were gray sheep and even jet black ones and periodically all heck broke loose. . .

"Whenever this happened, the parents of the village would shout 'Woe and disaster' and form committees. The Police Chief would pack a lunch and trudge from PTA to PTA pleading for more restraint, more restrictions — until things finally calmed down again.

"You might say that if the village had an Achilles heel, it was their pride in and their concern for, their children."

"One fine fall day," the fairy tale continued, a stranger came into their midst. . . a friendly Sociologist who represented a wonderful and powerful Giant with one eye who wanted to use his magic to let the world view this village. 'But why our village?' they asked.

"Because, continued the friendly Sociologist, the Giant here, believes that Teen-agers have been the victims of 'poor-press' and since your community has been designated a 'supportive community' in a report written by wisemen from the East, we hope to show the other side of the teen-age picture by picturing them — and you. Besides, we like your name — 'Webster Groves.' May we stay?

"Might they stay? The tornado, caused by so many doors opening wide all at once, almost blew the village flat. . . the Giant turned on the red light over his one eye and set to work. . . They worked with the same dedication as did those two who fashioned the Emperor's new clothes so long ago. . ."

Came the big night. "Every pair of eyes in the village was riveted on the Giant's One Eye. And what do you think they saw? An exquisitely constructed patchwork Crazy quilt, designed and executed with such skill and finesse that it appeared to be made of whole cloth.

"Little bits and pieces — plucked from here and tucked there. Questions asked, answers insinuated. . . And slowly but surely, all the

238

golden coaches of truth turned to pumpkins and the Friendly Sociologist into a lovely, fat rat! The villagers were at first confused, then disbelieving, flabbergasted and furious.

"Where was the 'supportive community'? There, doing the Watusi, very badly! Where was the 'good press' for the teen-agers? Their hard work and aspirations were tarnished. . . Where were their accomplishments? Unmentioned. . . The choir, the Y, the churches, the volunteer work — all cut — and in their places a contrived, concocted portrait of complacency.

"But most fundamental of all — where is the integrity of our erstwhile friend, the Sociologist? Where is the public responsibility and dedication to truth, bad indifferent, and *good* that the Giant with one eye holds so precious?"

The Giant — and other Giants — had been to other places, Selma, Alabama, Vietnam, Berkeley, Odie Dickens wrote. Did they, there, too, use the same formula of "deceit, duplicity and dishonesty"?

This probably was the biggest lesson learned by Webster residents from the visit of The Giant With One Eye. No one lost faith in Webster Groves. But a great many people lost faith in television documentaries.

In time it all blew over. A group of business men in an ad offered "16 in Webster Groves" — 16 reasons to buy there.

Half a dozen years later, an actor named David Hartman came to Webster to film a series — "Lucas Tanner" — and was well received. True, his show changed the name of the high school to Harry Truman High School, but they did use a real honest-to-goodness house, Judge Russell Doerner's, for the fictional school teacher.

And the fiction in "Lucas Tanner" seemed like realism, in fact like Simon pure truth, compared to the fiction in "Sixteen in Webster Groves."

Built by Robert Studley, this house later became the property of the Blackmer family and was moved to its present location on Blackmer place.

Big Bend and Lockwood, 1898.

Chapter Twenty-Five

Webster Looks to its Heritage

The 1960s saw many changes, some of which severed irrevocably the links to the past. Highway I-44, about as popular as the Berlin Wall, was fought with zeal by residents of south Webster, but eventually the State Highway Department prevailed, the road was carved through a lovely area of homes and the vroom and zoom of traffic reverberated day and night.

The Rockwood Apartments, where retired teachers and widows lived, was no longer "the apartment." First came those on Glen road and then Colonial Village in Old Orchard and The Algonquin on S. Gore. Each time, disturbed citizens protested the invasion of multiple housing into a community of single homes. But eventually it was conceded that the conservatively styled newcomers weren't too bad.

Commuter trains came to an end, too. As Wayne Leeman, Webster resident and train buff, wrote in the Post-Dispatch in 1961: "So ends an era of 100 years duration, as distinctive as steamboating, gas lights and old style trolley cars, which also succumbed to changing times."

Heading the list of mourners, he wrote, were "205 regular passengers and at least four times that number of 'foul weather friends'. . . one old timer said sadly in an advance memorial, 'Life may go on but it will never be the same.' "

The commuters were a close group. Some called themselves The Rattlers, had membership cards and a slogan, "Fight, fight for better equipment." Calling themselves The Oakland Limited, some of the commuters tried to keep the spirit going by riding the same bus downtown but life truly was not the same.

Social change was everywhere. The Viet Nam war, campus

demonstrations, the generation gap. Long hair and beards became the style; drugs became a problem, even in Webster. Young people seemed more serious. When they signed each other's Echo, it was no longer a flip two-liner but a page of open declaration and self analysis.

Some changes were happy ones. Forty Acres, though separated by the new highway, took on new life with an ice skating rink. Led by Jack Cooper, then Councilman, Mrs. Otis H. (Laura) Manchester and Mrs. Vernon (Maxine) Stromberg, many citizens had been active in arousing community interest in a proposed skating rink.

On November 3, 1964, 80 percent of the registered voters voted overwhelmingly in favor of building one. Dedication ceremonies were held on November 4, 1966. Director of Recreation at the time was Bill Kloppe, a man who had a hand in many of the fine recreational developments in Webster Groves. Architects for the rink were Hellmuth, Obata and Kassabaum. Mrs. Mary Ellen Young became the rink's first manager and soon the winter afternoons and evenings were bright with skaters and viewers as in the long ago days of Lockwood pond and Prehn's Hill.

"It's later than you think" was an expression popular in the early '60s. From time to time, residents who had an interest in history and heritage would remark that something really should be done to preserve the memories of the past in organized fashion.

Through the efforts of John W. Cooper, Jr., then city councilman and later mayor, the Webster Groves Historical Society was incorporated on March 31, 1965, and the city council passed a resolution endorsing its purpose on May 4.

The following February, 1966, an organizational meeting was held. Cooper was named temporary chairman and city attorney H. Jackson Daniel was appointed legal counsel. First elected directors included Mrs. Ralph H. Metcalf, secretary, Roy Brackman, treasurer, James R. Appel, William H. Copeland, L. Farrand Booth, Mrs. Robert G. Ellis, Mrs. S. Lester Ford and Mrs. E. Gary Davidson. The group agreed to accept charter memberships at $10 per couple.

By May, there were 131 charter memberships, representing 234 individual members and three institutional charter memberships. A competition was held to select an emblem and the winning design by Herschel R. Herman was adopted; its lines incorporated the sturdy trunks of trees and leafy branches so familiar in Webster.

One of the first projects planned was the marking of homes 100 years

First Century Home marked, 300 N. Gore.

old or older. Earl W. Hobbs was appointed to head the committee of Historic Sites.

On June 13, 1967, the first Century Home was marked. It was the home of Clarissa Start Davidson at 300 North Gore avenue, built by John and Mary Fulton. The two-story brick dwelling had had 11 owners, among them the William Lewis family, Charles Connons, Julian Lucketts and the Thomas H. Ward family. The Davidsons had purchased it in 1955; Mr. Davidson died in 1967.

Owning an old house can be a joy, not only in the challenge of renovation but in the delight of discovery as its owners delve into history to find out what kind of people used to live there. In the case of the Fulton-Davidson home, it was discovered that both John Fulton and Gary Davidson had been lawyers, both families had been interested in Mexico, and — for whatever astrology believers may make of it — that John Fulton and Clarissa Start both were born on March 28. This house was sold in 1970 to another antique collector and old home enthusiastic Mrs. Merle Campbell.

The Webster Groves Historical Society Bulletin made its debut in the spring of 1968 and subsequent issues described the marking of other Century Homes. The second home marked with the H. Jackson Daniel home, 225 Blackmer Place, on June 11, 1968. This house had been built in 1866 by Mr. and Mrs. Robert Page Studley; later it was owned by Mr. and Mrs. Lucien E. Blackmer. In the 1920s, Albert Blackmer inherited the house and moved it south. He built a new home on the corner and named the street Blackmer Place. Later owners of the home

At ceremonies marking the First Century Home (300 N. Gore) front row, Mrs. Robert Hansen, Mayor John W. Cooper Jr., Mrs. Clarissa Start Davidson and Mrs. Robert Ellis; From top, down stairs are Miss Julie Yarbrough, Miss Mary Yarbrough, Miss Judy Langenbach, and Mrs. Thomas Ward.

were the Clausen, Ford and Ackerman families.

The Helfenstein home, owned at the time by Mr. and Mrs. Schell L. Furry, was marked on December 14, 1968. On hand was Frank H. Simmons, a grandson of John Philip Helfenstein. Later homes marked were:

The Jotham Bigelow house, 1 Claiborne place, owned at the time by Mr. and Mrs. Gershon Ward and later by the Edgar Stemmlers; the Jackson home, 133 Gray avenue, now the home of Thomas J. Carroll; the Nathan D. Allen home, 23 W. Lockwood, now Mittelberg-Gerber; the John Richardson home, 318 E. Swon, owned by James S. White; the Richard J. Lockwood home, now Nerinx Hall; the Spencer home, 428 California, owned by Dennis Noonan; the Rock House, 330 N. Gore, now Edgewood Children's Center; the William D. Butler home, 5 Marshall place, owned by Mrs. Ben S. Lang; and the Peers S. Griffin home, 224 College avenue, now the home of Mrs. Bertram Elam.

The Chris Hawken house was of special interest because the Historical Society was desirous of renovating it as an organizational headquarters and landmark to be open to the public. Then at 9442 Big Bend road, it was the property of Church of the Open Door.

The church wanted to have the house removed so they could use the land. Through Mr. and Mrs. Chester Von Rump, members of both the church and the Historical Society, negotiations were begun.

William Bodley Lane, architect, was retained to handle the potential restoration of the house and the Society began to look into the possibility of a grant under the historic buildings preservation program. In the spring of 1969, a massive fund drive was begun to raise half the necessary $90,000 in order to qualify for matching federal funds from the Housing and Urban Development program. Adrian DeYong was chairman of the fund raising committee, assisted by John W. Cooper, Jr., Roy Brackman, Duane Yadon, Clarissa Start Davidson, Adele Stine, J. Marshall Magner, Chester Von Rump and Ted Reichardt.

A house tour was held May 25, 1969, a beautiful sunny day which produced a successful fund raising event. Houses on the tour included the Century Homes at 1 Claiborne place, 133 Gray, 300 North Gore and Hawken House, and the homes of Mrs. Ben S. Lang, 5 Marshall Place; George and Leone Cooper, 140 N. Rock Hill road; the Leland C. Shanles, 410 Hawthorne; Mrs. R. E. Bell, 458 Hawthorne; the Jack Roths, 104 W. Jackson; the James Whites, 318 E. Swon, and the Andrew Ries family, 30 Joy avenue.

Artists from Webster contributed their talents to decorate notepaper with sketches of landmarks; among them were Mrs. James (Metzy) Appel, Mrs. Helen (Nikki) Bottger and Mrs. Charles (Marilynne) Bradley.

A memorable fund raiser was the balloon race sponsored at one of the Community Day events. A Historical Society bulletin headlined its account: "SOME DAY THEY'LL ASK... REMEMBER THE BALLOONS?"

"Ideas are being sought for special events for the next Community Days but we'll have to go far to beat last year's stellar event," the story read. "Who will ever forget the balloon race and the dedication of one loyal member who boiled balloon after balloon on her kitchen stove in an effort to get one to blow up big enough for a display. (Someone had told her this would work. It didn't.)

"The Historical Society and Mac Hardware Store cosponsored the aeronautical event in which contributors purchased balloons, signed a name tag and then let the helium-filled ball soar away. Prizes were offered for those returned from the greatest distance.

"Tying for first place were V. Grossman whose balloon traveled to Enfield, N. C. and T. Wessel whose balloon traveled to Rocky Mountain, N. C., distances of 700 miles. Many were returned from lesser distances."

The Society had other Community Days projects, a picture taking booth with a Gay Nineties photoboard, a float in the parade with members in costume riding in antique cars.

A second house tour was held Sunday, October 11, 1970, this one a tour of Webster Park homes. An 1892 map was used on the tickets. Chairmen for the tour were Ann Cuntz, Pat Burton, Geneveieve Brackman, Sarah Muckerman and Marilynne Bradley.

Among the houses on tour listed on the program, were:

> 100 Orchard, built for Edward Lemoine Skinner, now the home of Mr. and Mrs. Lee C. Ferrenbach.

> 319 Oakwood, built in 1900 for the Weir family, now owned by the Victor Thompsons.

> 415 Oakwood built by Charles A. Baker in 1894, rebuilt after a fire in 1901 for W. C. Rumsey, now owned by Christopher Muckerman.

435 Oakwood, the home of David and Ann Boyce.

238 Park, built by the Joy brothers, owned by the Rice Greens.

424 Hawthorne, a newer home owned by the James Connors.

405 Orchard, the first home in Webster Park, built in 1892 for George K. Andrews, owned by his daughter, Mrs. Lewis W. Thomson.

103 Glen Road, the home of the Howard Bridges family.

Refreshments were served at the Bridges home and recipes from Mother Payne's Cookbook assembled by Sarah Ann Payne of Webster Park in 1908 were for sale. Flower arrangements were furnished by Webster Groves garden clubs.

Besides fund raising, there were many other activities of the early Historical Society. In a statement of purpose, Jack Cooper wrote:

"Webster Groves is a splendid residential community with many unique qualities, not the least of which are its traditions, heritage and ancestry. Since the founding of the Webster Groves Historical Society, it has been our aim to preserve the evidence of this history."

The Society, he continued, hoped to arouse interest through educational programs, and also to serve as custodian for written records and museum materials — pictures, furniture, clothing and objects illustrating life and conditions of the past.

Speakers at early meetings included Mrs. Robert G. Ellis and Mrs. Robert K. Hansen who showed their color slide program, "Our Webster Heritage," featuring old homes along with the legends and lore of the area; Mrs. Arthur Konzelman, museum curator, Jefferson Barracks; Mrs. Louis Farrand Booth, who spoke on Webster as she remembered it; librarian Helen Mardorf who showed her collection of old Valentines; Roy Brackman, speaking on street names; Wayne Leeman on trains; Ruth Ferris on steamboating; Elinor Coyle on the World's Fair era.

Contributions were coming in to the proposed museum as well. Books, pamphlets, atlases, maps, letters, diaries, photographs, postcards, toys, furniture, and clothing, items ranging from a rosewood piano to an antique fly swatter.

At last the necessary funds were raised for Hawken House, in contributions ranging from nickles and dimes to a check for $2000. The

Hawken House moves down the road a piece.

The move is completed and the house is restored.

Hawken House Dedication. Left, Mayor John W. Cooper, Jr., County Supervisor Lawrence K. Roos, and Congressman James W. Symington.

house was acquired from Church of the Open Door, approved by HUD as one of 20 houses in the U.S. which would receive funds to help in historical preservation, and plans and specifications went out for bid, the cost of restoration estimated at $53,000.

"Hawken House Moves Down The Road A Piece" was the title of a story by Kathleen Hays which appeared in the West County Journal on July 8, 1970. It described the moving of the L-shaped mansion in two sections from its Big Bend location to Southwest Webster Park on Rock Hill Road. Half was moved one week, half the next by the Schroll Moving Co. A basement with central heating, airconditioning and toilet facilities had been constructed as Phase One of the project. Phase Two was to be restoration and landscaping.

Many man and woman hours later, it was completed, beautifully decorated by Mrs. Walter J. P. Gibbs and Mrs. Ellis H. Hamel, who had chosen from the contributions of homes and friends in the area.

On Saturday, October 2, 1971, Hawken House was formally dedicated and opened for public inspection. Guests numbering 450 attended the champagne reception held under the canopy of a red-and-white checkerboard tent provided by the Ralston-Purina Co.

Presiding was the Honorable John W. Cooper, Jr., mayor of Webster Groves. Honored guests included United States Senator Thomas F. Eagleton, United States Representative James W. Symington (who had helped steer the project through the governmental formalities), Supervisor Lawrence K. Roos, St. Louis County; members of the Hawken family, William Bodley Lane, and Mrs. Gibbs and Mrs. Hamel. Piano music was provided by Russ David. Chairman of the dedication committee was the Mayor's wife, Betty Anne Cooper.

Last minute landscaping in the form of an herb garden had been done by the Webster Groves Garden Clubs Association. Hawken House was opened for tours, with volunteers serving as guides.

Mayor Cooper was succeeded as president of the Historical Society by A. Wellborne Moise. Present president is Marshall Magner.

Many Webster homes, some old and some new, have been seen on recent house tours.

On May 21, 1972, another Historical Society house tour was held. This one featured the following historic homes:

> 5001 Wilshusen, home of the John L. Banks family, built in 1842.
>
> 312 Hawthorne, home of the George Bishop Jr. family, a Webster Park residence built in 1902.
>
> 213 E. Lockwood, home of Mr. and Mrs. Lou Cariff, built in 1913.
>
> 216 N. Elm, home of the J. Richardson Usher family built in 1887 and originally occupied by the Clifford W. Darby family.
>
> 430 W. Swon, home of the Irvin Lanning family, built around 1900 for Woodson K. Woods.
>
> 314 Bristol Road, home of the David Fleisher family, built in 1938.
>
> 609 Sherwood, home of Mrs. Donald T. Wright; her beautiful azalea garden was a part of the tour.
>
> 133 Webster Woods, home of the Don Gerber family, also a newer home.

Refreshments were served at Hawken House.

Other groups have had house tours of historic Webster Homes. On Friday, December 8, 1972, Holy Redeemer Catholic Women's League presented a Festival of Christmas Candlelight Tour. On it were the Lennon house, 217 Arbor Lane, Moyle house, 365 S. Maple, Ferrenbach house, 100 Orchard, Perabo house, 335 Bristol, Campbell house, 300 N. Gore, Casey house, 406 Hawthorne, Shanle house, 410 Hawthorne and Peters house, 424 Belleview. Kappa Kappa Gamma had tour on April 30, 1974 with Edgewood, the Bergman house, 134 Gray, the Thomas Carroll house, 133 Gray and Helfenstein home, 135 S. Rock Hill (Dr. and Mrs. Henry Knock). Elinor Coyle was tour director for both.

In May 1975, the Historical Society held a house tour and added a new attraction, an antique show and sale, at Clark School.

Interest in old homes and their renovation has certainly been stimulated by the activities of the Historical Society. Three Webster Groves business men, Robert Graham, Jack Baringer, and William Woods, founded the Webco Corporation to renovate a series of homes. The first was the World's Fair Home, built in Buffalo, N. Y., shown at the World's Fair and moved to Webster Groves, on Clark avenue. It was given a face lifting and new landscaping and, as might have been expected, neighbors joined in the enthusiasm. Baringer stopped by one Sunday and found a neighbor watering the newly landscaped garden.

Webster Groves has been named a Bicentennial city and many projects honoring the nation's heritage will be carried out in 1976.

An encouraging new development in a city which prizes its heritage is the interest being taken in history by the young people. A course titled, "Adventure in American Social and Cultural History," taught at Webster Groves High School by Mrs. Wilda Swift, has resulted in an ongoing study of Webster Groves history and the collection of many nostalgic memories through interviews with longtime citizens.

The history project began as the germ of an idea in 1973 when it was necessary to find a new storage place for the many documents which had been collected by the Webster Groves Historical Society. Many volunteer hours had been spent in accumulating the memorabilia, but they had not been catalogued and were being stored in boxes on the second floor of the little house on Elm avenue which housed the Fire Department offices. With the building of a new firehouse, the documents had to be moved. Mrs. Swift, a member of the high school history department, and Jerry Knight, high school principal, offered to store them in a large closet at the school where they would be safe and dry. During the spring of 1974, a few of Mrs. Swift's history students began to sort the documents.

Mrs. Swift applied for and received a $14,060 federal grant from the National Endowment for the Humanities, which gave two such grants, one to Webster Groves, the other to the Oneida Baptist Institute, Oneida, Kentucky, an Appalachian community.

With the guidance of Mrs. Beryl Manne, Washington University archivist, senior student Phyllis Flick spent several hundred hours cleaning and sorting the documents. Other students went around Webster, getting taped interviews from long time residents in an effort to gather information about the period from 1896 to 1915.

Meanwhile, Webster Groves, which had been without any kind of newspaper for several years, had a community contribution in the form of The Acme Press, published and distributed free by Joseph Rath, owner of the printing company of the same name. Rath discovered that readers were interested in history so many of the issues contained excerpts from the studies the history class was doing.

At the end of the school year, Mrs. Swift's students published the results of their first year of work, a 70-page book, "IN RETROSPECT: Webster Groves, Missouri," Its editor was one of the students, Kathy Condon, and other students supplied art work, layout and articles. A charming example of nostalgia, it had a two sided effect, in preserving reminiscences for the future and giving the students an insight into the past. As Cheryl Bredin, one of the 21 students who participated, put it, "It's a lot easier to understand history when you're working in your own community and talking to people who remember."

Only a week apart from "IN RETROSPECT," was another important contribution to the preservation of Webster Groves history. Mrs. Marilynne Bradley who, for some time, had been making sketches of old homes in the area, published "ARPENS AND ACRES," a picture book of Webster Groves from 1850 to 1900.

Mrs. Swift's students are continuing their study and also continuing the big job of cataloguing the Webster Groves Historical Society collection. All of Webster Groves is indebted to the young historians for their efforts.

Chapter Twenty-Six

Who Lives in Webster Groves?

Many suburban communites would have little trouble in coming up with a profile of citizenry. Sociologists have analyzed and often decried the sameness of suburbia, with its rows of houses like peas in a pod, its insulation of young people who meet only one class, one kind of society.

This is not true of Webster Groves. An average citizen asked the questions, "What kind of people live in Webster Groves?" would be inclined to answer, "All kinds," though he might quickly amend it to, "All kinds of good people."

A city survey indicates, however, that there are certain characteristics of the Webster Groves family which might make up a profile. For example, of the families filling out the survey questionnaire, 33 percent were families of two, 18 percent families of three, 18 percent families of four, 11 percent families of five, 11 percent families of six, and 8 percent families of 1. In other words, a majority might be classed as small or medium sized families.

The age of the head of the household was 35 percent 60 years or older, 32 percent 45-59, 27 percent 30-44 and 7 percent 20-29. So one might conclude the average age is 30 to 60 with perhaps a larger than usual suburban percentage of senior citizens.

This would be explained by the answer to the next question, a statistic which would set Webster Groves quite apart from any other suburb. How long has your family lived in Webster Groves?

An impressive figure – 43 percent have lived in Webster Groves more than 20 years, 23 percent 10 to 20 years, 13 percent 6-10 years, 17 percent 1-5 years and 4 percent less than one year. Of these 74 percent had lived in the St. Louis area, 26 percent elsewhere before moving to the community.

Other questions had to do with shopping habits and opinions of city facilities and improvements. In a shopping query, 52 percent said they did some of their shopping in Webster Groves; 32 percent said they did most of their shopping there.

Reactions from strongly positive to very negative were requested on subjects ranging from cultural facilities to traffic control. Fifty percent or more of those who answered were strongly in approval of the city's residential character, its churches and "living in Webster" generally, while 25 to 50 percent expressed approval of people, cultural facilities, schools, apartments and city government services. Mild disapproval was expressed concerning streets, traffic control, lighting and shopping areas.

Programs for improvement which elicited enthusiastic response included the rehabilitation of commercial areas, private home rehabilitation aid, more trees, more organized recreation and other efforts to attract young people, street and sidewalk improvement.

Do you plan to move away from Webster Groves? Only 15 percent do. Those who plan to move, in 58 percent of the cases, will move (or be transferred) out of town.

When you retire, would you retire in Webster Groves if suitable housing was available? Yes, said 80 percent. Do you urge friends to move to Webster Groves? Yes, said 75 percent. Do you feel the city is making progress? A gratifying 85 percent said yes.

Statistics present a part of the picture but certainly not the whole picture of the Webster Groves resident. Somewhere it should be noted that it is a dog loving community where man's best friend has not been too restrained despite all those leash laws, that there are horse lovers as well (one man's horse regularly visited a Lockwood store to nibble feed) and that when the ban on leaf burning went into effect, cries of anguish could be heard to the County Courthouse.

Writer Dorothy Brockhoff found herself nonplussed in trying to pin down the Webster personality for a story in St. Louis Magazine.

"Webster Groves is a paradox," she concluded. "It is as old-fashioned as an antimacassar and as up-to-date as the latest wiggle — the Watusi. It has century-old houses and a thin-shell concrete pavillion that looks as if it had been dropped in the middle of Memorial Park by Picasso."

A merchant called Webster Groves a "town in transition" and added, "Of course there are many old families still here – third and fourth generation people, but there is a tremendous turnover of young people," a fact he attributed to large corporations encouraging their junior executives to settle in Webster.

"It's a typical suburban town," the St. Louis Magazine article quoted one resident. "It has a rural atmosphere," said another. "No, it doesn't," contradicted a third. "The charm of this place is that the people are extremely independent," went another analysis. But the comment heard "so often that it became as familiar as a TV commercial," was, "You just can't find better people."

Wrote Miss Brockhoff, "After wandering up and down Webster's pretzel-twisted streets, which we understand behave the way they do because Websterites 'would rather detour around a tree than cut it down,' we were inclined to agree."

There is a spirit of camaraderie in Webster Groves that is missing in many other parts of the county, the article continued.

"For example, where else but in Webster Groves would you find a street and a half, Marshall Place and part of North Elm with a 'mayor' all its own? He's one Jay C. Tipton who has a top hat with the title 'mayor' emblazoned on it in gold and a town crier's bell to prove it."

To outsiders, such neighborhood spirit might seem unusual, but Websterites are accustomed to belonging to everything from fraternal groups to Saturday Night Dance Clubs. "For Websterites are great 'joiners' – gather six or eight around a coffee pot, and the chances are they'll form a new group dedicated to this or that lofty purpose before the percolator cools."

St. Louis Magazine did not make a tally of such groups but the annual Lions Club yearbook does. And the variety is indeed amazing. Besides the schools, churches, old line organizations, civic and fraternal groups, there are specialized interest groups which fit no over-all category. For example, there is a China Painting Organization, a Needlework Guild, the Mound City Obedience Training Club, the Suburban Youth Boosters Club, a Toastmasters Club, Stamp Club, Saturday Night Dance Club, Dance Circle, Stephens College alumnae club, Junior Achievement society, American Association of University Women, and at least five senior citizens organizations, including the American Association of Retired Persons, Inc.

Apparently, variety is the spice which gives Webster Groves a part of its seasoning.

There are distinguishing characteristics to the average Websterite, too. The St. Louis Magazine feature termed Webster the "do-it-yourself capital of the suburbs."

"People here cherish these old houses," said one housewife. "And a good many of them do most of the restoration work themselves. It's a place where a young couple like Jack and Barb McKay take over grandmother's house to renovate — it's sort of a labor of love."

There's intense community pride. McCune Gill, insurance man whose hobby was history, wrote in one of his informative pamphlets of "150 Years at 743 Tuxedo Boulevard, " a summary of the past and also recollections of his own briefer period of habitation and the many things he had done to care for the house. In a social comment that applies to many in Webster Groves, he wrote, "If more people would keep their houses in repair and would remodel them occasionally, there would not be much of a problem of blighted areas."

Almost any project can go on in a Webster Groves backyard from the growing of a giant banana tree which attracted attention at one home to the construction of an open cockpit airplane which Wilbus C. Volker built in his Fairview avenue yard in 1967. But most "home work" has to do with the adding of wings and paint-up, fix-up remodeling of home exteriors.

The fact that there are so many dedicated do-it-yourselfers in Webster Groves may explain why there is more bloom than blight.

There are also a great many do-it-for-others people in the community. Far from an insular community, Webster Groves has had a greater than average interest in other countries, sending some of its students to other countries and welcoming other students and foreign visitors to Webster. One of these foreign interest groups was a group sponsoring visitors who came under the Experiment in International Living.

Among its Webster Groves sponsors were Dr. Frederick Sargent and his wife, Janet, who had met in Europe under an Experiment program in 1939 and had a sentimental regard for its work. The Floyd Reays, Richard Budlongs and William Laceys were others who arranged for exchange groups.

Students who have spent a year of study at Eden Seminary under a program started by Laura Olds Inglis in 1948 have also added considerably to the cultural exchange in Webster homes, starting with its first student, Marti Nortia of Finland and going on through the years with visitors from Austria and Germany, Japan and Lapland, France and England.

The Foreign Student Fund of the American Field Service has brought many students to Webster High School to spend a year. Like Rudy Vrugtman of Holland, who, according to a newspaper story, "did more to create a favorable image for his country than anyone this side of Hans Brinker and the boy at the dike."

Hosts and hostesses and homes offered for such programs have done much to create a favorable image for Webster. So have the students who have gone out to the Navajo reservations to do volunteer work for the American Indians, one of the popular teen-age projects in recent years, especially with the youth group of the First Congregational United Church of Christ. A pattern for work with Indians has been set by two couples with Webster backgrounds, Robert Roessel of Webster and his Navajo wife who pioneered in the work at Rough Rock, Arizona, and Mr. and Mrs. John Salyer, Mrs. Salyer being the former Ann Heap of Webster, who have spent their lives working on the Papago reservation near Tucson, Arizona.

There were young people from Webster in the Peace Corps, too. One of them was Gail Monroe who was part of a health and community development program for two years in a primitive area of North Brazil where she appreciated what her parents had always told her: "You kids don't realize how very fortunate you are." Gail and Betsy Hanger, who had spent a summer teaching children of migrant workers under an Office of Economic Opportunity program, were the sermon (the scripture lesson was "The Good Samaritan") at their church one Sunday.

Annually Webster teen-agers are among the YMCA group which supervises underprivileged children from Bogota, Colombia at Camp Bochica and Colombia youth come here to visit. Mrs. Jane Berry, of the Webster Y, supervised such a group in 1969.

In recent years, a Webster Groves church-YMCA summer project has made noticeable contributions to home rehabilitation and to bi-racial harmony. Started by Webster board members Dr. Frank Morley and Mrs. Elwood Hamsher in 1971, this group has worked to repair and improve the homes of aged, ill or financially limited individuals. In the summer of 1975, 35 Webster young people, most of them 15 and 16 years of age, worked for $2 an hour from funds which they themselves helped to raise, roofing a garage, doing house repairs, putting in new guttering and doing "lots of painting." One teen-ager who participated in the project summed up his reaction:

"I learned of the need for persons to get out and help those who can't help themselves and I learned to appreciate things I have that I've always taken for granted."

North Webster has had its share of residents who have helped others and helped themselves, too. One family, the Charles Thomas family, made headlines through their achievement of sending all nine of their children to college. Seven of the nine have made their homes in the area in which they grew up.

Lamar Kishlar was a Webster Groves resident who turned personal tragedy into concern for others. His son and daughter-in-law, Mr. and Mrs. Lamar Kishlar Jr., both contracted polio; the daughter-in-law died and Lamar Jr. (friends called him "Bud") spent the rest of his life in an iron lung.

Lamar Kishlar, Sr. devoted the rest of his life to helping, not only his son but other polio patients in iron lungs. His principal project was the servicing of all the iron lungs in the St. Louis area, some 20 in number in the 1950s. Vice president of the Ralston-Purina Company, he had heavy business responsibilities, but the friend who helped him, Milton

Custer, recalls that they would answer calls at any hour of the day or night if a lung was "down." At high noon or 3 a.m. they would go to the home or hospital to get the equipment going again.

An engineer, Kishlar also made many improvements on the machines used for polio patients. Young Kishlar had a portable respirator which allowed for greater mobility but the machine had a limited life of six weeks to two months. Kishlar designed a better one and outlined his idea to Custer. Then, one night on a parking lot while taking his grandson, Jimmy, and friends to the Muny Opera, Kishlar suffered a heart attack and died. It took a year but Custer finished the machine, which is now known as the Kishlar-Custer respirator, and "Bud" Kishlar used it until his death. One is now in operation at Deaconess Hospital in his name.

Another Websterite who turned her problem into help for others is Mrs. Corley Thompson. Peggy Thompson's daughter had a speech and hearing problem, so the Thompsons moved from Neosho, Missouri to the St. Louis area so she could have training. From a dedicated volunteer, Peggy Thompson turned into a professional, executive director of the St. Louis Hearing and Speech Center; she was named Outstanding Young Woman of 1962 by the St. Louis Jaycee Wives.

Many Websterites have spearheaded "help others" organizations – Virgie Barnett with the "Talking Books" program, Dick and Evelyn Budlong with the Frank Laubach "Each One Teach One" literacy efforts, Mrs. David (Eloise) Skilling with the Delta Gamma Tree of Lights project, Anthony DeMarinis, for many years executive director of the Family and Children's Service, Ralph Koeppe of Kingdom House, Bob Lance of the YMCA, and many other dedicated persons.

A Webster Groves Who's Who would be more likely to be made up of these names than of those that glitter on theater marquees. Webster has its number of "big names," too, as listed in the chapter on its "lively interest in the arts." And, as that chapter also detailed, it has a disproportionately large number of artists of the pen and of the palette.

It has its many home town boys and girls who "made good" on Broadway, In Hollywood and Washington, D. C. and every year the number adds a new star. Patti St. James, formerly of Webster High and Webster College productions, now tours with Van Johnson and is forming a new singing group.

It has had its sports heroes in years gone by and recent times – Allen Lincoln and Bud Sample and George Massengale and Jim Krebs and Joe

Ivory Crockett, "the fastest man on earth".

Clif and Nancy St. James,
Citizens of the Year, 1970.

Litzenich and Hank Kuhlman and Carol Pence; its father-son team,
Ralph Hart Sr. and Ralph Hart, Jr., both tennis champions; its
father-daughter team, Ted Young, who won the first St. Louis Silver
Skates and was president of the Amateur Skating Assn. of the United
States, and Gay Young, who won the national pair water skiing
championship with Rick McCormick in 1965 and has won many water
skiing competitions since then.

Its residents and former residents have included Charlie James and Tom
Redmond of the baseball and football Cardinals respectively, and Tom
Hornbein who climbed Mount Everest. And more recent Webster High
classes have produced Doug Wessel, of the Baltimore Orioles baseball
club and Ivory Crockett, "the fastest man in the world."

Hal Knight, Citizen of the Year, 1965.

Harry Gibbs, alias "Texas Bruce,"
Citizen of the Year, 1969.

These are the Who's Who names which make the news stories. A Who's Who too long to list would be the presidents of firms, the chairmen of boards, the doctors, lawyers, teachers, deans, professional people of high caliber such as Homer Jones, an advisor to several presidents of the United States. They were the kind who settled Webster Groves and like has continued to attract like.

Each year the Webster Groves Chamber of Commerce recognizes the work of someone who has made a special contribution to Webster Groves itself in the form of its Citizen of the Year award. This award has gone to the following persons:

1954-Dr. Raymond McCallister
1955-Dr. Leonard Steger
1956-John H. Carter
1957-The Rt. Rev.
   Monsignor Peter J. Dooley
1958-H. Jackson Daniel
1959-Hans Lemcke
1960-The Rev. Ervine Inglis
1961-William Chapman
1962-Mrs. John Stockham
1963-Clarence Appel

1964-Alfred Lee Booth
1965-Hal Knight
1966-Miss Esther Replogle
1967-John W. Cooper, Jr.
1968-John Gable
1969-Harry Gibbs
1970-Clif and Nancy St. James
1971-James Gordon Forsyth Jr.
1972-Warren E. Gerlach
1973-Cora B. Koenig
1974-Don Gerber

The very summary of their work may answer the question, "Who lives in Webster Groves?" and perhaps the right answer is: "All kinds – of good people."

Is it the pool. . . or the rink. . .

. . . or the trees. . .

Chapter Twenty-Seven
And Why?

"Why do you live in Webster Groves?"

The pretty young woman, wife, homemaker, mother, and, at that moment, ticket-taker for the block party being given on the night before July 4, in Webster Acres, had a quick reply. "It was my husband," Kathy LaBarge said. "He was in military service and we lived in Alaska and all over, but he had grown up in Webster Groves, and when he was ready to come back into civilian life, he said, 'We're going to live in Webster. It's the only place to bring up children.' "

This same question was asked of many residents, some young couples with families, some representative suburbanites who might be expected to choose a place like Webster. But it was also asked of professional theatrical people who might have chosen a showier life style, of retired people and widows who might have moved away, of world travelers who could have a more convenient jet port.

"Why do you live in Webster Groves?"

Some gave what Harry Gibbs called "the obvious reasons."

"The big, old barn of a house, walking distance to grocery store, church, school, YMCA, movies. . . the schools. . . community pride, and the advantage of raising four boys under the eyes of countless people who knew them by sight and knew who their parents are."

His wife, Jean, added another asset. Although a community of diversity, economically, sociologically, ethnically, politically, Webster is also "a place with a tremendous reservoir of good will," she said, a place where "no matter how marked or how heated differences may be, the good will is always there."

The Gibbses sometimes feel guilty, two people inhabiting a house which could accommodate eight, but their boys still think of it as "home."

"Webster seemed more home like than many communities," said Ted Young, whose wife, Mary Ellen, grew up in Webster. "Besides it had a superior school system, good churches, fine parks, friendly people, good fire and police protection, good civic government."

Oscar and Audrey Anderson moved to Webster because a friend, Walston Chubb, told them the schools "were very good." The children are grown now but they continue to live in a house just seven years away from its Century Home certificate. It's one reason they stay. . . "we're still working on it!" they explain.

Tom and Julia Yarbrough came back from Washington, D.C. where he had been administrative assistant to Senator Tom Hennings. They knew of Webster's reputation as a good place to bring up a family, of the reputation of its school system, found it a convenient place to get to downtown, Clayton, even Lambert Field, and liked the "sometimes elegant, mostly sturdy and historic homes that have given Webster its tone."

"I think I have accidentally found a word for Webster — tone," Yarbrough wrote. "Which is not to say tony or high-toned. Another word for it is flavor. The place has a richness and permanence about it. . . All of these qualities have made us wish to go on living here in retirement."

Grace and Keehn Spear, retired librarian and newspaperman, have found, "Other locations may be newer and more extravagant but the dignity and the concern for the past as well as for the present and the future give it a spirit of community that is matchless."

"Community" is a word that came up in many answers.

"We wanted our children to have a sense of community," Babs Ferrenbach said. "Many suburbs are just bedrooms. People don't really live there. We live in Webster Groves. Our children can walk to school, to church, we have a library close by. Their friends are within walking or bicycling range."

"And there are all kinds of people here," said her husband, Lee, "from very poor to very wealthy. It's a good mix."

Some answers were brief and matter of fact.

"I live here because I like it!" wrote super gardener Jessie Busch. "My family, friends, church and my own little half acre."

"Because I like it and because I want to," wrote Wayne Leeman. "This follows military service in the United States and Europe and extensive personal travel that includes three trips around the world. Governmental services have been adequate at reasonable cost. Five children have received an excellent education in the public school system. What do you want? An egg in your beer?"

Ray and Helen Behymer came to Webster to edit the News-Times in 1939 and feel they've been here all their lives. Their four children all graduated from Webster High, married and moved, and "now the nest is empty but we continue to enjoy Webster life through apartment occupancy," said Ray.

Irene Arndt, widow of a distinguished churchman, Dr. Elmer Arndt, is another apartment dweller and credits the Eden Seminary Family with keeping her here.

"I am fully in agreement with Margaret Mead that family is the core and center of our culture," she wrote. "As in any family, there's often a maverick and I think Eden is Webster's obstreperous, exasperating but loved maverick. . . For me, staying here is a great saving of time and energy that I don't need to spar around establishing my attitudes and stances. People know where I stand on racial discrimination, equal employment opportunities, civil liberty, social welfare, women's liberation, church world service and Christian faith."

Marshall Magner, who grew up in Webster, feels his childhood determined his life, professionally and personally.

"My earliest recollections are of spending as much time as possible outdoors in the fields and woods," he said. "I know when I was very young I thought there was nothing but country between Lee avenue and the North Pole. I roamed, fished and hunted as far north as Olive Street Road. I am certain that where and when I grew up influenced my thinking and learning. . . and my desire to become a professional biologist. . . Offers to move came over the years, one even to Cuba, but decisions to remain here eventually proved correct, especially the one to Cuba."

Some who have moved away from Webster still think of it fondly. Greg and Katherine Lucy retired to Tennessee but remember their 35 years in Webster. Why, "You've heard this before — schools, churches, trees, upper middle class conservative people, recreational activities. . . no industry, no saloons. . ."

... or the people?

"I love Colorado," wrote Mrs. George Helfrich, "but how I wish we had a place like Webster here. The friends we made, how we worked to improve our neighborhood. I think that's what we loved most. A community of people who worked together and played together."

That word "community" again.

The C. J. Wassilak family moved to Massachusetts but ten years later, they moved back to Webster... "to good schools, a good church and good friends. Webster Groves has that small town atmosphere on the fringe of a city that has so many things to offer. We chose to 'come back.' "

"We could've sold this property over and over again," said Mrs. Sadie Bauer, who lives on two acres of ground in the shadow of the Old Orchard business district, "but we like it this way. We still have our garden here."

There are two doctors in the Pennoyer family — James and Miriam. It was Dr. Miriam Pennoyer, school board member, who supplied a summary which includes most of the reasons "why" people live in Webster Groves... It appealed to them because it was... An established older town, not a subdivision... with a large representation of professional university faculty, people in the arts with interests similar to our own and enough of them to provide a wide choice of friends.

Yet at the same time a heterogenous community with all kinds of people to provide a natural rather than economically artificial mix. Glad that our youngsters had some opportunity for integrated experience in school.

A good school system which had a nation wide reputation.

Comfortable old homes and yards with space to breathe and at least a modicum of privacy yet without the isolation of many more prestigious areas.

For the kids. . . availability of activities and friends within bicycle range permitting them to be quite independent early on. . .

The same accessibility has been helpful to adults, particularly Grandma when she was alive and now with the energy shortage, it's great not to have to drive miles.

The lack of necessity to 'keep up with the Joneses' — anyone can feel free to do his own grubby jobs if he wishes without losing face. . . the ability of moneyed people to live quietly in the same neighborhoods as people of very limited means. . . the feeling of 'neighborhood' is strong.

Generally speaking, the stability of the community — probably fewer swingers, divorces, hanky-panky of all kinds. Kids rather expect parents to stay married and perhaps may be more inclined to keep their own partners."

Nancy St. James also feels this "air of permanence."

"It instills in children a sense of belonging to a community, becoming involved and developing a sense of responsibility," she wrote. "Our 13-year-old, Chip, in Mexico on vacation, was urged to stay but he insisted he had to be home — to be a party to July 4 activities in Webster Groves. When we first moved here, Mayor Cooper asked how we felt about living in Webster. My answer was: I feel it is not just a place to live but rather a way to live. I still feel the same way."

Jackie Hedgpeth studies Lockwood teacher Elizabeth Hughes.

Chapter Twenty-Eight

The End is the Beginning

How do you end something that has no end? For the history of a city is never written, never complete. Each day contributes a new page. The author-historian ponders about the proper last page, and then finds it. Someone else has written it. Our last word is taken in its entirety from the Board of Education publication, "Our Schools," for July 1975.

Graduation – always the same, always different

Assuming that graduation ceremonies can be held outside in June is the ultimate brinkmanship. This year thunderstorms predicted for June 5 grumbled for a while but finally relented and waited in the West. Ceremonies were held at Memorial Field as planned. As if on cue, blazing blue sky, brilliant sun, and brisk breeze set the stage for the appearance of the 469 graduates of the Class of '75.

By tradition, commencement exercises follow a prescribed format. Yet each year's ceremony manages to be indelibly etched with individuality.

Personalities of the graduates always assert themselves. The Statesmen Symphonic Band plays; the A Capella Choir sings. Their performances are poignant with seniors participating in these groups for the last time.

In this year's graduation ceremonies, the Rev. Paul Davis, father of graduate Mark Davis, gave the invocation and benediction. Two graduates, Dean Minderman and George Robnett, Jr., read the name of each of their fellow classmates as individual diplomas were awarded by Dr. G. W. Brown, superintendent of schools.

A quotation from Emerson was used in this year's printed program which captures the essence of the education which Webster Groves School District strives to provide: "The true test of civilization is not

Mary Tucker making commencement address.

the census, nor the size of cities, nor the crops — no, but the kind of man the country turns out."

The "kind of graduate" which Webster Groves High School "turns out" is very special. To illustrate, printed below is the commencement speech delivered by one of the graduates, Mary Shea Tucker, daughter of William J. Tucker Jr. and Patricia C. Tucker. Mary was elected by her fellow classmates to speak to them and for them. The speech, of course.., was prepared to be spoken and heard, not written and read. However, the wisdom of this young lady and of her peers is unmistakable in any medium:

COMMENCEMENT ADDRESS
June 5, 1975

"We have come to our beginning, full circle, from
one to twelve, now we're off the clock. With the sun shining and
the choir singing, I can't help being optimistic. There is
life, and hope, and the promise of greatness in this graduation
class. There always is.
"Graduation means leaving the comfort of things familiar:
admit slips, fire alarms, locker combinations, field trips,
Turkey Day, library fines, Steve Mizerany and home room — all
this, and the hundreds of faces and memories that go with it,
leaving it all for a 'Brave New World' for the rest of your
life. Graduation is an initiation ceremony, a rite of passage,
and the last hoop you are obliged to jump through.
"What was the purpose of it all? Twelve years I've
been in school: Henry Hough, Mary Queen, Bristol, Hixson,
Webster High. Only recently, within the past few days, have
I asked myself, 'What have I learned?' One of the most important
lessons, one I'm still learning, is to make myself do what I
have to do, when it needs to be done, and whether or not I
feel like doing it. I've learned that nothing can be taken for
granted, that people die, that love sometimes ends, and I've
learned much; I've grown through hurting. Troubles at home,
confusion about myself — unless you know me well, you'd
never know. And each of you is carrying some lonely sorrow.
A thing you long to tell the world about so they'll understand
why you are the way you are.
"As a class, on several occasions we've been jolted into an
awareness of how foreign, how unfair, and cruel life can be.
There is no escaping pain and suffering, physical and mental.
It is part of living, being human — the ache of loneliness,
poverty, disillusionment, fear of death, physical suffering.
When I hurt I can only tell myself that what does not destroy
me makes me stronger. Through suffering you come to know your
capabilities, your limitations. It is possible to learn through
pain — patience, restraint, courage, determination, independence.

"Pain is infinitely more desirable than apathy. Smug contentment is drugged indifference. The tragedy of life is not so much what people suffer as what they miss. Apathy, the national pastime. From front page events to the people next door. Who cares? So what. Big deal. I've been in classes where the teacher would struggle an entire quarter to spark interest, ignite curiosity, and couldn't even get a decent argument going. If you are apathetic about learning, you can be no better than mediocre.

"Zorba the Greek said, 'Life is trouble, only death is not. To be alive is to undo your belt and look for trouble.' I feel unbelievably alive today. I haven't undone my belt but I'm seeing things — my family, friends, Webster itself, all of you in a first-time way. The most important thing you should know after twelve years of school is that there is so much more to know.

"I'll finish with a passage from 'The Once and Future King'. . . Merlin is speaking to the young Arthur. 'The best thing to do,' he said, 'is to learn something. That is the only thing that never fails. You may grow old and crumbling in your anatomy; you may lie awake at night listening to the disorder of your veins; you may miss your only love; you may see the world about you devastated by evil lunatics, or know your honor tramples in the sewers of baser minds. There is only one thing for it then: to learn. Learn why the world wags, and what wags it. That is the only thing which the mind can never exhaust, never alienate, never be tortured by, never fear or distrust, and never dream of regretting. Learning is the thing for you.'

"All right, you no-mess, no-jive class of '75, go do your homework, and Godspeed."

What's so special about Webster Groves? Mary Tucker and 468 other graduates. And their parents and teachers and preachers and leaders and friends. And most of all, the younger children, the class of '85 and '95 and into another century, who will be writing this history of Webster Groves from now on.

C E N T R A L

LOUIS MONIER'S SUB.

Eugene Jaccard

Estate

N. D. Allen
13.03 a.

WARDER AVE.

W E B S T E R
10 11   12   13   3
C. S. Pennell Harriet Aug Pallis F. W. Thompson
            Pallis   5.50 a.
17.90 a.   4.74a. 4.74a.   4
        James F. Bruce Martha L. St. Louis Life
9   8   4.81a. Leonides Insurance Co.
                  Jane R. 10.15 a.
                  Murphy 161a. 5

BISMARCK   AVE.

Mary C. Marshall
26.79 a.
JAS. C. MARSHALL'S
1
Lucilla Marshall
26.71 a.

ROAD

WE
Emmerson
3a
S. E. Bailey
5 a.   5.50a.

Mary C. Flowence
33.17 a.

Dr. Stevens

Edmund N. D. Allen James
J. Bailey 4.19a. Clarkson
3.13a. 2
              ALFRED LEE'S SUBD.
Alfred Lee
3   4   5
11.48a.

BACON   AVE.

Elizabeth Barron M. A. S.
7a. Fishback Alfred Lee
9   8   8.85a.
4.80 a.

LEE   AVE.

Soldiers Orphan Home
10a.

COLLEGE

Soldiers Orphan
Home
9.73 a.

Mary Griffin

Mary E.
John M. Fulton
3.85a.

CHURCH HILL ROAD

WEBSTER

Emma L. Foote
4a.

Emma L.
Foote
3.4
3.75a.

Andrew & Ida
Birke

W E B
G. C. S. MARSHALL'S
33

German Sav.
Institution
4.93a.

SAM'L
TURNER'S
SUBD. 4

Stephen
Holland
Benj. R. Bonner

KIRKHAM

Henry P. Wyman
10.306 a.

S T E R
50
Joseph
Hafner
6.53 a.

James
Foster

Wm. Broderick

Mercantile
Bank of St. Louis
claimed also by H. A.
Haeussler
6a.

Calvin R.
Hunn
47
John
Flourney
1.58 a.

GRO
Jacob H. Clayton
48

John
Perceval
49
5.186 a.

R O

Charlotte
Holmes
5.6.17a.

Jane Thomas
3.45a.

Geo. P. Parsell
4 94 a.

PACIFIC

WEBSTER

SEC. 32
T. 45 N., R. 6. E.

COUNTY

Margaret Reilly

Jennie H. Marshall

R. W. Crittenden

Geo. E. Leighton
6.86a.

Chas. Parsons
4.50a.

Mettler

LYON'S

WESTERN BOUNDARY OF U.S. SURVEY 1953

Daniel Harper
9
44.86 a.

Samuel Jackson's
Est.
10
44.52 a.

PACIFIC RAILROAD

Mary
8
36.78 a.

A. Helfenstein

S A R P Y

J. P. Helfenstein
11
37.89 a.

19.53 a.

ROCK HILL ROAD

C. M. Avery
11.74 a.

Mary A. Bailey
3.55a.
N. C. Jackson
10 a.
Alfred Plant
3.59 a.

4.68 a.
M. P.
Studley

M. F. Studley
5.19 a.

M. C. Plant
8.94 a.

H. P. Wyman
4.83 a.

M. C. Plant
4.95 a.

12

M. F. Studley
5a.

F. P. Rice
5a.

JACKSON

Geo. E. Leighton   Charles Parsons   Josephine H. Ticknor

WEBSTER 1878

Scale 800 feet to one inch.

100 200 400 800 1000

SUBD.

T O W N S H I P

Stephen E. Holland   Cynthia S. Marshall   Wm H. Brown   Wm H. Brown   B. Webster

BROWN   ST.

Charlotte Holmes 9.13 a.

Joseph M. Cracken 6.81 a.

Jose L. Landy 3.14 a.

Saml L. Doyle
8.50 a.
1

Mary C. & Edw. R. Mason
22 a.
9

Jeff. Thos Payne 3 a.

Thomas J. Payne 19.75 a.
6

William Hoffman

Mary M. Paynes Est. 8.94 a.

C. M. Harding 24.43 a.

G L E N

12

Thos. J. Payne 10
4.572 a.
13
14

O.H. Payne
15

N.L. Payne
16
17

P A R K

Norton P. Chipman
18.59 a.
7

Edw. H. Payne
4.804 a.
30
33

PAYNE'S

S^uB.

Jefferson Payne 4.239 a.
34
35

E.H. Payne
18
6^t

Edward H. Payne
36
4.627 a.

NORTON

Robert H. Payne 1.063 a.
37

T. J. Payne 3.66 a.
19

4
Samuel H. White
40.39 a.
5

Samuel H White 5 a.

Lucy Wright 7 a.

Adele E. Miller 1.50 a.

N. D. Allen

Fidelia H. Wright 5 a.

Thomas J. Payne
39
3.75 a.
40

Fannie F. Payne 3.91 a.
Edward H. Payne

LOCKWOOD   AVE.

UNION

Board of Education Webster School 16.14 a.

Store

Harriet Vautier

Francis I. Plant 4.79 a.
17
18
19

Wm Ferrnish 2.52

10

Watson Acker

Adam Sutter 4.425 a.

Thos. Silence

Episcopal Church

Marq Woods 5.73 a. incl Roads
18

MARY GORE'S

Wm H. Gore

E.C. Barrett 7 a.

E.S. Barrett
24

Mary Ferrnish 3.49 a.

Thomas Geo Jones 3.52 a.

Elizab. Lancaster 1.51 a.

WOOD SILENCE &

SUB

EDMUNDSON'S

Henrietta Lehe

Edw. Lancaster 2 a.

James 1861 a. Lancaster 7

Thos. Silence

Margaret

Apel

Angelika Lockwood

William H. Gore

Sarah E. Plant 5.64 a.

E.S. Barrett

4
Elizabeth Richardson daughter
6.34 a.

Philip Jones
5
7.52 a.

J. S. Bants

Francis I. Plant

Francis I. Plant

SWON   AVE.

T R A C T

J. C. Swon 20 a.

Emeline E. Papin 7.094 a.
3.38 a.

1.094 a.

J. S. Bants

Julia E. Watts 20.34 a.

John R. Shelpey 20 a.

14
Mrs. S. V. Papin 20 a.

PAPINS ADD

TO WEBSTER

James Spencer Est. 24.50 a.
15

John W. Spencer 10 a.
16

T. B. Edgar

C. D. Yeager 14 a. 7.27 a.

ROAD

Wm Edmundson   Theodore Plate   Thomas Silence

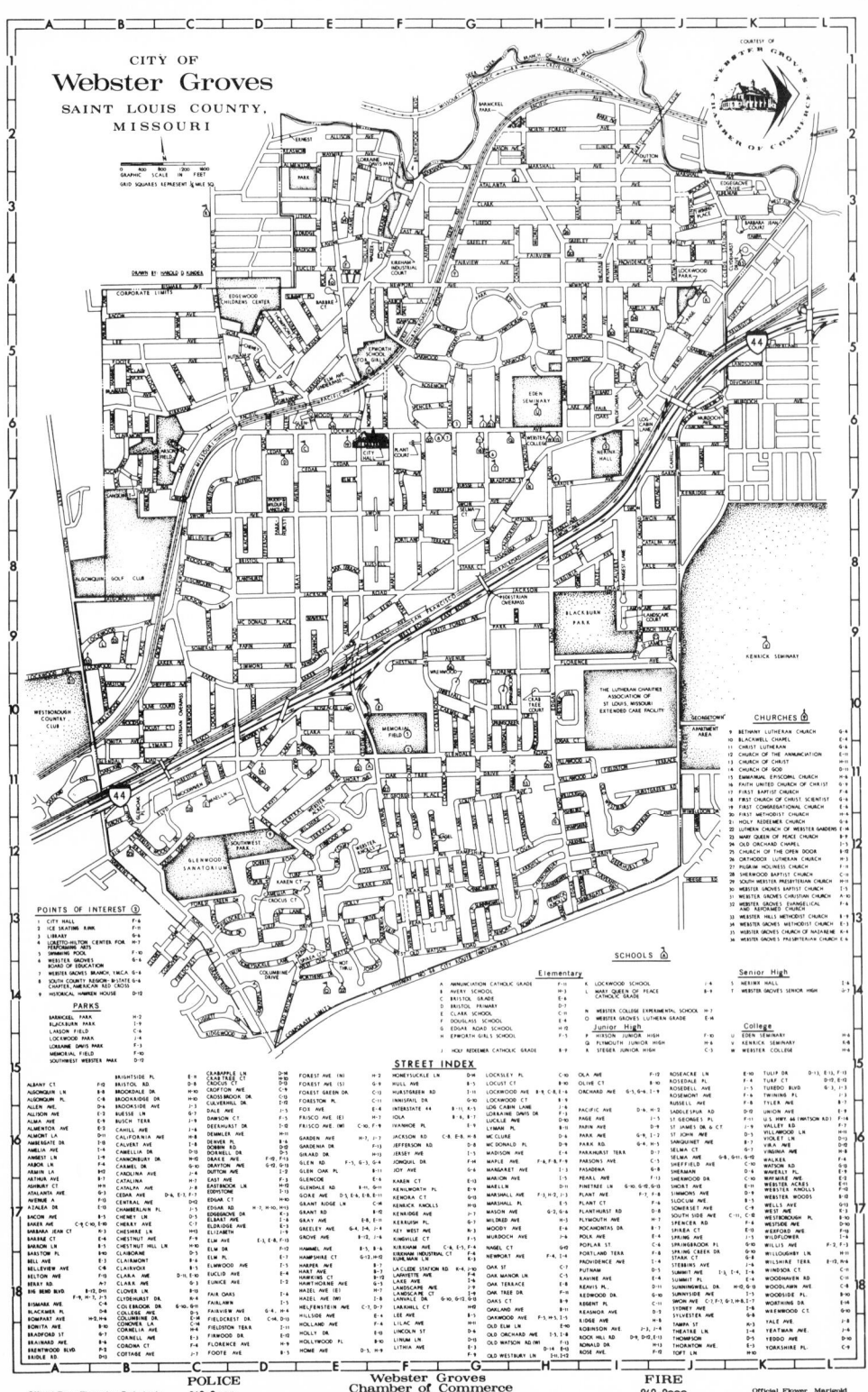

Index

Bibliography

The following reference material was used:

Webster Groves by Velma Benner;
Memories of The Old Home Town by Capt. Tom L. Gibson;
History of Kirkwood by Dahl;
The Octagonal Heart by Ariadne Thompson;
Old St. Louis Homes by Elinor Coyle;
The Golden Age by Elinor Colye;
Arpens and Acres by Marilynne Bradley;
In Retrospect: Webster Groves, Missouri by members of Mrs. Wilda Swift's Webster High
    history class;
Scharf's History of Missouri;
Thomas' History of St. Louis County;
History of St. Louis by McCune Gill;
The First Hundred Years by Sylvia Stevens Schmid;
Webster Groves Presbyterian Church history;
Emmanuel Episcopal Church, 85th and centennial histories;
A Profile of a Congregation: Evangelical U.C.C.;
Kate Moody papers, Missouri Historical Society;
Gore-Helfenstein papers, Missouri Historical Society;
Father Robinson's diary;
St. Louis Magazine, Webster Groves issue, March 1965;
Webster Groves 35 years ago by Ruth Owen;
Webster News-Times, 1950 special historic issue;
Webster Groves Historical Society Bulletins;
Speeches by Roy Brackman, Helen Booth, Dr. Marshall Conrad and Miss Ruth Ferris to the
    Webster Groves Historical Society;
Stories from the *St. Louis Globe-Democrat, Watchman-Advocate, Acme Press;*
Stories from the *St. Louis Post-Dispatch* by John Archibald, John Brophy, Wayne Leeman,
    George McCue, Clarance Olson, Russell Roth, and Clarissa Start;
St. Louis Public Library, Webster Groves Library and Mercantile Library clipping file on
    Webster Groves;
Know Your City booklets by Webster Groves League of Women Voters;
Year books of the Webster Groves Lions Club.

Acknowledgements

THE AUTHOR EXTENDS GRATEFUL THANKS TO THE MANY PEOPLE AND ORGANIZATIONS RESPONSIBLE FOR MATERIAL AND PICTURES IN THIS BOOK, ESPECIALLY:

Mayor John W. Cooper, Jr.;

Mrs. Mary Lou Paillou, city clerk;

Mrs. David Drinkhouse, Webster Groves City Council;

Mrs. Frances Stadler and Gail Guidry of the Missouri Historical Society;

Miss Lillian L. Hubbell, Noel Holobeck, Mrs. Melba Browning and Miss Virginia Rosenmeyer, St. Louis Public Library;

Miss Helen Mardorf and staff members, Webster Groves Public Library;

Miss Elizabeth Kirchner, Mercantile Library;

Miss Lillian Drese, U.S. Veterans Administration;

Evarts Graham, managing editor, St. Louis Post-Dispatch, and Post-Dispatch staff members Gene Pospeshil, Jim Rackwitz, Nancy Stoddard, Thelma Montgomery, Harry Behnen, John Pelly and Wayne Leeman;

Mrs. Adele Trembley Wilson for the use of her scrapbooks;

Mrs. Wilda Swift and Miss Phyllis Flick for assistance with Webster Groves Historical Society pictures being catalogued at the high school;

Mr. and Mrs. J. Marshall Magner, Mr. and Mrs. James McMillan, Miss Edna Carroll, Mrs. Louise Rutherford, Mr. and Mrs. Ray Flint who provided pictures from personal albuns;

Mrs. Robert Ellis, Miss Adele Stine, Mrs. Cora Koenig, Otto Zinke, Mrs. May Killian, A.J. Klien, Mrs. Sally Hennies, Frank McGrath, Mrs. Rita Claypool, Mrs. Paul Crow, Frank Corbett, Mrs. Fred G. Carpenter, Mrs. Harvey Doerr, Mrs. John Clayton, Fred Zinn, Henry Kuhlman, William Bodley Lane, Fred Entrikin and many others who contributed material and reminiscences.

Mrs. Charles MacVeagh for assistance with photographs.

OUR SINCERE APOLOGIES to those persons whose names and stories do not appear. Material for this history was collected, for the most part during summer months when many were out of town. It is the author's hope that this book will serve as a first edition, which will be revised and augmented many times with omissions and errors corrected.

OUR FINAL THANKS to the professionals who assembled this book: Miss Georgia Colombo, James K. Thompson and George Nicks;

To Dr. Max Wolfrum who checked the manuscript for grammar;

AND ESPECIALLY to Mrs. Harriet Davidson who generously contributed her time, expertise and services to reproduce the pictures used in this book.